Soul A

Soul
Astrology

How Your Rising Sign Reveals
Your Soul Path and Life Purpose

Ruth Hadikin BSc.

ISBN-13: 978-0995559301
ISBN-10: 0995559309

Published by Ruth Hadikin Associates
Contact info@RuthHadikin.com

Cover image:
"Galactic Space Sunrise" Stock image. GraphicStock.com

Dedication and Acknowledgement

This book is dedicated to all my teachers. I have been extremely fortunate to meet knowledgeable, wise, and skilful teachers throughout my whole life, from even before I started school when my mother and grandfather taught me to read. Right up to the present day there have been countless teachers, too numerous to mention, to whom I am deeply grateful. In particular I would like to thank Master Astrologer Alan Oken for generously sharing his insight and wisdom, especially in the refined art of astrological delineation, which has greatly facilitated my own skill at interpreting the mandala that is our birth chart. I am also grateful to Esoteric Astrologer Candy Hillenbrand for her succinct descriptions of the Soul Purpose of each sign, which have inspired my own writing, and which I have quoted often.

My good friend and mentor, Master Visionary Intuitive Anya Sophia Mann deserves a special mention for her major contribution to my understanding of the energetics of astrology, and my ability to describe them. It is very rare to meet someone with such an exquisite ability to discern and describe subtle energies, who is also a master teacher and facilitator. Above all not only has she has taught me how to discern subtle distinctions in the quality of energy, but she has also given me the precise language to describe those distinctions.

I am deeply grateful to her for her kindness and generosity in sharing her unparalleled skill of discerning energy and her precision of language in describing subtle energetic distinctions. Her teaching and support is invaluable as I continue learning to identify, define and understand the energies of astrology more deeply and precisely. I aspire to be able to discern and describe energy to the degree that she can. Her language is evident throughout the whole book. Her influence has not only changed the outcome of this book, but in fact without her input it probably would never have been written.

Ruth Hadikin
August 2016

Contents

Foreword

Ruth Hadikin and I share three very important life interests: the journey on the Spiritual Path, the expression of that journey through the study and teaching of astrology, and the subjective guidance in these two respects of the same Master Teacher, the Tibetan, D.K. In this respect, D.K. advises the following to his students in his great work, *"Esoteric Astrology"*:

"If, in the presentation of this vast subject (of astrology), and in the process of indicating the attitude of the Ageless Wisdom to this new and coming (yet very ancient) "science of effective energies," as it has been called, I may present a new approach...

I am hoping that some astrologers may be found who will be sensitive to that which is new. I am believing that there are investigators along astrological lines who will be open-minded enough to recognize possible hypotheses and then to make fair experiment with them...

I am looking for these fair-minded astrologers to make experiment with the factors and suggestions which I may indicate."

- The Tibetan, D.K., Esoteric Astrology

Several of the Tibetan's students have come forth in response to this mandate, among them are Michael Robbins, Errol Weiner, Kurt Abraham, Frances Moore, Phillip Lindsey, Torny Jansson, Risa D'Angeles, and me. I am now very happy to add one more name to this grateful group: Ruth Hadikin.

We are grateful because we have been led to the door of an ancient science, one whose inner purpose is to help link the Soul with the personality, the inner life with the outer, and that which is by nature of the Spirit to that which is by manifestation of the Earth. This gratitude expands and extends into the realm of service as each one of this small group of esoteric astrological writers holds service to humanity and the Hierarchy of Teachers as the primary impulse in our hearts and in our small contributions to the One Work of expanding consciousness in these times.

In this collective endeavor, Ruth Hadikin in her well formulated, informative, precise but easy-to-grasp book, Soul Astrology, adds to these contributions in "modern" esoteric astrological literature. It is a most welcomed addition indeed as Ruth's gift combines not only accurate and useful information, but also contains the soul-generated energy of healing as the source-matrix through which her writings flow. This is perceptible and is an essential part of the beauty contained in her pages. Thus the book is an example of "thinking in the heart" and the fusion of intuition with mind.

In short, Soul Astrology is a wee treasure. It is one that is easily accessible to those with little or no esoteric training and a lovely reminder of truth to those of us already steeped in the Ancient Wisdom Teachings of which the true astrology is an integral part.

The reader will obtain many benefits from Ruth Hadikin's work. I add my love and blessings to your journey.

Alan Oken, author Soul-Centered Astrology
Bali, Indonesia
24 August, 2016

Introduction

Some of the biggest questions that we ever ask ourselves as we walk though this journey of life are "Who am I?" and "Why am I here?" The deep search for meaning and purpose is so innate in all of us. It is part of the human condition.

Yet a part of us is almost afraid that these questions are so big that they are unanswerable. Many of us go through life seeking and wondering, but rarely finding answers that we are truly satisfied with.

This is where the 'split' between our Soul and our personality begins. If we listen deeply we can hear that soft, still, voice inside calling us to listen more deeply and to follow our Soul's path. Yet on an everyday level, as our attention gets eaten up by tending to the business of the day, our personality finds it hard to even find a moment to pay attention to our Soul's calling.

If we were totally free of our everyday responsibilities, and had the time to go deep into meditation like the yogis of ancient times who spent many years meditating in the isolation of a mountain cave, the deeper answers to these profound questions would eventually arise in us, just as it did with them.

However for most of us that is simply an idea that we can hardly relate to. In our busy information and technology-driven society, even having time to simply sit and be yourself for five minutes without the demands of the outside world is becoming a rare luxury. So if we don't have the time to tune in and listen to the deeper stirrings of our Soul, how can we possibly begin to answer those profound questions for ourselves? Who am I? Why am I here? This is where Soul Astrology can be a helpful tool for us on our journey of self-exploration.

The truth is that we can never really become separated from our Soul. Even though we may not always be aware of it, because of the distractions of our everyday lives, it is nevertheless an inherent part of who we are. In fact it is more than that. It IS who we are and because of that, we can see its reflection - if we know where to look.

If you were able to see the fullness of your own being, you would be amazed. You would look like a beautiful rainbow, with myriad different colors representing different energies in constant movement, flowing in and through your energy field as 'you'! At the simplest level, you are a magnificent field of intelligent, conscious, Universal energy having an individual experience.

Your birth horoscope (birth chart or natal chart) is like a snapshot of your own energy field taken at your birth. Although it seems to depict things that are outside of you, like planets and Zodiac signs, as you read this book you will begin to understand how they are really just reflections of who *you* are (and who you are becoming) as an energetic being. Ultimately you are not separate from the Universe, and are therefore part of a continuous flow of Universal Energy having an individual expression. We call this individual expression of energy our Soul.

According to *"Esoteric Astrology"* by Alice Bailey[1] our Soul's journey begins in the first Zodiac sign Aries as *"a point of light in the mind of God"* and travels on a journey through each of the twelve Zodiac signs culminating in the twelfth sign of Pisces. Some astrologers believe we spend up to eight lifetimes in each sign.

You are born at a time when your Soul Sign is rising on the horizon (in astrology this is called your Rising Sign or Ascendant) because it

---

[1] Alice Bailey (A.B.) is said to be an 'amanuensis' of sorts to a spiritual teacher who referred to himself as The Tibetan. An amanuensis is generally someone who is hired to take dictation, but in this case the Tibetan and A.B. had a telepathic relationship. At the time The Tibetan said he was abbot of a monastery in Tibet, which some scholars now believe to be Tashi Lhunpo monastery at Shigatse, in the Tibetan region of modern-day China. The work known as "A Treatise on the Seven Rays" (of which Esoteric Astrology is volume III) was transmitted by the Tibetan through Alice Bailey.

is already a vibrational match for your Soul. The Rising Sign creates a 'window of opportunity', a portal if you like, when your Soul can 'beam in' on a matching wavelength!

So if someone has Cancer Rising for example, it's not so much that they have Cancer Rising *because* they were born at that particular time, but rather that they were born at a time that Cancer was rising on the horizon *because they are a Cancer Soul*. It was their time. The energy matched their vibration and so it was the perfect time for them to incarnate. This is why I refer to the Rising Sign as your Soul Sign. Throughout this book, whenever I refer to your "Soul Sign" I'm talking about your Rising Sign (Ascendant).

> *"Know thyself.*
> *If thou canst learn the true nature of thine own self,*
> *thou wilt know the reality of the Universe"*
>
> - Swami Abhedananda

Your horoscope is therefore a symbol of your individual energetic field, your own personal mandala, and therefore your Soul. Because you are a spark of creation it is also something quite sacred. The whole Universe is like a hologram where the whole is contained in each of it's parts and if you can really understand this, you can understand yourself at the deepest level, and you will understand the workings of the Universe.

The key to Soul Astrology is really self-observation. The more you observe these Universal energies as they express themselves through you, the more you get closer to the answers to those big questions (who am I? and why am I here?).

Astrology is simply a language that helps us to understand and make subtle distinctions in the energies that we are experiencing, observing and understanding. Through self-observation and a basic understanding of your birth chart you can begin to understand who you really are and why you are here.

It sounds like a pretty huge claim to suggest that the answers to such deep questions can be found in a birth chart, but I believe that is exactly what we can see, once we understand energy, and know how to look.

At the simplest level all you really need to know to begin to explore this idea for yourself, is your Sun, Moon and Rising Sign[2] (Ascendant). Then you can start using Soul Astrology as a practical tool in your daily life to support you in understanding yourself, knowing your Soul's Path and realizing your life purpose. Your Rising Sign represents your *subtle Soul light* (your Soul Sign), your Sun Sign indicates how you flow your *prana or life-force energy*, and your Moon Sign indicates *how you flow your emotional energy*. How you express your Soul light in the world depends on various factors such as your level of consciousness and your ego-personality (we'll say more about that later)!

If you are a relatively awake, aware, spiritually-oriented person you may express a finer, more altruistic, essence of your Soul Sign. If you are more down-to-earth and worldly-oriented you may express a more conventional worldly quality of the same energy.

For example, if you do have Cancer Rising a more spiritual expression might be to bring higher degrees of empathy and compassion into the world (The Dalai Lama has this placement). A more conventional focus might be to simply nurture those around you to the best of your ability.

In addition to your level of consciousness, your Soul Sign is also expressed through the 'lens' of your personality signs: mainly your Sun and Moon signs. Imagine a crystal prism. As light shines

---

[2] On your birth chart the Rising Sign will usually be indicated by the letters AC or by Asc. which is an abbreviation of it's astrological term "Ascendant".

through a prism it is *refracted*³ which allows us to see the colors of the rainbow that make up the light. In a similar way we could say that the light of your Soul is *refracted* through the lens of your personality, mainly your Sun and Moon signs. In other words it is your personality that molds, shapes and colors the different facets and expressions of your Soul light. So your Soul Sign indicates *what* you came here to do and your Sun and Moon signs show *how* you will do it!

In my experience our lives follow a definite path that, if we have the courage to follow, will eventually lead us where we want to go. There is a pattern to life that is not fate, or destiny, but our innate potential unfolding. Just as, given the right conditions, an acorn will become an oak tree, so our lives are following a true path of growth and development that our Soul is always calling us up to... the next best iteration of ourselves.

You are here to be the best version of you that you possibly can be. How can you know what that next iteration will be? Your heart will tell you. If you follow your heart's desire, your own great adventure, it will lead you exactly to where you need to be to shine your light in the world. Your Soul is calling to you through your heart. If you look at some of the key events in your life, you'll see a pattern emerging. The purpose of this book is to support you in having a deeper understanding of your Soul Sign by helping you to understand the characteristics and quality of the underlying energy that creates this pattern, and some of the factors affecting it's expression, so that you can use Soul Astrology as a tool in understanding yourself.

While there is much new material in this book, many of the Soul Sign descriptions were originally published as a series of articles for

---

³ Refraction is a process of 'bending' or causing rays of light to deviate, thus making visible the multiple rainbow colors that make up our everyday experience of light such as ordinary daylight (otherwise known as *white light*). In a similar way, even though you may have the same Soul Sign as another person, you will each express your light uniquely as it shines through your different personality 'lens'.

RealAstrologers.com, in Life Coaching Magazine (LCM) and some were broadcast on LCM Editor Anya Sophia Mann's YouTube Channel, so they will already be somewhat familiar to readers of LCM. Having said that, it felt important to bring all those pieces together and weave them into one cohesive whole, together with additional commentary, for the purpose of deeper understanding and for new readers. This was my overall intention in putting the book together in this way.

Also some quotes are intentionally repeated. When this happens take note: it is not an editing error, it is either because I felt they bring a deeper insight that is particularly relevant to the sign in question and/or that they are especially pertinent to our individual and collective journey of spiritual awakening. Whenever you come across a quote for the second or third time, it may be worthwhile to take a moment and contemplate it again on a deeper level.

A note about internet research in general, and Wikipedia in particular: throughout the book I have provided links to definitions and resources for further study. These should be taken simply as a starting point for further exploration and not as hard fact. The very nature of the internet means there is much misinformation 'out there', and one of the challenges for the Aquarian Age for us all will be in learning discernment, especially in the art of discerning 'good' information from 'bad' information. In the case of Wikipedia, it is an open 'wiki', which means everybody can join, and anyone can update the content. It is still a very helpful starting point for research, because content is checked, modified and moderated, but care must be taken because there can still be religious and cultural bias, and inaccuracies. It is wise to always cross-reference content from at least two or three reliable sources before depending upon 'facts'.

I know many readers will want to dive straight into the sections about their own Rising Sign, and that's perfectly natural (that's exactly what I would have done before I started studying astrology in depth)! But I invite more serious students of astrology to start at the beginning and follow the book through its logical progression, at least once. That way you will get a feel for how the energy of one sign flows into the next, and a sense of our Soul's growth as a developmental process unfolding through stages. This developmental process is reiterated and reinforced as we go through three 'cycles' of the signs in Chapters 3, 4 and 5.

You might also find it very helpful to read *"Your Essential Guide To Soul Astrology"* as a companion to this book. You can get a free copy by signing up for my weekly newsletter *"Life's Greatest Adventure"* at RuthHadikin.com The weekly insights in my newsletters are also designed to support you in going deeper in your self-exploration, and understanding your Soul's journey.

One thing I have learned from the Tibetan tradition, is that even the greatest spiritual masters will apologize upfront for any errors and omissions in their work. I would like to continue in that vein here by pointing out that each of us, myself included, is interpreting spiritual teachings according to our own level of consciousness. In this book I am merely sharing my own insights and impressions, and in so doing apologize for any errors or inaccuracies there may be due to my own ignorance, misunderstanding, or lack of consciousness. Each student on the path is encouraged to keep going deeper in their own spiritual journey and to trust their own intuition and insights first and foremost, above all else.

Finally I hope you enjoy your journey into Soul Astrology and that it inspires you to go even deeper into your own journey of Self-exploration, whereby you discover your own true nature as a spiritual being.

1. Your Healing Journey: Duality, Polarity and Wholeness

"You live in illusion and the appearance of things.
There is a reality, but you do not know this.
When you understand this,
you will see that you are nothing,
and being nothing you are everything.
That is all."

- Kalu Rinpoche

Astrology and Healing

It might seem odd to begin the astrological story of your Soul with a Chapter on healing, but as we shall see it is important to understand precisely what is meant by healing in this context, and to have some understanding of the background of reincarnation and wholeness upon which Soul Astrology rests. In this Chapter we will explore what is meant by healing, why astrology can be a powerful tool for healing, and why healing is an inherent key to your Soul's journey.

We live in an illusory world that we believe to be real. In *"Esoteric Astrology"* the Tibetan Master DK refers to this as 'glamour'. The dictionary definition of glamour is:

1. Exciting or mysterious attractiveness usually associated with striking physical beauty, luxury, or celebrity.

2. Archaic Magic cast by a spell; enchantment.

Source: TheFreeDictionary.com

This reflects how we think of glamour in our modern age: a glitzy quality of sparkling attractiveness, champagne celebrity lifestyle, and/or high fashion, but the true meaning of glamour (and the meaning which I believe the Tibetan was trying to convey) goes much, much deeper. They both share one thing in common: illusion. We know the glamorous lifestyle of our celebrities is all illusion, but it's an illusion we buy into. We know that in 'real-life' they have their own problems as much as anyone else. What we don't know, is that our so-called real-life is also itself a kind of illusion.

According to consciousness researcher Steve Taylor in his profoundly inspiring and groundbreaking book "Waking From Sleep", our current everyday state of consciousness (where we think of being 'awake' as the opposite of being 'asleep') is in fact a kind of sleep[4]. He compares this to higher states of consciousness and peak experiences where people have a kind of 'spiritual awakening' and experience a more vivid and expanded perception of reality, which they often describe as being more 'real'.

Often these higher states of consciousness, or awareness, last for a few days or possibly even months before the individual eventually returns to a more *conventional* (ordinary, everyday or worldly) level of consciousness. In rare cases it becomes a permanent state of being, in which case the individual is then said to be 'awake' or 'enlightened'.

---

[4] He also makes important distinctions between true spiritual experiences and drug or chemical-induced experiences which, although pleasurable, can have an illusory quality to them and be lacking in the immense feelings of warmth, love, nurturing and the experience of crystal clarity that accompany true spiritual experiences.

When the Tibetan speaks of glamour he is speaking of this 'spiritual sleep': the tendency for us, in our everyday lives, to get caught in illusory ways of thinking and behaving, where we live our lives in a kind of dream-like state unaware of the spiritual and energetic reality of our own nature, and the Universe. This happens for various reasons but the two main factors that contribute to our state of illusion are *social conditioning* and *the way our human brain is wired* to enable us to learn!

It might seem as though the very things that we depend upon for everyday functioning in the world can become obstacles when it comes to our own spiritual awakening, yet all is not lost. The greatest spiritual teachers and master yogis throughout the ages have recognized these 'obstacles' and have been showing us various ways to get through them to wake up to our true reality. One of these ways is through the study and practice of Soul Astrology, but before we get into the details of your own Soul Astrology let's take a deeper look at how this illusion happens.

Social Conditioning and Karma

Most of our behavior is learned behavior. Western sociologists and psychologists debate on just exactly how much of human behavior is learned from our environment (our family, friends, the society we live in) and how much is genetic (inherited from our parents). When we introduce the idea of reincarnation it swings the debate strongly in favor of everything being learned.

Many eastern traditions have the concept of 'karma'. This is a difficult concept to convey and I won't go into too much depth here, but it might be helpful for the purpose of understanding Soul Astrology to simply think of karma as *everything we have ever learned in this and past lives*. For example if a young child starts playing the piano at age two and nobody in the family is musically inclined, Western science would say he had a 'genetic tendency'.

In some eastern traditions it would be said that he had learned the skill in a previous lifetime, and it had carried forward as part of his 'karma'. There is so much more to karma than that, but if you just hold this simplified idea as you read on, it can help you to understand what we mean when we start talking about the distinctions between personality and Soul.

The Human Brain

The thing that sets us above most animals and other species is our powerful, intelligent, and adaptable, human brain. Yet it is the very thing that keeps us in an illusory version of reality and prevents us from seeing the Universe the way it really is!

Our brain loves to 'learn', and we get through our everyday existence because we have learned so much: walking, talking, reading, writing, driving and so on. There is nothing wrong with learning, but the very way that the brain functions also keeps us in illusion.

Neuroscience is only just discovering what ancient yogis and spiritual teachers have taught for centuries, which is that we are actually living in an illusory world created by our brain. We don't experience reality 'as it is' at all. What we experience as reality is actually a *projection from our brain based on past experience*:

"we generally think of 'seeing' as the result of processing information that comes through our eyes, but the truth is that several times more of what we "see" consists of information produced within the brain.

All of us carry around internal models that the brain uses to construct, from endless perceptual fragments, what we call reality.

In other words,
much of what we experience of reality
is, in Eagleman's words,
a 'beautifully rendered simulation'".[5]

Separation

So what does all this have to do with Soul Astrology? Your social conditioning from this and past lives, contributes to your sense of being a separate 'me', apart from everyone else in the Universe. Your brain serves to project your own version of reality and helps to keep this idea of a separate 'me' alive and kicking. Each one of us has our own 'story of me' running like a computer program in the background. It is who we think we are: "I'm someone who likes this or that, can do this or that, can't do this or that" and so on ...and on ...and on!

This projection of thoughts, feelings, behaviors, likes, dislikes, talents and flaws, is who we *think* we are. In Soul Astrology we refer to this 'idea of me' as your *ego-personality*. It is not who you *really* are, but it is who you *think* you are, based upon your everyday experience.

In conventional astrology we use the symbolism of astrology to describe the energy dynamics of your ego-personality. In your horoscope (natal chart) these characteristics and tendencies will show up in the positions of the personal planets by sign, house and aspect. Our personality, ego-personality, or identity are one and the same: how we think, act, and feel about ourselves on a daily basis, and who we generally believe ourselves to be.

---

[5] *"The Cosmos Inside Your Head: Neuroscientist David Eagleman Tells The Story Of The Brain On PBS"* by David DiSalvo for Forbes.com Online at http://www.forbes.com/sites/daviddisalvo/2015/10/13/the-cosmos-inside-your-head-neuroscientist-david-eagleman-tells-the-story-of-the-brain-on-pbs/#167447eb65f2

The specific 'set' of thoughts, ideas, beliefs, skills, talents, strengths and weaknesses that we think of as 'me'. What we like, what we don't like, what we can do, what we can't do, what we will and what we won't. All are wrapped up in this package that we call 'me'.

This 'idea of me' (what we call our personality) is part of the overall illusion created by our brain that keeps us living in *separation* and *duality*. When we are personality-oriented our life is all about getting the needs of our personality met and we live in a 'dualistic' state: me-you, us-them, him-her, up-down, black-white, Aries-Libra, Virgo-Pisces, Scorpio-Taurus, etc. In our dualistic state everything appears to be separate and polarized into opposites.

Healing: the Integration Process of Personality-Soul Fusion

Whenever we are thinking in terms of 'me' or 'I' this is our *personality* (our identity). It is an illusory *idea* about ourselves, which we have constructed over our lifetime (and probably over past lifetimes) and it is largely the result of continuous, pervasive, *conditioning*. Our Soul on the other hand, is our connection to the Divine. It is said to be a vehicle for Divinity to experience itself in matter.

It is through direct perception and experience of our Soul that we can go beyond the limitations of social conditioning and even our brain wiring, and access the greater universal consciousness that lies beyond. When this happens we start 'waking' up from the big sleep that has humanity enthralled in a collective illusion.

Having some kind of regular meditative practice is essential to this process because it is only through meditation that we can access and experience the greater part of our being that we call our Soul. Why does this matter, on a practical level? Because the whole point of our spiritual journey is to integrate the two. Not that they are really separate but, due to our over-identification with our personality traits, and general lack of attention to our spiritual world, we perceive them as two separate things.

In *"Esoteric Astrology"* the Tibetan Master refers to this integration process as personality-Soul *fusion* and it is essentially a process of *self-awareness*.

**"Astrology is the science of
wholeness, unity, non-duality"**

– OSHO, Indian Mystic

The word "heal" comes from the Old English word *haelan*, which literally means, "to make whole." In essence, there is no separation. Our perceived separation is part of this illusion generated by our social conditioning and our brain.

The solution is to *cultivate our awareness to the point where we can perceive reality as it really is*: a complete, whole, and unified 'hologram' of intermingled, intertwined, dancing energy and light. The very thing that makes us whole is *pure awareness*. Awareness is therefore the key to our healing journey, and the method for cultivating awareness is meditation.

What Energies Are You Healing and Integrating In This Lifetime?

In Astrology energy is described in terms of its *quality* (*modality*) and *element*. Each Zodiac sign has a unique combination of quality and element, and therefore has a unique energetic signature, characteristic and purpose.

The Three Modalities
The three modalities describe the *mode* or *way* an energy flows. In astrological terms an energetic quality, or modality, is either *Cardinal, Fixed or Mutable*.

Cardinal energy has a creative quality to it. It is the energy of Spring and creation. Cardinal signs usher in new ways of doing things, and carve out new pathways.

Going 'where man has never gone before', exploring new frontiers, being at the forefront of evolutionary processes, are all qualities of cardinal consciousness. The challenge for cardinal signs is they may experience restlessness if they have to stay with one idea, plan, job or project too long. The cardinal signs are Aries, Cancer, Libra, and Capricorn.

Fixed energy has a stabilizing quality to it. It is the energy of Summer: a place-holder energy that stabilizes forms for the duration of their lifespan. Fixed signs have the ability to create structures and hold them in place. If water needs to be channeled from A to B we need a structure, a canal, to get it there.

This ability to create structure, channels, frameworks etc. is a hallmark of fixed consciousness. The challenge for fixed signs is change, getting stuck in a rut or fixed way of thinking is a possibility, and stubbornness can be a problem. The fixed signs are Taurus, Leo, Scorpio, and Aquarius.

Mutable energy has a dissolving, changing, quality to it. Mutable signs are agents of change. It is the energy of Autumn, as old forms are broken down to release their energy. Flexibility, changeability, movement and adaptability are qualities of mutable consciousness. The challenge for mutable signs is to create structure and stick at something to completion. The mutable signs are Gemini, Virgo, Sagittarius, and Pisces.

The Four Elements
In Western Astrology[6] the four elements are Fire, Earth, Air and Water. In terms of your spiritual growth and development:

> **Fire** signs are about Mastery of Action (Aries, Leo, Sagittarius)

---

[6] In other astrological systems, for example Tibetan Astrology, a fifth element of 'space' or 'spirit' is included.

Earth signs are about Mastery of the Physical (Taurus, Virgo, Capricorn)

Air signs are about Mastery of the Mind (Gemini, Libra, Aquarius)

Water signs are about Mastery of Emotions (Cancer, Scorpio, Pisces)

Within each element there is a sign for each *modality*, so there is a cardinal, fixed and mutable fire sign; a cardinal, fixed and mutable earth sign; a cardinal, fixed and mutable air sign; and a cardinal, fixed and mutable water sign. This makes up the total of twelve signs.

Personality-Soul Fusion and The Three Crosses

In addition to the modalities and elements, in *"Esoteric Astrology"* the Tibetan describes the process of personality and Soul fusion in terms of the 'three crosses'. The three crosses are describing three clearly defined *stages in the evolution of human consciousness*, and are distinct from the modalities described above. For example by modality an individual can have a chart dominated by cardinal signs, and yet be on the 'mutable cross' in terms of their own level of consciousness[7].

The Mutable Cross is where the majority of humanity is at this present time. This is where the individual is totally personality identified and personality driven. There is little or no personal experience of a spiritual life. Although the person may believe in a Soul, they have not yet experienced it for themselves.

The Fixed Cross is where the individual is becoming aware of, and aligned with, the Soul life. They are aware of personality and Soul, but the two are still seen as separate and so there is duality.

---

[7] The three crosses in this context do not refer to individuals with a cardinal, fixed, or mutable grand cross in their chart, but rather refer specifically to levels of consciousness.

It seems that a significant growing minority of people on the planet at this time are currently experiencing this Soul awakening at the level of the Fixed Cross.

Finally the Cardinal Cross describes individuals where personality and Soul are fully integrated. The illusion of personality has dissolved and the individual leads a Soul-centered life.

Become a Player

It is important to make a distinction between *studying* spirituality or metaphysics, and actually *practicing* meditation. It is the difference between knowing *about* something, like being a tennis fan, and actually *having personal experience* like being a tennis player.

Many people like to read, study and learn about spiritual and metaphysical topics (including astrology), yet they do not practice. They are more like 'fans'. In their everyday lives they still experience fear, anger and other disturbing emotions because study alone does not heal our underlying sense of separation.

In fact, due to the objective nature of study with its intense intellectual focus at the expense of our other senses, it is likely to add to our brain wiring and increase our sense of separation! To have real spiritual experiences where you have an opportunity to 'wake up' and experience reality as it really is you have to become a player, which means engaging regularly in some form of meditation or mindfulness practice.

Through meditation, where we observe ourselves with care and attention, we notice the energies at play in our body and mind. We notice from our own experience just how much we are driven by our conditioned responses: the habitual unconscious drives of our personality that keep us from experiencing our true spiritual nature.

As we become more adept at meditation our intuitive capacity becomes more developed and fine-tuned. Meditation opens our heart, expands our consciousness, and thereby develops our intuition.

"Intuition is the ability to perceive that quality of energy
—the true essence of meaning—
within any form of expression"

- Alan Oken

Intuition is an enhanced form of perception in which we develop our ability to perceive subtle qualities of energy and light. Over time, as our intuition develops, we notice increasingly subtler qualities of energy and light that lie beyond our conditioning, which are the very essence of our Soul. Once we have perceived our own Soul qualities directly, through our own experience, there is no turning back. Then we are truly on the path of healing through personality-Soul fusion.

Soul Astrology and Your Healing Journey

In this chapter we have presented a very brief overview of the path to healing that each of us walks on our individual journey back to wholeness.

Here's what we've covered so far: because of our social conditioning and our brain wiring we live in the illusion of separation. All disease results from this illusion of separation. Through pure awareness we recognize the illusion and return to wholeness (healing). The method for developing awareness is meditation, which cultivates intuition (our ability to perceive energy).

The Tibetan Master in *"Esoteric Astrology"* describes this healing journey to wholeness as *personality-Soul fusion*. Soul Astrology gives us a language to describe the energy dynamics of this universal healing process (See Chapter 6 for more discussion on Soul Astrology as a holistic science to support our process of healing).

The following chapters will therefore focus on two levels:

1. How the energy of your Soul Sign is expressed through your personality (as it is 'filtered' through your brain wiring and social conditioning) and

2. The purer expression of the sign as it is experienced at the level of your Soul: the pure awareness, or consciousness, that lies beyond your brain wiring and social conditioning. We might sometimes refer to this as higher vibration, higher octave, higher mind, or your Higher Self.

What is Soul Astrology?

What sets Soul Astrology apart perhaps from other forms of astrology is the emphasis on intuition. One cannot really understand the language of Soul Astrology without a highly developed intuition. In *"Esoteric Astrology"* the Tibetan states that astrologers of the future will be highly intuitive.

Intuition is essential for developing the heightened awareness necessary to perceive the subtler qualities of the Zodiac signs and planetary bodies, and that degree of intuition is only cultivated through meditation. Thus meditation is an important foundation in the study and practice of Soul Astrology.

Whenever I refer to Soul Astrology I am talking about a complete holistic approach which includes the study of astrology, astrological language and how that relates to our Soul's journey, and *also* includes practices such as meditation to expand our consciousness and awaken our intuition so that we can cultivate our ability to describe subtler energies, based on our own experiential learning (learning from our experience).

> *"The basis of the astrological sciences is*
> *the emanation, transmission, and reception of energies*
> *and their transmutation into forces by the receiving entity ...*
> *it is all a question of developed reception and sensitivity."*

– The Tibetan

Once your awareness expands to the point where you become aware of the ongoing interplay of energy and light, then you will truly understand the value of astrology as a language to describe subtle distinctions in the quality of light and energy.

Soul Astrology *is* the study of love and light expressed as you! The healing process of personality-Soul fusion described by the Tibetan is one of waking up to your own true nature by developing your intuition through meditation, and then using the language of Soul Astrology to describe the subtle qualities of light and energy that become part of your awareness.

In the next chapter we'll look more deeply at why your Rising Sign can be considered an indicator of your Soul's journey and purpose in this lifetime.

2. Your Rising Sign: Your Soul's Purpose

"The Soul is our individual link to the
essential substance of the Creative Source ..."

- Alan Oken, Soul Centered Astrology

The purpose of any spiritual path or practice is to support us in integrating our Soul and personality by developing Soul awareness, recognition, and identification.

Soul Astrology supports us in this process (and on our spiritual path) by helping us to use our intuition to discern which of our personal qualities, traits, and tendencies are true expressions of our Soul, and which are learned behavior (personality-based).

When we begin to look at our natal chart from a spiritual perspective, it is important to remember that we are always talking about energy. If you could see your natal chart in 3D (or better still multi-dimensionally), you would see a glorious rainbow-colored mandala – indicating all the dynamic energies that combine to make up your energetic field! If you could see that visually, you would be able to detect a core vibration, a pure essence, almost like a fabric into which all the other energies are woven. This "fabric" would be your Soul and its nature would be that of your Rising Sign. A beautiful sight to behold!

The Dawning of Your Life

Your Rising Sign (Ascendant) is the essence of your Soul, and so it comes first. It is because your Soul is already resonating to a specific vibration that it can incarnate at a specific time and place, which matches that vibration. As we mentioned earlier, in astrology the Rising Sign is the sign that was rising on the horizon at the time of your birth (which is why it is called the Rising Sign). It therefore creates a window of opportunity for your Soul to incarnate at that precise moment, in that precise location, *because it is the same frequency.*

When the time of your birth is approaching, and your Soul Sign rises on the horizon, this 'window' (or portal) opens and because it already matches your Soul vibration, you are able to 'beam in' on that frequency to begin a new incarnation. I like to think of your rising sign as the 'beam of light' that you rode in on!

"A child is born on that day and at that hour
when the celestial rays are in mathematical harmony
with his individual karma"

- Sri Yukteswar

In the introduction we gave the example of someone with Cancer Rising. This is such an important point it is worth emphasizing here, so that you have a clear understanding. So for example, if you have Cancer Rising it is *because you are already a Cancer Soul* that you were able to incarnate when Cancer was rising on the horizon. Your Rising Sign is your Soul's energetic signature and so, because like attracts like, you were able to tune in, latch on, and "beam in" on this frequency. It is *your* frequency. Your wavelength. Your resonance.

Your rising sign is also indicating the pure vibrant spiritual energy that you brought with you to be expressed in this lifetime, which serves the dual purpose of fulfilling your own personal spiritual development, while at the same time making your own unique contribution to the spiritual upliftment of humanity and our beautiful Earth home.

This is why birth is a very exciting time! Just as the rising Sun marks the dawn of a new day, so your Rising Sign marked the 'dawn' of your life, and the birthing of new life on Earth is always filled with potential and possibility. All newborns carry their own unique and Divine energy signature so there will never be another you, throughout all of eternity. You are part of a group of Souls who share the same Rising Sign and Soul purpose, yet you will express that purpose uniquely depending upon other factors in your chart, including your Sun and Moon signs.

The moment of your birth is therefore a very sacred and special time. Not only does it mark the dawning of your life but also it is *the beginning of your Soul's experience in this incarnation.* In other words, at the precise moment you were born a being of light began a specific and purposeful journey into this physical incarnation (that would be you). You are not here by accident. Your Soul is unfolding in a very particular and specific way. Just like in a forest there is a reason for every noble oak tree, gentle fern, and delicate flower, there is a precise and exact reason why your life is unfolding right now, exactly as it is.

> *"The entire theme of the Zodiac*
> *can be approached from the angle of light*
> *and its unfolding and increasing radiance."*

- The Tibetan, *"Esoteric Astrology"*

Soul Astrologer Errol Weiner, explains in his book *"Transpersonal Astrology"* how your Soul stays in the same sign for seven or eight incarnations, and that it is possible, by noting the degree of the

Rising Sign (Ascendant), to estimate how many lifetimes your Soul has been in this sign. There are 30° in each sign, so simply divide 30 by seven or eight to get a sense of where you are up to now. So using our example, if you have 14° Cancer Rising, you are about half way and may have been a Cancer Soul for three or four lifetimes.

Your Soul is growing, changing, and passing through *stages of development*, just like your physical body does. When you were an infant and as a young child, you went through *developmental stages*. These are the milestones that marked significant stages of your growth and development: such as eating solid food, teething, sitting, standing, walking, and talking. Similarly, according to the Tibetan Master DK, in *"Esoteric Astrology"* by Alice Bailey (AB), your Soul also passes through significant developmental stages. In the case of your Soul, each stage is a significant milestone in the development of your light body.

As we navigate our inner journey, we become more familiar with our inner world. The dedicated Master Yogi's and Saints that have trodden this inner path before us described their experiences in various scriptures, leaving a kind of map, so we can know what to expect on our own journey. Some scriptures describe our spiritual journey in terms of 'stages', while others describe it in terms of individual experience. Although each journey is unique, and descriptions vary due to cultural and language differences, there is still some 'common ground' that we can all expect to experience.

Patanjali, one of the founders of modern Yoga, described five 'bodies'[8] we can experience on our inner journey. He related these to five elements of earth, fire, water, air and ether. These he called the physical or 'earth' body (annamay kosh), the energy 'fire' body (pranamay kosh – this is also known as the 'vital' body in other traditions), the mental 'water' body (manomay kosh), intuitive 'air' body (vigyanamay kosh), and the bliss 'ether' body (anandmay kosh). Our journey is one of awareness and movement through each

---

[8] *"Mastery Over The Five Elements"* by OSHO. Online document available at http://www.OSHO.com/library/default.aspx

of these inner 'bodies'. Once all five have been transcended, we attain 'Universal Mind'.

Each Zodiac sign represents one significant stage in your Soul's development. Below I have given an overview of the developmental stage at each Zodiac sign and in further Chapters we will be looking in more depth at your Soul's current stage of development specifically, as indicated by your own Rising Sign.

What is a Soul?

Before we continue maybe we should take a moment to define more clearly what we mean by Soul. For our purposes here Soul can be thought of as an *individualized expression of Divinity*. If the whole of existence (seen and unseen; physical and non-physical) were an ocean, then we may consider our Soul to be like a glass of water taken from that ocean. It is still part of the ocean, it still has all the qualities of the ocean, it will eventually return to the ocean, yet for a short time it is having an individualized experience.

In reality, we are of the nature of light. The whole of existence is one huge experience of light, dancing through different forms of expression. You are one form of that expression. So you are actually light, having an individualized experience. In order to have this individualized experience, *light manifests as form*. When we talk about developmental stages, we are talking about the development of a 'light body' from being what the Tibetan describes as a spark or "point of light in the mind of God" to being a fully developed individual *light being* - or Soul.

> *"The Soul is our individual link to the*
> *essential substance of the Creative Source...*
> *Astrology is a system that seeks to interpret*
> *the nature of the Universal Life Force*
> *as It moves, shapes, and creates human life and all events.*

> *The planets, signs, and houses, are not*
> *the causal elements of manifestation.*
> *They are, rather, the reflections of*
> *a transcendental synchronicity*
> *manifesting through the rhythms*
> *and timing of a cosmic clock."*

- Alan Oken, Soul Centered Astrology

Soul Development: Preparation, Crisis and Service

In addition to looking at what your Soul experiences at each of the twelve stages of development[9] indicated by the Zodiac signs, The Tibetan further groups the Zodiac signs into three **major stages of development** which he calls signs of **'preparation'**, **'crisis'** and **'service'**.

This helps us to understand the overall picture and get a sense of what is actually unfolding. As you read this remember your ascendant is the indicator of your Soul's journey and you may have the same Soul Sign for up to eight incarnations. That gives a sense of overall perspective in terms of your own Soul journey. That said now let's take a look at each of these three stages of preparation, crisis and service in turn:

Preparation

The first four signs are said to be signs of preparation: Aries, Taurus, Gemini and Cancer. In all aspects of our growth and development, there is a stage of preparation in which we must simply wait,

---

[9] In *"The Labours of Hercules: An Astrological Interpretation"* by Alice Bailey the Tibetan uses the mythology of Hercules to describe the stages of Soul development in each zodiac sign. Much insight can be gained about the current stage of your Soul's development, by meditating upon the appropriate 'Labor of Hercules' in this book.

experience, and grow. This is a vitally important stage when much is happening to prepare us for who we are becoming. This is like the embryonic stage of development in the womb.

During the embryonic stage something very amazing and miraculous happens. It is a process of cell division and definition. What I mean by that is that following the initial sperm and egg coming together, not only do the cells multiply fast, but they *take on form appropriate to purpose*. At first it's difficult to tell the difference between the embryo of a fish, a puppy, an elephant or a human! In those very early stages they are all similar, but it is during the first 12 weeks of pregnancy that the embryo defines itself. Its cells not only grow and multiply but they become distinctly human.

This is not a matter of conscious awareness or anyone 'thinking' about doing anything: it is a process that is guided by the Soul[10] that began before the incarnation, and unfolds naturally. The incarnating entity is in blissful ignorance of what he or she is about to become!

A very similar process is unfolding with our Soul's development in the first four Zodiac signs. We may or may not be consciously pursuing a spiritual path. We may be in blissful ignorance. However, at a Soul level we are still taking form and shape: in preparation for who we are to become as fully awakened beings of light.

Crisis

Then we come to the signs of crisis: Leo, Virgo, Libra and Scorpio. The word crisis is very interesting. We often think of a crisis as something traumatic, or bad, happening. However, one dictionary defines crisis as "*A crucial or decisive point or situation; a turning point.*" Indeed our modern word crisis has its origins in the Greek word *krinein*, which means 'to decide' and refers to a 'decisive point'.

---

[10] Modern science might say it is genetics, but then how did our consciousness incarnate and therefore inherit the genetics of a fish or a puppy or a human? That part of the process is driven by our consciousness at Soul level.

A crisis forces us to act or to move. It pushes us into the next stage of our development that is necessary for our growth. Imagine our infant growing nicely in the Mother's womb. He or she can't stay in there forever! Soon the day of 'crisis' will come, when that decisive turning point arrives and it is time to be born into the next phase of our existence outside the womb.

So it's appropriate that the first sign of crisis is Leo: because our first 'crisis' is the crisis of individuation and that is the path of Leo. Our journey of independence and individuation begins with birth. So it is at Soul level, when one has Leo Rising, one's whole life is about the journey of individuation.

Indeed this theme of individuation continues through Virgo and Libra until we reach the final stage of crisis in Scorpio, where we undergo another major transformation. The Tibetan says we 'do battle' in two signs: Leo and Scorpio. In Leo we battle for our individuality, in Scorpio we battle for our Soul. Scorpio brings a crisis between the temptations of our lower personality and the higher calling of our Soul, which 'pushes' us into the final stage of our development.

Service

The final four signs, Sagittarius, Capricorn, Aquarius and Pisces, are said to be the four signs of service. As a result of the experiences and development through the stages of preparation and crisis, the Soul now has *capacity*[11]. The preparation is done, and the Soul is now 'fit for purpose'. So what is this capacity and purpose? It is *the capacity to bring greater degrees of light into the world through the body of humanity, for the purpose of evolving consciousness through the evolution of human consciousness*. No small task!

If you ever felt at any point in your life as if *you* don't matter,

---

[11] Capacity: The ability to do, make, or accomplish something; capability. For example a comedian's *capacity* for making people laugh. Source: thefreedictionary.com

remember you are on a very important journey. Even though you may not be aware of it at times, you ARE a being of light, and your journey IS unfolding in perfect, Divine, timing!

The Rising Sign (Ascendant) is therefore considered by Soul-centered astrologers to be the most important sign in astrology, precisely because it indicates your Soul's path, it's purpose and expression in this lifetime, *and* the current stage of your Soul's overall development.

If you don't know your Rising Sign there's a calculator on my website that can tell you. Just enter your birth details at: http://ruthhadikin.com/whats-my-soul-sign.html

"The Soul is the reality lying behind the persona,
the mask of the Soul. It is the Soul or higher self
that comes first, as does the Rising sign.
The Rising sign, the Soul and the Soul's purpose
are therefore one and the same"

- Errol Weiner, Transpersonal Astrology

As we have seen, your Soul is on an unfolding journey in which it will eventually pass through each sign. The Soul's journey through the 12 signs of the Zodiac is explored by The Tibetan Master in "The Labours of Hercules: an astrological interpretation", where each of Hercules' 'labors' is a metaphor for a stage of our Soul Journey. At each 'stage' we can see how the Soul is growing and developing in a specific way. If the Soul spends up to eight incarnations in each sign, we can see that it would take the Soul up to 84 incarnations to complete one cycle through the Zodiac.

It's not really such a simple linear progression from A to B, the Soul's journey is much more complex than that, but for our purposes here it's a good analogy as we try to gain some understanding of the bigger picture with our 'small' minds!

The Soul's Purpose Through The Signs

In this fantastic journey, the Soul begins in Aries as *"a point of light in the mind of God"*. In Aries we see the initial spark of inspiration: the first impulse to exist. A Divine Idea that eventually translates into the *pulse of Life*. An original concept[12]. This point of light then becomes a beam of light in Taurus, multiple rays of light in Gemini, the 'diffuse light of form' in Cancer, and begins to individuate in Leo.

Your Rising Sign can therefore give you a sense of what your Soul has come to learn and do in this lifetime. With Soul Astrology we're always thinking on two levels:

- what might be happening at the level of our Soul-light, and
- how this is being refracted and/or expressed in our physical experience through the 'lens' of our personality.

This dual 'purpose' we might sum up as our overall *Soul Purpose*.

Your Soul Keynote

The Soul Keynote (from *"Esoteric Astrology"*) is something for you to contemplate. It has layers of meaning that will be revealed as you progress along your path. Read it slowly and contemplate it often. It is to be treated with respect, since it carries a sacred resonance that can align you with your Soul's essence. As you return and contemplate it from deeper levels within your own consciousness you will see new meaning in the words each time. The more you contemplate and meditate upon your Soul Keynote, the more its esoteric (inner) meaning will be revealed to you. It will awaken your own Soul's resonance.

What follows is a brief summary of what the Soul wants to express

---

[12] Concept: from Latin *conceptus* (a thought, purpose, also a conceiving, etc.), from concipere, present active infinitive of concipi (to take in, conceive); see conceive. Definition from http://wiktionary.com

(including the keynote for each Soul Sign), and what personality challenges this may present, at each stage of development through the twelve Zodiac signs:

ARIES RISING: THE ARIES SOUL

> *"The Light of Life Itself. "*
> - The Tibetan, *"Esoteric Astrology"*

If you have Aries Rising you are here to inspire others with Divine ideas. Your challenge is to tame your mind, cultivate your intuition and cultivate self-awareness to the point where you can distinguish Divine inspiration from the needs and drives of your own personality.

Soul Keynote:
> *"I come forth and from the plane of mind, I rule"*

TAURUS RISING: THE TAURUS SOUL

> *"The penetrating Light of the Path. "*
> - The Tibetan, *"Esoteric Astrology"*

If you have Taurus Rising you are here to release personal attachment and develop your senses for their highest purpose: to lead you to freedom, liberation, illumination and eventually enlightenment. Because Taurus resonates with peace, you tend to relax once you have all your creature comforts around you. Your biggest challenge is to stay awake, and not become complacent!

Soul Keynote:
> *"I see and when the Eye is opened, all is light"*

GEMINI RISING: THE GEMINI SOUL

> *"The Light of Interplay. "*
> - The Tibetan, *"Esoteric Astrology"*

If you have Gemini Rising you are here to teach right human relations. To do this you have to 'marry' the head-mind and the heart-mind and deeply understand relationship as the interplay of light. Because Gemini is so curious you are interested in everything, so your biggest challenge is to stay focused on your Soul path and not become distracted by conventional affairs.

Soul Keynote:
> *"I recognize my other self*
> *and in the waning of that self,*
> *I grow and glow"*

CANCER RISING: THE CANCER SOUL

> *"The Light within the form."*
> - The Tibetan, *"Esoteric Astrology"*

If you have Cancer Rising you are here to find your inner light, keep it lit, and flow greater degrees of compassion into the world. Because Cancer is the sign of mass consciousness, you feel the fear of the masses. The biggest challenge for you is not to succumb to fear but to allow it to move through you and become transmuted into compassion.

Soul Keynote:
> *"I build a lighted house and therein dwell"*

LEO RISING: THE LEO SOUL

"The Light of the Soul."
- The Tibetan, *"Esoteric Astrology"*

If you have Leo Rising you are here to usher in an era of heart-centered leadership. Your biggest challenge will be to not become identified with your actions. You are NOT what you do. There is a real self, and a false self, and it is your job to figure out which is which. Once you do this you align with your Soul purpose and your life becomes an expression of Divine Will.

Soul Keynote:

"I am That and That am I"

VIRGO RISING: THE VIRGO SOUL

"The blended dual Light."
- The Tibetan, *"Esoteric Astrology"*

With Virgo Rising you are here to be of service by flowing pure Divine love into the world through your work. Your biggest challenge is to not become discouraged and disheartened by the imperfection of the conventional world, which could leave you feeling anxious and critical. The perfection you seek is the perfection of the Soul. Let go of ideas of how things 'ought to be' and flow your love anyway.

Soul Keynote:

*"I am the Mother and the child.
I, God, I, matter am."*

LIBRA RISING: THE LIBRA SOUL

"The Light that moves to rest."
- The Tibetan, *"Esoteric Astrology"*

If you have Libra Rising you are here to bring in greater degrees of harmony and balance into the world through right relationship. In your case this comes from a deep understanding of the relationship between all things: including people and the beautiful planet we live on. Your biggest challenge is finding the balance between self and other in your own relationships. You matter as much as others. Not more, not less. Finding the point of balance that honors both is part of your life's work.

Soul Keynote:
*"I choose the way which leads
between the two great lines of force"*

SCORPIO RISING: THE SCORPIO SOUL

"The Light of Day."
- The Tibetan, *"Esoteric Astrology"*

If you have Scorpio Rising you are here to transform darkness into light through your own personal journey of healing and transformation. I've never met a Scorpio Soul who had an easy life. You are learning about energy and how to flow energy in ways that are beneficial to all concerned. It often feels like your life is one big struggle, but it is a struggle which makes you stronger, and comes at the appropriate time. Like a chick pecking it's way out of an egg, it's time now to hatch. Your biggest challenge is to not get caught in confrontation but to transmute the energy of any potentially volatile situation, which transforms you and lifts you to your highest potential.

Soul Keynote:
> *"Warrior I am and from the battle
> I emerge triumphant"*

SAGITTARIUS RISING: THE SAGITTARIUS SOUL

> *"A beam of directed, focused Light."*
> - The Tibetan, *"Esoteric Astrology"*

If you have Sagittarius Rising you are here to uplift humanity through the revelation of truth and wisdom. To do this you have to know truth for yourself, the deeper spiritual truth that lies beyond mind and mental concepts. Since Sagittarius is the sign of the philosopher you love to think and formulate philosophies to guide our way of living. Your biggest challenge is to release all man-made mental concepts, go beyond opinions and philosophy, and discover the underlying truth of your existence.

Soul Keynote:
> *"I see the goal.
> I reach that goal
> and then I see another"*

CAPRICORN RISING: THE CAPRICORN SOUL

> *"The Light of Initiation."*
> - The Tibetan, *"Esoteric Astrology"*

If you have Capricorn Rising you are here to express your vocation for the greater good. Your 'vocation' is your spiritual calling. You are here to listen to your spiritual calling and thereby make the sacred manifest in the world. At the highest level the Capricorn Soul is an engineer of light. You have an innate knowing of alchemy and how to manifest 'heaven on Earth'. Your biggest challenge is to use your talent and energy for spiritual purposes: to aspire to spiritual heights rather than becoming lost in the trappings of worldly wealth and achievement.

Soul Keynote:

> *"Lost am I in light supernal,*
> *yet on that light I turn my back"*

AQUARIUS RISING: THE AQUARIUS SOUL

> *"The Light that shines on Earth, across the sea."*
> - The Tibetan, *"Esoteric Astrology"*

If you have Aquarius Rising you are here to flow the dual waters of love and life into the world in ways that benefit humanity. Your biggest challenge will be to get out of your head and into your heart. The spiritual energy of which we speak flows through the heart and, as the fixed air sign, Aquarius is very much a sign of the mind. It is too easy for you to be lost in ideas. When you access the power of your heart you will use your mind as the vessel, the vase of Aquarius, through which you steadily direct the love and light that flows from your heart.

Soul Keynote:

> *"Water of life am I,*
> *poured forth for thirsty humanity"*

PISCES RISING: THE PISCES SOUL

> *"The Light of the World."*
> - The Tibetan, *"Esoteric Astrology"*

If you have Pisces Rising you are here to flow universal love into the world. The biggest challenge for you is to create appropriate boundaries, and not take things personally. Because you can feel what others feel, it is easy for you to take on other people's feelings. It is important for you to realize that everything you feel isn't yours, and that other people are responsible for their own feelings. Allow others to learn their own lessons, and stay in the place of love. This way you become a 'spiritual pacemaker', striking a heart-tone that others can follow.

Soul Keynote:

> *"I leave the Father's home*
> *and turning back, I save"*

What you are here to do and how you will do it.

From the twelve developmental stages above you can see how your Rising Sign points to *what* you are here to do in this physical lifetime! *How* you will do it, depends upon other factors in your chart, in particular your Sun and Moon signs. In astrology the Sun and Moon are known as the two 'luminaries', in other words the 'two lights'. They are thought of as the most personal planets in any birth chart because they have the most impact upon our lives. Their energy is therefore the most obvious and easiest to observe, and their

characteristics form a large part of what we call our personality. For this reason I often refer to them as the 'personality signs'.

For example if you are a Cancer Soul with a Gemini/Leo personality (Gemini Sun/ Leo Moon) you are here to flow compassion into the world (Cancer Soul) through writing, speaking, communicating (Gemini) and creative self-expression (Leo).

Whether you will experience and actualize the full spiritual potential of your Rising Sign or not, depends upon your *level of consciousness*. This is why meditation is so important. If you are spiritually asleep, you will naturally experience the qualities of your Rising Sign as part of your personality. As you awaken to your spiritual purpose you will feel a quickening, experiencing the subtle stirrings of your Soul's calling, through your Rising Sign. The Rising Sign bridges the worlds between spiritual sleep and awakening.

From Aries at the beginning through to Pisces at the end, the whole Zodiac can be viewed as developmental stages in human consciousness. What happens when a Soul reaches the end of the Zodiac (the twelfth sign of Pisces) and thus completes a cycle? It begins again at the first sign of Aries, progressing upwards through an endless spiraling, unfolding, blossoming, of human consciousness.

The Soul is a vehicle for spiritual energy, and so your Soul Sign indicates your innate core essence. It is the essence of who you really are, and your true nature as a spiritual being, but this all remains latent while you are identified with, and driven by, the needs of the ego-personality. Your spiritual awakening involves realizing this core energy and expressing it into the world, thereby becoming a fully Soul-Centered individual.

3. The Twelve Soul Signs

In Soul Astrology we are often speaking on two levels. It is important to understand the difference between the ego-personality expression of our Soul Sign and its higher, Soul-Centered expression. The 12 Zodiac signs represent 12 Divine Intelligences. In their purest form these energies carry a high vibration and Divine Purpose. By the time this energy has filtered its way through our foggy, confused and conditioned, egoic human mind, its original "tune" is distorted somewhat. This 'distorted' expression of the energy is our ego-personality and once we have fully 'healed' by clearing our conditioned behavior we are said to be *fully integrated*. In other words the process of *personality-Soul fusion* as described in Chapter 1 is then complete. We can then fully express the Soul Centered vibration of our Soul Sign.

Whether you will experience and actualize the full spiritual potential of your Soul Sign or not, depends upon your level of consciousness. If you are spiritually asleep, you will naturally experience the qualities of your Soul Sign as an inherent part of your personality. As you awaken to your spiritual purpose you will feel a quickening, experiencing the subtle stirrings of your Soul's calling, through your Rising Sign. The Rising Sign bridges the worlds between sleep and awakening.

"This physical awakening experience is directly related to the fact that the Rising Sign is the central factor connected to spiritual awakening. We incarnate into a new life, we awake each morning into a new life; and we are born again into a new life when we awake to spiritual purpose in our lives."

– Errol Weiner, Transpersonal Astrology

If we think of the octaves of the musical scale, we can get an idea about the lower and higher vibrations of each sign. The lower octaves are fear-based and come from externally imposed ideas about how we ought to be, while the higher octaves are love-based and arise purely from within our own heart. This is an important key, not only to understanding the lower and higher expressions of each sign, but for knowing how to shift from lower to higher expressions. The shift is from fear to love, but this is meaningless until we experience the shift in perspective that comes from navigating the octaves on the spiritual spectrum. When you come from a place of love within, you will naturally express the highest octaves of your Soul Sign.

Each Soul Sign is here to learn and develop in specific ways, in this lifetime. You are here to grow into what you may become: your full potential as a spiritual being. Just as an infant that is learning to speak isn't learning a 'lesson' as such, but is rather *unfolding his natural potential*, so it is the same with your Soul work. Likewise your Soul work shows up naturally, as major themes throughout your life, calling you to awaken, live, and rise to the highest octaves of your Soul Sign.

"The Rising Sign is the powerhouse – the central electromagnetic centre of one's life (chart) and this energy begins to be released when one awakens."

- Errol Weiner, Transpersonal Astrology

Aries Rising - The Aries Soul

If you have Aries Rising you can consider Aries to be your 'Soul Sign' and consider yourself to be an 'Aries Soul'. Simply put, if you have Aries Rising you are here to express the highest 'octave', the highest spiritual potential of Aries that you possibly can in this lifetime.

At Soul level Aries is a sign of *higher mind* and plays a vital role in the development of the antahkarana[13], or "Rainbow Bridge" between higher and lower mind. This is why Aries is associated with the brow, forehead, eyes, and is symbolized by the horns of the Ram. It is commonly believed that the eyes are the windows of the Soul and it is through the eyes that we can glimpse higher mind, or Soul. This is why Aries is also highly intuitive and the type of intuition associated with Aries is that of *direct knowing*. Once one can attune to subtle spiritual energy at Soul level, wisdom reveals itself fully and completely without having to go through the lower mental process of thought, which is relatively slow by comparison. So this Arian type of intuition is an *immediate direct knowing that is beyond thought*.

To be aware of knowledge at this level one must cultivate awareness through *direct perception* of the full spectrum of energy, from the grossest energetic movement to the finest spiritual subtle ripples. Yet at personality level Aries can be anything but subtle and may even develop a reputation for being direct to the point of bluntness, self-absorbed, and oblivious of the needs of those around them! In fact, this is all normal and is part and parcel of what Aries is learning at this stage of Soul development.

---

[13] "In Hindu philosophy, the antahkarana (Sanskrit: the inner cause) refers to the *totality* of two levels of mind, namely the buddhi, the intellect or higher mind, and the manas, the middle levels of mind which (according to theosophy) exist as or include the mental body. Antahkarana has also been called the link between the middle and higher mind, the reincarnating part of the mind." - from https://en.wikipedia.org/wiki/Antahkarana

As the first sign of the Zodiac Aries is, in many ways, the 'baby' of the Zodiac. There can be an innocence and naïveté around Aries, with an expectation that life events should just be easy and somehow simpler than they often turn out to be in practice. It's as if they have no experience of life which, in a sense, is true at Soul level. In *"Esoteric Astrology"* the Tibetan describes the Soul in Aries as a *"point of light in the mind of God"* and this simple phrase can tell us much about the Soul experience in Aries.

Remember Aries is a sign of the mind, so Aries comes filled with excitement, ideas, inspiration and enthusiasm for the journey. The whole blueprint for the journey ahead is mapped out in his (or her) mind and Aries brings the drive and the impetus to get started. It's like that stage of a vacation or trip where you know where you are going and why, and the day has finally arrived. The time is now! You are full of enthusiasm, brimming over with excitement, and you take your first eager steps down the road.

That is the energy of Aries. Nothing has happened yet to dampen your enthusiasm. You haven't hit any obstacles or glitches, and because you can't even foresee that there could possibly be any, you haven't planned or prepared for them. Because you have never walked this path before, you can't possibly imagine what could happen, which also means you have very few coping skills.

Arians are great people to have around at the beginning of a project because their innate inspiration and childlike enthusiasm can really put a light under the fire, ignite the project and get it started, but if you leave Aries managing the dull, day to day problems that will inevitably arise, you will soon see his feathers droop and his light go out, like an Eagle caught in a rainstorm pathetically sitting dripping in a tree waiting to dry out before he can majestically soar again.

Often Aries has the initial idea or impulse and may lack the next step. He can also be childlike in his expectation that ideas should just instantly manifest into reality, with no further effort on his part. It's as though the idea of cake should be enough in itself.

"I just thought of it, so where's my cake?" Like a small child he seems oblivious to the reality of what resources, skill and effort may be required to create cake!

Associated with this is Aries tendency to just put out ideas and expect others to pick up the ball. There is an important balance needed whereby Aries tends to his own creative projects (the 'seeds' of his inspiration) long enough for them to manifest and become established, before he hands them over too quickly to others. This way Aries learns to add skill to his amazing vision.

Aries is a sign of vision, courage, boldness, leadership and drive. Imagine the military commander who can see a way forward through the forest. He isn't personally going to cut down the trees! He'll order someone else to do that because he is keeping his eye on the horizon, on the vision, and his concern is on driving through, pushing ahead, reaching that goal. Also, in his narrow focus, he may have given little thought with regard to the wider implications of cutting down trees and what that could mean for the ecosystem in the long term. So we can see that Aries may also sometimes have a tendency towards blinkered vision: being preoccupied with only his own immediate issues and not considering the wider implications of his actions on others and his environment.

Aries is not a loner, he is a leader and a leader needs someone to lead. That is why Aries is the sign of the Ram. A Ram needs a flock and wherever Aries goes, people follow. Because of his innate intuition and inspiring vision, people are naturally drawn to Aries. His confidence and vision are contagious and people naturally want to follow. So this brings Aries a vital lesson in responsibility. As much as he would like to be a free individual, Aries is part of the flock and wherever he goes others follow. So he needs to carefully review his motives, raise his sights, and ensure that he is leading his flock onto the highest path, and not the lowest.

When Aries awakens spiritually and listens to his highest calling, he is an inspiring spiritual leader. Guiding others with his altruistic vision towards the highest goals of all: self-realization, spiritual awakening and enlightenment. If he is sleeping (in a spiritual sense) he may be mis-leading people, taking actions and decisions that are either selfish impulses from his own ego, or simply leading others from ignorance, by being too caught up through his own conditioning in a materially-driven, selfish and destructive society.

Your Aries Soul work shows up as major themes throughout life, which may relate to these areas:

- Cultivating self-awareness: awareness of both your own energy field, and the effects and impact of your energy and actions on those around you. This will also awaken awareness of your spiritual energy.

- Taming your mind: evaluating the billions of ideas that pass through your mind and learning to exercise judgment about which ones are most beneficial to pursue.

- Focusing, effort, and tenacity: sticking with your creative projects and ideas long enough to birth them into reality, and applying the necessary personal effort to make it happen.

- Expanding your mind. Look deep within to see where your own worldview may be limited, and be limiting you. You are on a fantastic journey from lower to higher mind!

- Becoming familiar (through self-observation) with the *Rainbow Bridge* from lower to higher mind, so you can distinguish between an 'impulse to act' that arises from your lower egoic mind, and one arising from higher, Divine mind.

"The Ascendant is directly concerned with the purpose and the plan, and the more one is prepared to attune to and co-operate with the higher self the more one can unfold and manifest the energies of the Rising Sign and thus fulfill one's purpose"

- Errol Weiner, Transpersonal Astrology

If you have Aries Rising you are here to ignite and inspire others with an infusion of Divine ideas, sacred fire, and spiritual energy so they may realize their own spiritual potential. Before you can do this you must cultivate self-awareness and realize your spiritual potential, so you can skillfully navigate the full spectrum of the Rainbow Bridge at will: accessing the highest realms of consciousness that are currently humanly possible, and living your life as the true spiritual "Rainbow Warrior" that you are.

Key Points:

- If you have Aries Rising you can think of yourself as an Aries soul.
- Cultivating self-awareness will support your awakening to your spiritual purpose.
- Expand your mind. Look deep within to see where your own worldview may be limited, and limiting you.
- Be aware of how your energy, thoughts and actions affect others.
- You are here to ignite and inspire others with an infusion of Divine ideas, sacred fire, and spiritual energy.

Taurus Rising - The Taurus Soul

If you have Taurus Rising you can consider Taurus to be your 'Soul Sign' and consider yourself to be a Taurus Soul. Simply put, if you have Taurus Rising you are here to express the highest 'octave', the highest spiritual potential of Taurus that you possibly can in this lifetime.

According to *"Esoteric Astrology"* if you have Taurus Rising you are here to realize the freedom that comes with releasing personal desire and attachment. This sacred sign is associated with the opening of the third eye, and the highest spiritual illumination and realization, right up to full enlightenment. The Buddha was born, became enlightened and passed into parinirvana[14] during the time of Taurus.

The association between Taurus and enlightenment cannot be ignored and the power of this sign to bring spiritual illumination cannot be underestimated. But what do we mean by releasing desire and attachment? It sounds a bit impoverished and miserable, especially when you think that most Taureans love to indulge their sense-pleasures! More cake anyone?

To understand the spiritual path of Taurus, true freedom, and the liberation that the release of attachment brings, we can simply look to the teachings of Buddha himself. Why not? He was a Taurus after all! Dynamic Buddhist Nun Ven. Robina Courtin actually uses the analogy of chocolate cake to provide a clear, humorous, and eloquent explanation of what Buddha meant by attachment. It is not the *pleasure* of chocolate cake that causes us suffering, but our *attachment* to it.

When we are attached we experience an exaggerated idea about the object of attachment, for example chocolate cake. Yet we believe this exaggerated idea to be true. Then if we don't get the object of our attachment (in this case chocolate cake) we feel upset and if we get too much of it we feel sick! Too little, and we suffer, too much, and we still suffer. This is because our distorted exaggerated idea leads us to believe that the cake itself is the *source* of pleasure.

If this were absolutely true, then the more cake we had, the more pleasure we would have, but this is clearly not so! Anyone who has ever eaten too much at Christmas can vouch for that! More cake leads to suffering, not pleasure. This is the nature of attachment. In other words it is not the *objects themselves* that cause our

---

[14] "In Buddhism, the term parinirvana (Sanskrit: parinirvāṇa; Pali: parinibbāna) is commonly used to refer to nirvana-after-death, which occurs upon the death of the body of someone who has attained nirvana during his or her lifetime." - Wikipedia at https://en.wikipedia.org/wiki/Parinirvana

unhappiness and suffering, but rather our conditioning and our *exaggerated and distorted ideas* about what will really make us happy.

Without this false exaggerated idea called attachment, we would enjoy the pleasure without the pain. Without attachment we wouldn't be upset if there was no chocolate cake, and we wouldn't over-indulge if there was. The cake would have no power over us, and we could simply take it or leave it. In this example we're using cake to keep it simple, but you can substitute any of the things we humans get attached to: our homes, our friends, lovers, spouses, jobs, money, food, alcohol, tobacco, drugs, gambling, pets, etc. Even our closest loved ones and family.

When we apply this same principle to our family, we can see that it is our *attachment* that causes most of our problems. Our exaggerated and distorted ideas about *how things ought to be* are at the root of most of our suffering. Imagine if we could release all of our false ideas and expectations and simply enjoy things, and people, *exactly as they are*?

Releasing personal desire and attachment is only the beginning of a journey that takes Taurus into the depths of our true nature as spiritual beings.

Releasing attachment is just the beginning. In many spiritual traditions releasing attachment would be considered to be a *preliminary practice*. Preliminary practices are for the beginning stage of the spiritual path, and they prepare us for the later stages. In many traditions releasing attachment is considered a preliminary practice because it prepares you for more advanced practices, which you would be unable to focus on if you were still distracted by (and preoccupied with) your everyday attachments!

On an everyday level, most of us organize our lives around our attachments: When we will have our next cup of tea, coffee, meal, cigarette, drink, cake, movie, TV show, game, etc. If we are not aware of what is happening, our whole life simply becomes one of pandering to our attachments, and getting them met. So first freeing ourselves of these attachments is seen as a necessary step that creates the space and freedom to pursue a serious spiritual path. So what might be the more advanced experiences of Taurus once we have freed ourselves from personal desire and attachment?

The spiritual path of Taurus involves the skilled and masterful use of your senses to explore spiritual experiences and help you to realize your true nature. Once you stop hi-jacking your own senses with attachments, you are able to use your sense-perception for deep self-exploration. Releasing attachment is essential if you are to develop clear perception. You then become capable of examining the true nature of reality through *direct perception*. With this capacity you can see that the whole of humanity is one body, and the nature of that body is light. This is why the sign of Taurus is associated with illumination.

As we mentioned in Chapter 1, we live most of our lives caught in the illusion of ourselves as a separate entity, rather than anchoring our consciousness in the truth of our being as a unique individual within this body of humanity. This illusion of separation causes fear to arise. We all experience fear and it is part of our human journey from being an innocent newborn, to pass through the experience of fear and separation, to once again return to a deeper spiritual connection. The form that fear takes is different for each of us, depending upon our karma[15] and Soul Sign.

For Taurus, fear comes with attachment, as we try to hold on to the things we fear to lose. Taurus Rising brings the capacity and predisposition to experience the physical world mainly though the senses. Sense perception is an innate ability. Sensuality is a way of experiencing life. When that beautiful and natural sensuality is tainted by attachment, the so-called 'negative' (or fear-based) expressions of Taurus arise (acquisitiveness and possessiveness).

In Chapter 2 we discussed how our spiritual development passes

[15] See "Social Conditioning and Karma" in Chapter 1.

through several growth (developmental) stages, which were described by the great yogi Patanjali as 'bodies'[16]. As we collectively experience the intellectual stage of our spiritual journey (Patanjali's mental body), fear arises as a side-effect of our capacity to create mental concepts. Basically the more we can think, the more we can experience fear. One such mental concept is the idea that 'I' am separate, which we described in Chapter 1. This concept then branches off into ideas of ownership: that this separate 'I' possesses things. For example 'I' leads to 'me', which leads to an *idea* of "mine".

When Taurus experiences fear, she becomes more avaricious and possessive, as though having more things would make the fear go away. When she releases fear and lives from love, she is able to enjoy all her senses without the pain of attachment.

Once the process of releasing attachment is complete, fear no longer arises and is replaced be the deep inner peace that Taurus so desires. Then the deeper journey of Taurus begins. Once all habitual 'grasping' and 'aversion' has ceased, it is possible to rest in a state

known as 'calm abiding'. This is where your attention rests calmly in full awareness of the present moment. You simply rest in the state of *awareness* itself.

---

[16] Patanjali associated manomay kosh (mental body) with the element of water and we can see that throughout the Piscean Age (astrologically Pisces is the mutable water sign), which spanned from around the time of Christ to our modern era, the body of humanity has largely been cultivating, developing and refining the intellect and, more recently, acknowledging and cultivating emotional intelligence. In some eastern traditions intellect and emotions are not considered separate but both are seen as aspects of the mental body.

"Rest naturally, like a small child.
Rest like an ocean without waves.
Rest with clarity, like a candle flame.
Rest without self-concern, like a corpse.
Rest unmoving like a mountain."

- Milarepa

From this resting place, all is observed. When your energy is no longer invested in chasing after objects outside of you, your inner world begins to open up, through your senses. Sights, sounds, smells, tastes, sensations, all become sharper and clearer. Eventually you even let go of desiring sensual stimulation, and simply rest in the awareness of things exactly as they are.

Through this awakening of awareness, you begin to realize that your senses are actually portals of light. It has been written that every pore of your body is a 'buddha eye'. This refers to the realization that all your sensory experiences are actually allowing more light to enter into, and emanate from, your physical body.

This experience of simply resting in the state of awareness allows a natural process of 'enlightenment' to unfold, leading to an extremely advanced spiritual level where you can actualize what is known as the light or *rainbow body*[17]. The path of enlightenment and

illumination is particularly associated with the sign of Taurus. We'll say more about that in Chapter 4.

If you have Taurus Rising you are here to release attachment and develop your senses for their highest purpose: to lead you to

---

[17] There are many well-documented accounts from the Tibetan tradition (and others) of yogis attaining spiritual realization to the degree that their physical bodies shrink and/or liberate as their consciousness forms a non-material *body of light* know as a *rainbow body*, at the time of their 'death'. Read more at https://en.wikipedia.org/wiki/Rainbow_body

freedom, liberation, illumination and eventually enlightenment. Then your full spiritual potential will blossom, you will truly live from love and all around you will benefit from basking in your pure fragrant light.

> **Key Points:**
> - If you have Taurus Rising you can think of yourself as a Taurus soul.
> - Cultivating sense-perception without attachment will support you in awakening to your spiritual purpose.
> - Look deep within to see the difference between love and attachment.
> - Watch your own thoughts, words and actions, to check your motivation.
> - You don't need to 'lose' the things you love, only your attachment to them! Then you can enjoy the pleasure of your senses without the pain of attachment.

Gemini Rising - The Gemini Soul

If you have Gemini Rising you can consider Gemini to be your 'Soul Sign' and consider yourself to be a Gemini Soul. Simply put, if you have Gemini Rising you are here to express the highest 'octave', the highest spiritual potential of Gemini that you possibly can in this lifetime.

The sign of Gemini is associated with all aspects of communication: speaking, talking, writing, thinking, and all at lightning-fast speed. Fast-talking, fast-moving, fast-thinking, ever-moving, restless fidgety Gemini! Conventionally Gemini is associated with gossip and fickleness yet there is so much more depth to this highly significant sign, than first meets the eye.

According to *"Esoteric Astrology"*, Gemini is the only sign that is connected to the remaining eleven signs of the Zodiac. Well wouldn't that make sense from the sign of connection? If we think weaving, connection, and *communion*, we are starting to touch upon the deeper spiritual significance of Gemini. Gemini takes the threads of Life, the threads of the Universe, and weaves them all together into one cohesive whole. No small task.

> *"I cannot too strongly reiterate the constant necessity*
> *for you to think in terms of energies*
> *and forces, of lines of force, and energy relationships...*
> *The whole story of astrology is, in reality,*
> *one of magnetic and magical interplay for the production*
> *or externalization of the inner reality"*

-The Tibetan, *"Esoteric Astrology"*

Yet we can go even deeper. In his book *"The Self-Aware Universe"* quantum physicist Dr. Amit Goswami explains how consciousness is the basic 'building block' of the Universe (and all Universes). Everything is 'made' of consciousness. So the very *'threads of Life'* that Gemini is weaving, are therefore *threads of consciousness*. Now we're talking! (Or not, as the case may be)! Gemini knows that words are powerful, but that thoughts are even more powerful, and consciousness beyond thought is even more powerful again.

The deeper purpose and motive[18] underlying Gemini's sometimes incessant chatter, is an innate need: not only for connection but for deeper communion. Gemini is the sign of *holy communion* in the simplest and most sacred sense of *communing with all that is healthy, healed and whole (holy)*. Gemini can be thought of as the 'connective tissue' of the Universe: permeating, weaving through, and touching, everything and every no-thing! It is in Gemini that consciousness becomes aware of itself, by reflecting itself back to itself, through the illusion of another. This is one of the deepest esoteric mysteries of Gemini.

---

[18] Motive: *"that which inwardly moves a person to behave a certain way"* from Online Etymology Dictionary at http://etymonline.com/index.php?term=motive

As the mutable air sign Gemini is a sign of mind, and changeable mind at that! If we observe closely (and intelligent Gemini is excellent at noticing things!) we can see how it is the everyday working of the mind that divides and separates. From the all-inclusive experience of this eternal present moment, the mind steps in and begins separating and categorizing: "That is a tree". "There goes a plane". "Here is my computer". "There is a cat". "This is my house". If you really watch your own mind you will see it does this constantly. From the eternal Universal dance of interconnected energy, the mental mind isolates and labels 'things', and this becomes a habit until all we see are 'things' and we lose sight of the continuity of the Universe.

The Gemini mind divides and separates, creating polarity and duality. Me and You. Male and Female. This and That. Yet we are only ever a moment away from stepping outside of this mental dialogue and becoming aware once more of the Universal consciousness that is all that is. This awareness would also be a function of Gemini, through which he has an innate understanding of relationship. Because Gemini is connected to everything, he can see how everything fits together. Gemini can see the big picture and the finer details at one and the same time.

Here then is the key to understanding both the highest spiritual purpose of Gemini, and his lower fear-based expressions. One of the (many) dualities that Gemini needs to resolve, is the separation of the head-mind, and the heart-mind. Remember, in reality there is no separation. As we mentioned earlier, the separation is an illusion created by the mental aspect of mind. If we really understand Dr. Goswami's hypothesis of *everything being consciousness* then we could in fact say that, in a sense, everything is also 'mind'. We also mentioned earlier that Patanjali, one of the founders of modern yoga,

referred to this 'Higher Mind' as *Universal Mind*. Perhaps it is also analogous to what psychologist Carl Jung called the *collective consciousness*. This all-inclusive Universal Mind encapsulates the wholeness of our being. In Universal Mind there is no separation.

If you have Gemini Rising you can consider yourself to be a Gemini Soul and you are here to learn *right human relations* yourself so you can teach it. To do this you have to 'marry' your head-mind and your heart-mind and deeply understand relationship as the *interplay of light*. Because Gemini is so curious you are interested in everything, so your biggest challenge is to stay focused on your Soul path and not become distracted by conventional affairs.

The highest octave of Gemini accesses the intelligence of the heart through higher love. You learn this from experience when you spend more time in your heart and realize that when you are heart-centered, there really is no separation. It is the illusion of separation itself that creates fear. The danger for Gemini is that you may weave your own web of thoughts, and then get caught in them yourself. Always remember how the Gemini mind separates, labels and categorizes. This is a brilliant device that you have created, which allows you to process vast unimaginable amounts of information.

You are an ace at mental processing, but mental processing is only a tool. It is a device that we use for our everyday living, not the essence of our being. If you become identified with your mental processes, you begin to feel lifeless. When you spend too much time thinking, not only do you become identified with your thoughts, but you also begin to notice something is 'missing' in your life. You become 'disconnected' from your heart, spirit and Soul, and the playful light of Gemini begins to grow dim.

When Gemini gets 'lost' inside his own head the illusion of separation becomes exaggerated. You can become fearful and may spend too much time talking about, and processing, mental information in a scattered and unfocused way. This can lead to mental overwhelm, burnout, anxiety and even fatigue. The solution is to go deeper in meditation, learning to focus your attention in the heart, resting peacefully in your heart center. From this place of peace within, you realize that there is no separation, that we are all one and, indeed, all mental concepts arise from the one source.

Energy follows attention and through the practice of meditation (in other words learning to focus your attention) you begin to access Universal Mind and set yourself free from the 'prison' of lower mind and mental processing. Universal Mind includes your heart and Soul. Mental processing excludes everything else. Once you perfect the art of keeping your attention in Universal Mind you resolve the final duality of Gemini: that of personality and Soul.

"I recognize my other self
and in the waning of that self,
I grow and glow"

- The Tibetan, *"Esoteric Astrology"*

If you have Gemini Rising you are here to recognize and teach the interrelatedness of all things through loving awareness. To do this you must first release the fear-based expression of Gemini, which comes as a result of being over-identified with your thoughts.

You are not what you think. It is vital that you meditate or take up some similar practice for focusing your attention, so you can go beyond mental processing, and realize for yourself the reality of Universal Mind.

From this higher perspective you will experience your Soul as the truth of your Being and experience the highest wisdom that comes through deep connection and communion with higher Love, and all that is.

> **Key Points:**
>
> - If you have Gemini Rising you can think of yourself as a Gemini Soul.
> - The deeper purpose of Gemini is communion: reconnection with all that is, and realization of Universal Mind.
> - To realize (and live) from Higher Mind Gemini has to resolve polarity and duality, by recognizing that all is one.
> - Through observing the workings of the mind as it creates and resolves duality, Gemini awakens an innate knowing of right relationship.
> - Energy follows attention, so one of the main skills that the Gemini Soul is mastering, is the art of choosing where you place your attention, and holding focus.
> - Regular meditation is vital for expanding your awareness and developing the necessary focused attention.

Cancer Rising - The Cancer Soul

If you have Cancer Rising you can consider Cancer to be your 'Soul Sign' and consider yourself to be a Cancer Soul. Simply put, if you have Cancer Rising you are here to express the highest 'octave', the highest spiritual potential of Cancer that you possibly can in this lifetime.

The sign of Cancer is associated with home, food, nourishment, family, nurturing, childbirth, Motherhood, empathy, compassion and emotional intelligence. Symbolized by the Crab it is also associated with the ocean, and like a crab it is associated with being near the ocean, yet living on the land. Esoterically there are deep mysteries associated with the 'quiet' sign of Cancer.

Cancer is a small constellation, but that shouldn't lead us to underestimate her power. Cancer is the *cardinal water* sign, and all cardinal signs are here to take the lead in some way: to pioneer, introduce enlightened ideas and new ways of being into a specific area. In the case of Cancer, that area is emotions. All water signs are about mastery of emotions so as the cardinal water sign, Cancer is here to take the lead in terms of our personal emotional development and lead us into a new era in the evolution of human consciousness through emotional intelligence.

Not only does our Rising Sign indicate our Soul's journey of awakening (how we 'awaken' into our spiritual reality), but also it indicates how we 'awaken' or are born into the world, and indeed how we awaken and flow our energy into the world each morning. With Cancer Rising you are learning how to nourish yourself and others, on a daily basis and throughout your life, with your Soul-light. You are learning about spiritual light on many levels, developing awareness of it, and understanding the healing and nurturing qualities of light.

The whole journey of your Soul through the twelve Zodiac signs is a story of light, building up the volume of light in your light-body (your Soul), while simultaneously increasing the amount of light that can be held and processed in your physical body. When your Soul is in Cancer there is the potential for you to become more aware of your Soul-light. According to *"Esoteric Astrology"* all incarnations happen in Cancer. Taking into account that Cancer is the light within the form, it also seems that the formation and building of your light body also happens at this stage, hence the Soul keynote for Cancer referring to a 'lighted house':

"I build a lighted house and therein dwell"

-The Tibetan, *"Esoteric Astrology"*

Your Rising Sign indicates how you awaken into our world, into new situations, and into stages of consciousness. According to the Tibetan in *"The Labours of Hercules: An Astrological Interpretation"*, Cancer is the last of the four signs of 'preparation' (see Chapter 2) and as a cardinal sign, 'leads' you into the next phase of your Soul's development. If you have Cancer Rising you are about to 'leave the womb' in a spiritual sense, and be born into the next phase of your Soul's development. It marks a 'rite of passage' where you are maturing into your Soul's awakening.

So not only does your Rising Sign indicate your path of awakening, but also the sign of Cancer is about birth and awakening. In Cancer you experience the first glimmer of your Soul's presence. You begin to realize that you have a Soul and are so much more than just your physical body. You awaken to a greater aspect of your being. If you have Cancer Rising you are here to find your Soul-light and, like a lighthouse-keeper, keep your light lit, no matter what is going on in the world around you. Even if it sometimes feels like trying to keep a candle alight in a howling gale!

The Zodiac uses animal symbols to convey an impression of energetic qualities. The energy of Cancer is crab-like in many ways, for example walking sideways! Cancerians tend to approach new situations side-on, as they feel their way forward. If you have Cancer Rising you may have a tendency to approach new people, places and situations with caution, possibly a little trepidation, and maybe come at it sideways until you can establish a feeling of safety for yourself.

This caution is not without reason. Just like you would cup your hand around a candle flame in the wind, to prevent it from being blown out, so a Cancer Soul has an innate knowing that your inner light has to somehow be protected from the outer world, to preserve it's sacred qualities until it is strong enough to shine like the Sun irrespective of outer conditions. Just as a mother is protective of a vulnerable infant, until the child has grown into independence, so with a Cancer Soul you have a built-in sense of the importance of protecting and nurturing your emerging Soul-light within.

Have you ever watched crabs near the ocean? They have the ability to quickly bury themselves in the sand and 'hunker down' to wait until the most dangerous tides have passed. We can use this symbology to understand the Soul's journey in Cancer. It is about where you place your attention. Because Cancer has the ability to attune to mass consciousness, it is too easy for Cancer to be swept away on the current tide of mass consciousness, fear and emotional over-reacting. This is where the Cancer Soul needs to learn how to 'hunker down' and ride out the tide. You do this by keeping your attention on your own light, and not the tsunami of mass human emotion that is (apparently) heading your way. When you do this you learn how to keep your Soul-flame alight, and by so doing you realize that this is the real key to changing the world.

> *"Every jewel is intimately connected with*
> *all other jewels in the universe,*
> *and a change in one jewel means*
> *a change, however slight, in every other jewel"*

- Stephen Mitchell

As the sign of mass consciousness Cancer has a built-in radar, which you can send out to sense the mood and feelings of the collective. Your innate sense of connectedness with all of humanity is the source from which your deep empathy (and ultimately great compassion) arises. This ability to feel what others are feeling, is the key to understanding both the highest spiritual purpose of Cancer and the ego-based challenges at personality level.

Part of the journey for a Cancerian Soul is to cultivate intuition. When you can tap into mass consciousness, it isn't easy to hear your own voice over and above the many. This is another reason why the sign of Cancer is associated with fear and caution. If you have Cancer Rising, it is likely that you are aware of fear on waking each morning. This is because when you first awaken and your mind is quiet, this is the time that you are most tuned-in to the consciousness of the masses, and it is a simple fact that there is a lot of fear rippling through humanity at the moment. You are aware of it. You feel it.

All cardinal signs are courageous signs of leadership. This may not be how you initially think of the sign of Cancer, but imagine the courage that is needed to stay focused on compassion in the face of a tide of human suffering and fear. On a very practical level, with Cancer Rising your first act of courage is to get out of bed in the morning, in the face of all fear, and to stay focused on your light throughout your day!

As the sign of emotional intelligence, part of your work in this lifetime is learning how to 'navigate' through emotional frequencies so you don't keep your attention on the wavelength of fear, but are able to transcend it and hold a higher emotional 'tone' within your own being. You understand the truth of our connectedness, by experiencing for yourself that the changes you make within your own being, have a definite ripple-effect in the consciousness of humanity, and that you have the power to reduce fear in the world by first and foremost transforming it into compassion within yourself. This process of emotional evolution through the water signs begins in Cancer (cardinal water), is consolidated in Scorpio (fixed water) and culminates in Pisces (mutable water).

"Love and compassion are necessities, not luxuries.
Without them humanity cannot survive."

- HH XIV Dalai Lama

Through your own experience you begin to learn that compassion is not just an idea or a philosophy, but a real tangible energy that you can consciously flow through your own heart-center, and by doing so you change the 'flavor' in the ocean of human consciousness. The Dalai Lama has Cancer Rising and has spent a lifetime teaching, demonstrating and transmitting compassion and unconditional love across all cultures and boundaries. This is the true nourishment that Cancer brings to the world: spiritual nourishment. When you transcend fear you will come to know that the 'Divine nectar' of compassion, which flows through your heart, is what truly nurtures and nourishes humanity on our journey of evolving consciousness. If you have Cancer Rising you are here to bring compassion and unconditional love into the world in ways that you possibly cannot imagine. You do this by overcoming fear and attachment, cultivating emotional intelligence and fine-tuning your own intuition. Your spiritual home is the light that you always carry within, the whole world is your family, and you selflessly nourish others primarily through the emanation of your inner light.

Key Points:

- If you have Cancer Rising you can think of yourself as a Cancer Soul.
- The deeper purpose of Cancer is to selflessly nourish others through compassion and unconditional love.
- To realize the highest purpose of Cancer, the Cancer Soul needs to transcend fear and cultivate intuition.
- This is achieved by keeping one's attention on one's inner light, and cultivating emotional intelligence to the degree that you can navigate through emotional wavelengths.
- Energy follows attention, so one of the main skills that the Cancer Soul is mastering, is holding focus on your inner light, which encourages it to grow.
- The true nourishment that Cancer brings to the world is spiritual nourishment, by flowing compassion and unconditional love into the world.

Leo Rising - The Leo Soul

If you have Leo Rising you can consider Leo to be your 'Soul Sign' and consider yourself to be a Leo Soul. Simply put, if you have Leo Rising you are here to express the highest 'octave', the highest spiritual potential of Leo that you possibly can in this lifetime.

The regal sign of Leo is associated with Kings, royalty, nobility, drama, theater, actors, children, creativity and play. Leo is the sign of Self-realization: the path that takes us from self-consciousness, through self-awareness, to ultimate Self-realization. Along the way we may develop a misguided sense of self-importance but this is understandable when we consider our experience as we pass through the Leo stage of our Soul's journey. If you have Leo Rising you are part of the group of Leo Souls who are here to usher in an era of heart-centered leadership through creative expression of Divine Will. Before you can reach this highest potential, you need to overcome the fear-based expressions of Leo so you may live your life through the highest love-based expression of Leo. This means fully understanding the ego-personality so that you can rise above it. There is a false self and a real Self and it is Leo's job to figure out which is which. The Leo stage of our Soul's journey is a highly significant developmental milestone in the evolution of human consciousness. Leo is indeed very important, but not in the self-important way that the ego would like to think!

Whether we have personal planets in Leo or not, this stage of Soul development is relevant to us all because right now we are all at varying stages of the *individuation process* symbolized by Leo. Because the whole of humanity is awakening through this process Leo can be thought of as very much a sign for our times[19].

In *"Esoteric Astrology"*, the Tibetan Master explains that we 'do battle' in two signs: Leo and Scorpio. In Leo we are fighting for our individuality while, at a later stage, the battle in Scorpio is for our Soul. The journey of Leo is very much one of individuation, and recognizing the *importance* of the individual is a vital step in this process. It is Leo's job to stand up and say "what about ME?"

A newborn infant is a bundle of pure awareness. They are aware that they are hungry, they cry, they get fed. They are aware that they are uncomfortable, they cry, someone (hopefully) comes to make them feel comfortable again. At this stage there is no idea of 'me' yet. This is an important point to recognize, if we are to fully understand the individuation process.

*"No-one is free who has not obtained
the Empire of himself"*

- Pythagoras

---

[19] Read more about the significance of Leo for the current stage of the evolution of human consciousness in this special feature article *"The Age of Aquarius: Evolving Consciousness"* online at: http://lifecoachingmagazine.net/age-of-aquarius/

You might be able to remember back in your own life to a time when you were so young, there was just experiencing without labels. If you have been fortunate enough to spend some time with young infants you'll notice this exploring stage. When they pick up a flower, a building block, an insect – anything. The process is the same. They touch. Feel. Look. Probably put it to their mouth. If left undisturbed they will spend a long time getting to know the object. They are immersed in pure experience without mental concepts.

A new baby can't think "this is a flower". Labels are given later by those around him who will tell him "that is a flower". It is important to recognize that even before he had the capacity to think "this is a flower" he was still experiencing, and his experience was *individuated*. It was his experience, nobody else's.

> *"Realization is not knowledge about the universe,*
> *but the living experience of the nature of the universe."*
>
> - Chögyal Namkhai Norbu Rinpoche

It is a normal part of our intellectual development that we will quickly learn language and labels. It is an essential stage because it

is how we relate to the society into which we have been born. We initially connect with others and begin to relate in non-verbal ways with our parents, but very quickly as our social circle grows, we begin developing social skills, one of the most important of which is language.

This process hints at both the fear-based ego-personality expressions of Leo and the highest love-based Soul expression. The biggest ego-challenge for Leo is not to get caught in the labels that society puts upon us. When the society tells a Leo that he IS a banker, nurse, actor, fire officer, police officer, dropout, genius, addict, executive, scientist, slob, etc. he is likely to play the role full out. With great integrity, responsibility, and deep sincerity Leo will play the part that the society has conferred upon him, whether he be a prince or a pauper.

The danger is when he comes to believe that role is who he really is. Deep down he knows he really IS a 'somebody' but the mistake is in thinking that the 'somebody' is his role in society. This is why sometimes Leo can appear stuffy or pompous. There can be a sense of being 'unnatural' as Leo wholeheartedly throws his life and Soul into the role he has been given. When our Leo friend is gripped by fear he can fall into a vicious cycle where he clings even tighter to his externally imposed roles and titles, from a false sense of security, only to find that those very roles are taking him further away from experiencing his real self.

"Know Thyself.
If thou canst understand the nature of thine own self,
thou wilt know the reality of the Universe."

- Swami Abhedananda

Self-Conscious

At this point our Leo friend is self-conscious. At some point our infant began to develop the idea of 'me'. There is a point in child development where an infant will just look into a mirror and giggle. At first there is no 'self' recognition, then one day it arises. Suddenly the infant looks in the mirror and realizes they are looking at their individual self, which they will soon come to call 'me'. This is the arising of self-consciousness. From this point, as the child grows he will be comparing 'self' with 'other' to find his place in the world. To see where he 'fits' into the society in which he was born.

"A man's true life is the way in which he puts off
the lie imposed by others on him.
Stripped, naked, natural, he is what he is.
This is a matter of being, and not of becoming"

- OSHO

Until recent times, people rarely went beyond this stage. In communist countries we can see there is very little emphasis on an individual self, as one is expected to be a 'good citizen' and do one's duty to contribute to the society. This was also the case in the West before 1945. Since then, in the West at least, we have seen the emergence of the individual.

People no longer want to be seen as cogs in a machine. We can also see this in the current wave of revolutions in the middle east as people are standing up and saying "What about ME?" Individuals are demanding to be acknowledged and this is a vital stage in the evolution of consciousness because it is individuals who awaken, not societies. Society itself is merely a label that we have given to a group of individuals.

"Egoism, the limiting sense of 'I',
results from the individual intellect's
attributing the power of consciousness to itself."

- Patanjali

Self-awareness

For Leo, the way home to his authentic Self is the pathway to his Soul. Leo's spiritual path is to keep asking, "Who am I?" and not to stop until he has the answer. Through this process he cultivates deeper awareness of himself as an individual: self-awareness. Authentic Self is the one who was there before all the labels. The one who was experiencing as a baby, before the development of conceptual thinking and language. You don't have to do anything to be a somebody. You always were. Even before the label "I". Even before you 'thought' you were you. You were. You existed. Existence itself was experiencing Life, as you. This is what Christ meant when he said "be as children".

> *"There are no levels of Reality,*
> *only levels of experience for the individual.[20]"*
>
> - Ramana Maharshi

Self-realization

On our spiritual path there comes a time to drop all labels and recognize reality for what it is. In meditation we might return to the state of pure experiencing, where we can spend time with a flower simply experiencing it's essence without the sense of separation that comes with thoughts such as 'this is me' and 'that is a flower'.

If you have Leo Rising you are here to awaken. You are here to remember the state of pure being that is beyond all labels and concepts. Once you have returned to this childlike state you will recognize yourself as awareness itself, and awareness will be aware of itself. This is the ultimate Self-realization. You recognize your Self as the essence of all existence. Then you will live Life through your heart-center and be a pure expression of Divine will in the world. You will know your will and God's will to be one and the same.

---

[20] Some quotes are intentionally repeated throughout this book, either because they are particularly relevant to the sign in question and/or they are especially pertinent to our journey of spiritual awakening, and deserve additional contemplation. This is one such quote.

Key Points:

- If you have Leo Rising you can think of yourself as a Leo Soul.
- The deeper purpose of Leo is Self-realization through the process of individuation.
- To realize the highest purpose of Leo, the Leo Soul needs to release identification with externally imposed labels and roles and re-connect with his own vital essence.
- This is achieved by cultivating awareness, expanding perception, and deep understanding of the true nature of Self and the Universe.

Virgo Rising - The Virgo Soul

If you have Virgo Rising you can consider Virgo to be your 'Soul Sign' and consider yourself to be a Virgo Soul. Simply put, if you have Virgo Rising you are here to express the highest 'octave', the highest spiritual potential of Virgo that you possibly can in this lifetime.

The sign of Virgo is associated with health, healing, wholeness, the harvest, purity, the Divine Feminine, the Mother, Mother Earth and... service, one's vocation or spiritual calling. The simplest way to summarize the purpose of a Virgo Soul is *"to be an expression of Divine Love through one's vocation or dharma"*. In other words if you have Virgo Rising your Soul's purpose is to bring greater degrees of love into the world through your *sacred* work.

In modern times the meaning of work becomes distorted when we think we have to accept jobs that are 'Soul-destroying' because we need the wages. In contrast, our true vocation is actually our spiritual calling. It is our Divine work and our very reason for being. It is the purest expression of our life and Soul, and finding our vocation, discovering the place of wholeness where we can fully be and express ourselves through our life's work, is the highest purpose of Virgo. Before we can do this we have to 'purify' the fear-based expressions of Virgo and access the highest love-based expression of this beautiful sign.

Ruled by Mercury, the Virgo mind is perceptive, discerning, detailed, incisive and analytical. These attributes combined with an inherent desire for 'perfection' can lead to many of the challenges that our Virgo friend experiences at the fear-based personality level. If left unchecked your mind can go into overdrive, run you around in circles like a dog chasing it's tail, and leave you feeling jaded, anxious, disheartened and somewhat overly critical as you become cynical about the 'imperfect' world around you. Yet ironically, in *"Esoteric Astrology"* Mercury is also associated with the development of Higher Mind. The action of Mercury may seem to be Virgo's downfall yet it actually indicates the pathway to the higher purpose of Virgo. The real 'purification' that Virgo needs is purification of the mind and the true perfection that you seek is perfection of your Soul.

The word 'pure' comes from the Latin 'purus' which derived from the Greek 'pyr' meaning fire. The words pure and pyre (as in a funeral pyre) originate from the same root. Originally the word 'purification' meant *cleansing by fire* and this is a clue to the deeper esoteric mysteries of Virgo and her highest Soul purpose. The 'cleansing' that happens when the Soul is in Virgo is a spiritual cleansing, and the 'fire' of which we speak is the cool spiritual flame of awareness that 'burns off' all ignorance and reveals the light of awareness.

> *"Once your awareness becomes a flame,*
> *it burns up the whole slavery that the mind has created."*
>
> - OSHO

Once the flame of awareness has arisen in Leo, it is Virgo's job to bring that pure awareness to the 'real' world in practical ways. At the personality level Virgo has a brilliant, sharp, analytical mind. Let's pause for a moment and (in true Virgo style!) examine the word 'analyze'. At around 1600CE the word analyze meant 'to dissect'. So when we are analyzing something we are 'cutting it up'. Figuratively speaking (and sometimes even literally) we are taking it apart so we can examine all it's component parts more closely. While the sign of Virgo is often associated with brilliant research and detailed analysis, the true gift of Virgo (and her association with healing) lies in the way she *puts things back together again*!

To an analytical mind, the characteristics of Virgo themselves may appear as separate 'things': health, healing, wholeness, the harvest, purity, the Divine Feminine, the Mother, Mother Earth, one's vocation or spiritual calling, research and analysis. Yet when we reverse the analytical process they lead us back home through a process of purification or spiritual cleansing. We return to 'the Mother' and reap the 'harvest' by becoming healed, healthy and whole, from where we can be of true service in the world. This process of 'putting things back together again' is called *synthesis*.

For synthesis to happen there must be separate parts that require synthesizing, so we can see that by nature, during the process of

synthesizing there is still a sense of separation. Once the separate 'parts' become whole again, the highest octave of Virgo has transcended separation and returned to wholeness. The very word 'heal' comes from the Old English 'haelan' which literally means 'to make whole'. That which 'makes things whole' is pure awareness itself. At the highest level, the Virgo Soul already knows that all 'things', all phenomena in material existence, arise from pure awareness (or consciousness) and resolve back into pure awareness itself.

"Consciousness is the ground of all existence"

– Dr. Amit Goswami

Your Virgo Soul knows that it is pure awareness itself that resolves all. So we can see that it is not analysis itself that heals (because by nature analysis dissects and separates) but rather it is the quality of the *awareness that we bring to something* that heals, because it brings us back to an awareness of wholeness and in this wholeness, we find love. Cold analysis, without the presence of love, only increases separation and dis-ease.

One of the deepest sacred mysteries of Virgo is the knowledge that it is actually our loving awareness that heals. We 'heal' by bringing our loving, aware, conscious presence to something. By doing so, we return to the wholeness from which all arises and therein we find the purest Divine Love. Flowing this pure Divine love into the world by bringing pure awareness (presence or consciousness) into our everyday work is the highest Soul purpose of Virgo.

"We bring the Being to the doing"

- Anya Sophia Mann

Some spiritual traditions refer to a 'Mother and Son' awareness. The 'son awareness' would be our everyday fear-based mind made up of thoughts, stories, fantasies, ideals, concepts, fears, strategies, plans, emotions and so forth. The 'Mother awareness' would be the ocean of pure loving awareness from which, and within which, everything else that we know (including ourselves) arises.

In meditation, as we observe the activity of the everyday mind rising and falling, we may come to realize that we are none of those things, and that who we really are is the ever present pure awareness that observes all. At this point it is said that the son has returned to the Mother's lap. This succinctly points to the process experienced by the Soul in Virgo. In *"Esoteric Astrology"* this process of 'all things returning to the Mother awareness' is reflected in the Soul keynote for Virgo:

"I am the Mother and the child.
I, God, I, matter am"

- The Tibetan, *"Esoteric Astrology"*

So now we can begin to see that when we talk about our vocation or spiritual calling, we are not talking about searching high and low until we find some special kind of 'perfect sacred work', but rather it is about making the ordinary things that we do every day sacred, by bringing the purest quality of our loving awareness to them in deep recognition that all things really are sacred. We 'purify' the things we do, with our conscious awareness. This is the true meaning of Virgo. This reminds me of the proverb:

"Before enlightenment, chop wood, carry water.
After enlightenment, chop wood, carry water!"

- Zen Proverb

If you have Virgo Rising, your Soul's purpose is to bring Divine Love into the world. When you become fearful, it is too easy for you to become lost in mental activity, and exhaust yourself by trying to find perfection in the outer world. The key is to recognize, through your brilliant clear direct perception, that the source of your exquisite discernment and analysis IS awareness itself, and within that awareness is Love. When you realize that you ARE that awareness, you also know without doubt that you ARE Love. You realize that you are the embodiment of loving awareness. At that point all work becomes your vocation as the quality of your loving awareness brings perfection to everything you do, by making it sacred. This is the Soul's journey through Virgo.

Key Points:

- If you have Virgo Rising you can consider yourself to be a Virgo Soul
- The fear-based expressions of Virgo can include worry, anxiety, workaholism, criticism, and cynicism.
- To key to transcending fear and rising to the love-based expression of Virgo is to realize ever-present awareness as yourself.
- Within pure awareness you naturally find the presence of Divine Love, and realize this as your true nature.

Libra Rising - The Libra Soul

If you have Libra Rising you can consider Libra to be your 'Soul Sign' and consider yourself to be a Libra Soul. Simply put, if you have Libra Rising you are here to express the highest 'octave', the highest spiritual potential of Libra that you possibly can in this lifetime.

As we continue our Soul's journey through the twelve signs of the Zodiac, through which we are coming to understand the fear-based

reactions and highest love-based expressions of each Zodiac sign, we arrive at the beautiful sign of Libra. Symbolized by the scales, Libra is associated with balance, harmony, justice, ethics and the law. Esoterically Libra is associated with the Law of Harmonics, and the whole of Nature is governed by harmonics. Perfect balance. Ecosystems depend upon it.

> *"There is geometry in the humming of the strings,*
> *there is music in the spacing of the spheres."*

> - Pythagoras

After the Soul has found love in Virgo, Libra now realizes the power of choosing the highest expression for that Divine Love. If you have

Libra Rising your purpose is to bring greater degrees of harmony and balance into the world through *right relationship.*

The Libra Soul resonates with *harmonics* and Libra's innate sense of harmony comes from deep inner knowing of this universal law. This is an important key to understanding both the lower fear-based expression of Libra and the highest love-based expression, so we will take a moment to explore the nature of harmonics and how it relates to the sign of Libra.

The Universe is made of consciousness, which expresses itself through various frequencies. We can think of a human being as an instrument of perception created for detecting some of those frequencies, within a specific range. We do this through our five senses. We *feel vibration* at a physical level, then once this vibration speeds up we experience it as *sound.* When it becomes even faster again, we experience it as *light.*

In this way consciousness experiences itself through a human being and in turn we are aware of the conscious universe through our five senses. By fine-tuning our 'instrument' and increasing our 'sensitivity' (our ability to perceive through our senses) we become

aware of subtler and subtler levels of awareness. We are on a journey of experiencing conscious awareness through our senses and then recognizing that conscious awareness as ourselves. We call this our spiritual journey.

"I wonder if anyone else has an ear so tuned and sharpened
as I have, to detect the music, not of the spheres,
but of earth, subtleties of major and minor chord
that the wind strikes upon the tree branches.
Have you ever heard the earth breathe?"

- Kate Chopin

Experienced meditators tell us that once we are able to sense subtle frequencies beyond thought and mental activity, then we enter a different state of consciousness where there is a natural state of peace and joy and even more subtle vibrations can be detected. The pathway to this innate natural peace and joy requires navigating the energetic scale from the lower frequencies such as strong painful emotions to the higher frequencies of love and light. We do this in much the same way as climbing the musical scale from the lower octaves to the higher octaves. Before we can navigate any scale we first need to understand the relationship between the different levels and this is where harmony enters the picture.

Harmony exists wherever there is *right relationship*. For example, in music there can be 'consonant' (congruent) sounds and dissonant (incongruent) sounds. Contrary to popular belief harmony doesn't happen only when there are consonant sounds, but where there is a *balance between consonant and dissonant sounds*.

So when our Libra friends focus only on having pleasant (consonant/congruent) experiences to the exclusion of what might be causing discomfort (dissonance/incongruence), they actually move farther away from the very harmony that they so deeply desire.

Harmonizing means bringing both the pleasant (consonant) and unpleasant (dissonant) 'notes' in our lives into right relationship with one another. This is an ever-unfolding process whereby we open ourselves to greater degrees of harmony and congruence.

"Happiness is when
what you think,
what you say,
and what you do
are in harmony."

- Mahatma Gandhi

We can now see why the themes of harmony, peace, higher thought, natural law and right relationship are important for the Soul's journey through Libra. In order for humanity to make beautiful music together, rather than just noise, there needs to be right relationship between our consonant and dissonant notes! The true inner peace that Libra seeks is the result of harmonizing all our experiences, both pleasant and unpleasant, into one cohesive whole so we experience right relationship with ourselves, others, and the whole of Nature.

The purest 'essence' of Libra is higher love, peace, beauty and harmony. Anyone with personal planets in Libra innately resonates at this frequency and therefore not only has an innate ability to detect subtle nuances of disharmony and incongruence, but also has a deep inner knowing of what needs to happen to restore harmony, balance and congruence. However this spiritual essence is filtered through the 'lens' of a fear-based human mind which colors it's expression.

When our Libra friends experience fear, they may try manipulating the people and environment around them in a misguided attempt to 'keep the peace' by avoiding incongruent experiences. The underlying motivation beneath this behavior is their desire for peace but this will only happen when they embrace that which is incongruent, thereby bringing it into harmony, balance and congruence.

This is why a major theme for Libra is balancing relationships, especially the relationship between self and other. One of the skillful ways in which Libra 'hides' to avoid dealing with uncomfortable issues is by keeping their attention on others and on meeting other people's needs. While this seems to work for a short time it isn't really a firm foundation for a healthy relationship because in itself it is incongruent and ultimately leads to resentment.

For there to be balance in any relationship our Libra friends have to learn to bite the bullet and look at the root causes of discomfort and incongruence. This involves going within, looking closely at themselves and at the role they are playing in other people's lives.

Then our Libra friends will have a precious opportunity to fine-tune their skills of harmonizing through right relationship. Right relationship means being at peace within ourselves first, and then we will always be in right relationship with others.

"He who lives in harmony with himself
lives in harmony with the universe."

- Marcus Aurelius

Libra is a cardinal sign after all, and cardinal signs are pioneering signs of leadership. If you have Libra Rising your Soul's purpose is *pioneering in the field of right relationship*, bringing innovative solutions that contribute to world peace and harmony. When you become fearful you have a tendency to avoid discomfort and seek only pleasant experiences but this cannot bring the true harmony you

so deeply desire. By having the courage to look directly at the causes of discomfort, and then taking inspired action to harmonize them, you can access the power of higher love and express your Soul's purpose in the real world through effective relating skills.

Key Points:

- If you have Libra Rising you can consider yourself to be a Libra Soul.
- The highest Soul purpose of Libra is bringing greater degrees of harmony into the world through right relationship.
- You do this not by avoiding uncomfortable situations but by fine-tuning your skills of relationship so you can bring the 'consonant' and 'dissonant' notes into accord with one another. This is the art and science of harmonizing.

Scorpio Rising - The Scorpio Soul

If you have Scorpio Rising you can consider Scorpio to be your 'Soul Sign' and consider yourself to be a Scorpio Soul. Simply put, if you have Scorpio Rising you are here to express the highest 'octave', the highest spiritual potential of Scorpio that you possibly can in this lifetime.

As our Soul's journey continues we arrive at the beautiful and enigmatic sign of Scorpio. The intense sign of Scorpio is most commonly associated with sex, death and regeneration. It is also associated with other people's money and resources, and even cruelty, so why beautiful? Because when we understand the underlying Soul dynamics in Scorpio we see that there is a beautiful, natural, and inevitable process of integration, healing and transformation happening.

Before we can connect the dots and see what these seemingly diverse associations have in common, we have to understand a little about the stages of development of our Soul through the signs and

what particularly is happening at this stage of our Soul's journey. As mentioned earlier, *"Esoteric Astrology"* speaks of the Soul's 'battle' in two signs: Leo and Scorpio. We saw why, in Leo the battle was for our individuality, now in Scorpio the battle is for our Soul.

Esoterically what happens in Scorpio is the culmination of the process of personality-Soul fusion. This explains the depth and intensity of Scorpio for it is in this sign that we need to face the depths of our own Soul, and succumb to the surrender of the ego that happens as a result.

"The Woods are lovely, dark and deep.
But I have promises to keep,
And miles to go before I sleep,
And miles to go before I sleep."

- Robert Frost

The 'individuality' that we fought so hard to gain in Leo appears in Scorpio to be dissolving in the light of the Soul and, at the ego-personality level of instinct, when we feel threatened it is natural to fight. To onlookers this can also appear cruel. When our Scorpio friends feel fear, it is felt at a depth and intensity that few of us can even imagine – as though their very survival is at stake which, from the ego's perspective, it is!

When we instinctively fight for survival things can become really vicious. If you have ever tried to take a terrified cat to the vet you'll know what I mean. The claws come out, there's hissing and spitting, and it will grasp and claw at anything to try and get away. This is an instinctive fear-based reaction and in the case of the cat we can clearly see that it isn't personal. The cat doesn't even know who you are, it will just scratch anybody or any thing that is getting in the way! This is a clue to the solution and the power of healing and transformation in Scorpio.

To get beyond our fear-based reactions we need to look at the roots of fear itself and this is why Scorpio will often merrily go where angels fear to tread – to go as deep as possible and uncover the root of an issue. The root cause of our fear is actually our inability to tell illusion from reality. The ego, our personality as we know and think about ourselves, is actually a complex illusion created by our mind[21]. In our earlier section on Leo we outlined the process whereby at a certain point in early childhood development we form a mental concept of ourselves that we call 'I'. This is the idea that there is a 'person' in here, that we call 'me'.

When our Scorpio friends, or indeed any of us,　are attacking, grasping, and clawing, we are suffering from a false sense of separation where we feel we have to defend our illusory sense of self by attacking an illusory 'other'. Going deeper, beneath this illusion of 'me' to discover the underlying reality of our existence, and hence the Universe, is the Soul purpose of Scorpio. This is how we

---

[21] See Chapter 1 for a reminder of how your mind creates the illusion of a separate self that we're calling your *ego-personality*.

discover the point of light in the darkness, and discover that ultimately everything is light. The higher purpose of Scorpio is to transform darkness into light but first, our attachment to the idea of 'me' must finally be overcome.

"You live in illusion and the appearance of things.
There is a reality, but you do not know this.
When you understand this, you will see that you are nothing,
and being nothing you are everything. That is all."

- Kalu Rinpoche

When our frightened Scorpio is fighting for survival other people's money and resources seem to be of great importance. It can feel as though we have to 'fight' or compete with others to get our share. One of the ego challenges of Scorpio can also be a tendency to become overly dependent on other people's resources to meet their needs.

This is part of the illusion: that what we need is outside of us, and under the control of others. When our Scorpio friend discovers the true nature underlying the illusion there is a softening, and a realization that there is nothing and nobody to 'fight'. We are only ever fighting reflections of ourselves.

"Contemplate life as infinite,
undivided, ever present, ever active,
until you realize yourself as one with it.
It is not even very difficult,
for you will be returning only
to your own natural condition."

- Nisargadatta

In Leo we experienced the process of self-realization. In Scorpio that self-realization turns to self-reliance. Everything we need is already within us. We have heard that phrase so often it can seem like a cliché yet it really does point to a deeper spiritual truth. Once our Scorpio friend discovers the reality that everything they have really is already within them, they will have discovered the very thing that they can always rely on: their own Divine presence.

There are many names for this unchanging presence that we can always rely on: awareness, God, Great Spirit, Quantum Intelligence, the Divine, consciousness, the Self, existence or even simply Life itself. Whatever we call it, if we go deep enough in our journey we find that it is always there. It can always be relied upon, and it IS who we are. This is why Scorpio is also associated with birth, death and regeneration because it is in Scorpio that we have the potential to discover within ourselves this everlasting presence that permeates and supersedes all forms and all lifetimes. In other words, things may come and go, but consciousness itself never dies.

If you have Scorpio Rising you can consider yourself to be a Scorpio Soul and your Soul's purpose is to *transform darkness into light*. You do this by confronting the apparent darkness within yourself. When you have the courage to face your fear directly, the illusion dissolves and what remains is your light. You recognize 'the point of light' in the darkness as your own awareness, and you realize once and for all that your true nature really is one of light.

You realize oneness with 'all that is' and clearly see that there is no 'enemy' outside of yourself. There is no-one to fight. All fear naturally subsides (for there is nothing left to fear) and you are transformed. Then, as a result of your own personal journey of healing and transformation, you naturally become an inspirational source of healing and transformation for others.

Key Points:

- If you have Scorpio Rising you can consider yourself to be a Scorpio Soul.
- The highest Soul purpose of Scorpio is the transformation of darkness into light.
- When you succumb to fear you feel as though all the power and control is outside of yourself and you have to fight for it. This is an illusion created by our egoic mind.
- The solution is to continue going deeper on your inner journey until you find your true inner power. From this place you clearly see there are no enemies outside of yourself.

Sagittarius Rising - The Sagittarius Soul

If you have Sagittarius Rising you can consider Sagittarius to be your 'Soul Sign' and consider yourself to be a Sagittarius Soul.

Simply put, if you have Sagittarius Rising you are here to express the highest 'octave', the highest spiritual potential of Sagittarius that you possibly can in this lifetime.

As we continue our journey we arrive at Sagittarius, the sign of the seeker. Sagittarius is associated with seeking, searching, teaching, learning, travel, philosophy, wisdom, religion, idealism, optimism, purpose, freedom, goals and truth. These all seem like worthy higher pursuits, yet when viewed through the lens of the fear-based ego-personality they can become badly distorted.

Higher truth, freedom and spiritual goals can become fear-based dogma, opinions, freedom for selfish pursuits, and ego-driven materialistic goals, yet esoterically Sagittarius is a sign of liberation. The lessons that begin in one sign are carried forward by the next so like his predecessor Scorpio, Sagittarius is also learning the balance of power.

In *"Esoteric Astrology"* we are told that the fire signs bring three gifts. In Aries we have the *gift of existence*; in Leo we have the *gift of opportunity through individuality* and in Sagittarius we have the *gift of power* .- This is a higher power of which we speak. Not power over others, which would be the egoic idea of power, but rather the power of *Self-Mastery*. The Self-Realization which was attained in Leo, that became Self-Reliance in Scorpio is now set, in Sagittarius, to become Self-Mastery.

> *"We may define "Esoteric Astrology" as that side of the subject which views all stellar phenomena from the standpoint of unity; whilst Exoteric Astrology begins its study from the side of diversity and separateness. The Esoteric Astrologer looks upon the whole expression of life as proceeding from one central and primal source, and therefore seeks to understand the subject from the point of view of the One flowing forth into the many."*

– Alan Leo

All fear comes from the illusion of separation[22]. Understanding this is key to understanding the higher wisdom of Sagittarius, because the highest wisdom comes from oneness. From unity consciousness. The awareness that all really is one. As long as our Sagittarian friend is caught in illusion and duality, his power will be directed towards self-advancement. There is a key distinction for Sagittarius to understand: whether the freedom he seeks is truly freedom from the illusion of ego, or whether he is simply seeking freedom for his ego!

The freedom to be oneself is one of the highest values in our western culture, yet for the most part what we really mean is the freedom to do as we please. Yet doing as we please can keep us firmly stuck in our own conditioned behaviors and fear-based ego responses. When we really get everything we desire, we can become truly miserable and realize that none of it had the power to bring us deeper satisfaction and fulfillment. That can only come from within.

---

[22] See Chapter 1.

*"There are two great disappointments in life.
Not getting what you want and getting it."*

- George Bernard Shaw

Driven by innate curiosity and a thirst for knowledge about life, the universe, and everything, our Sagittarian friend is on a lifelong quest for truth. Yet Sagittarius is not called the sign of the philosopher for nothing. Philosophy is all about taking ideas and applying them to life in meaningful ways. In other words taking an idea and turning it into a rule or guide by which we 'should' live.

On the surface this might seem like a good thing. Having idealistic standards to strive for and moral codes to live by can only improve our lives, right? Yet that has been the story of human history from the onset. Each generation seeks to impose it's own set of rules,

codes and standards onto society for the purpose of 'improving' it. Mental concepts taken to extremes become dogma and there is a not-so-very fine line between philosophy and dogma.

*"A man's true life is the way in which
he puts off the lie imposed by others on him.
Stripped, naked, natural, he is what he is.
This is a matter of being, and not of becoming."*

- OSHO

When our Sagittarian friend becomes fearful he clings to his mental concepts, has difficulty distinguishing personal opinion from truth and may cling to dogma from a false sense of security. The highest wisdom that Sagittarius truly seeks is far beyond words, language and mental concepts.

The Universe has the power to create mountains, move oceans, grow rainforests and fill them with a myriad of living beings, while simultaneously keeping the solar system orbiting around the Sun and maintaining the delicate inner workings of a human body, from digesting your food to making sure the oxygen levels in your cells are in perfect balance. All in 'silence' and all without a single 'philosophy', 'moral code' or 'standard' about how things ought to be done. Do you ever wonder how it coped before humans arrived on the scene to 'think' about the 'best way' to 'do' life? Amazing!

The real power of Sagittarius comes when he realizes Self-Mastery, which begins with mastering his own thoughts and actions. When the archer turns his arrow inwards, he focuses on the 'correct' goal: the journey to seek his true nature. Our true nature as human beings lies well beyond our capacity for thought, and is discovered through direct perception. It is the difference between experiencing ice cream and thinking about ice cream!

"There are no levels of Reality;
only levels of experience for the individual"

-Ramana Maharshi

Through deeper meditative or spiritual practices Sagittarius begins to realize his deep connection with life itself. Feeling the pulse of life force energy surging through his veins, and when his busy mind becomes quiet, our Sagittarius friend wakes up to the realization that he is one with the very life force that is moving planets and creating universes. Through direct perception he realizes that these universal forces are running through him and that he and the Universe are one and the same. Through his own expanded perception and awareness he arrives at the ultimate goal.

"Realization is not knowledge about the Universe,
but the living experience of the nature of the Universe"

- Chögyal Namkhai Norbu

The Tibetan Buddhist tradition speaks of 'clear-light' wisdom, which is a higher wisdom, beyond conceptual thinking, that we can access when we have become stable enough in meditation to experience the true nature of mind, which is said to be clear light.

Through meditative practices the everyday mind is transcended and the true nature of our clear light mind can be accessed. It is said that all wisdom can be known at this point, but it is not what we would normally think of as knowledge. It is not information. It doesn't come in the form of words or thinking. It is through direct perception and resting in clear awareness that such wisdom is known.

Once there has even been a glimpse of recognition of the clear-light wisdom that lies beyond the chatter of our everyday mind, we have identified the 'true' goal. This is the highest wisdom and deeper

spiritual truth that our Sagittarian friends really seek. Through deeper contemplative practices it is possible to abide continuously in this awareness and by doing so, ever-deeper insights into the true nature of the Universe will arise. We may realize that our awareness, and the awareness of the Universe, are one and the same and that the nature of the Universe is awareness itself. In Tibetan Buddhism this is said to be the ultimate wisdom.

"Once your awareness becomes a flame,
it burns up the whole slavery that the mind has created."

- OSHO

If you have Sagittarius Rising you may consider yourself to be a Sagittarian Soul and your Soul's purpose is to *uplift humanity through the revelation of truth and wisdom*. To attain this highest of goals you first need to transcend your own fear-based reactions, which may cause you to cling to opinions and man-made dogma as though they were spiritual truth.

When you are free of such man-made concepts and self-imposed dogma, you are truly liberated. This is achieved by going deeper within on your own journey of self-exploration, where you realize your true power, recognize your true nature as oneness with all that is, and have access to the ultimate wisdom of the Universe!

Key Points:

- If you have Sagittarius Rising you can consider yourself to be a Sagittarius Soul.
- The highest Soul purpose of Sagittarius is to uplift humanity through the revelation of truth and wisdom.
- When you succumb to fear you may take refuge in opinions and dogma from a false sense of security.
- The solution is to employ meditative and contemplative practices that take you beyond conceptual thinking and lead you to direct experience of the clear wisdom of your mind's true nature. From there you realize your true power, recognize your true nature as oneness with all that is, and have access to the ultimate wisdom of the Universe!

Capricorn Rising - The Capricorn Soul

If you have Capricorn Rising you can consider Capricorn to be your 'Soul Sign' and consider yourself to be a Capricorn Soul. Simply put, if you have Capricorn Rising you are here to express the highest 'octave', the highest spiritual potential of Capricorn that you possibly can in this lifetime. Capricorn is associated with achievement, practical application, method, ambition, material resources, finances, government, initiation and discipleship. Esoterically it is said that the spiritual 'goal' is identified in Sagittarius and then in Capricorn we choose to walk the path. The highest Soul purpose of Capricorn is to *create heaven on Earth*[23] and it is no accident that we celebrate Christmas and the birth of the Christ during Capricorn season.

---

[23] What do we actually mean by 'heaven on Earth'? Well it can mean different things to different people. In this context, we are referring to the idea that according to Esoteric Astrology Venus is a sacred planet, while the Earth is a non-sacred planet. Yet they are said to be 'sister' planets.

The words 'discipline' and 'disciple' both have their origin in the Latin verb *discere*, which simply means *to learn*. So if Sagittarius has identified the spiritual goal, Capricorn's job is *learning how to get there*. The whole idea of 'discipleship' implies that there is a *practical methodology to achieve a tangible result*. Through our Soul's experience in Capricorn we learn to build a very real "stairway to heaven". So what would this 'heaven' look like? Rather than thinking of it as a physical location, it can be thought of as the blissful state of nirvana or Samadhi that comes after many years of applied discipline in a yogic or monastic tradition.

Capricorn is the sign of mindfulness, method, and skill, cultivated through *patient application and practice*. The power that was gained in Sagittarius must now be applied in practice. The essence of Capricorn lies in the most appropriate use of resources, in particular spiritual resources, to achieve success. This is the key to understanding both the fear based reactions and love-based responses of Capricorn. Esoterically Capricorn is said to be the most mysterious sign of all, the true meaning of which we will only fully come to understand when humanity has made great leaps in consciousness.

"The basis of the astrological sciences
is the emanation, transmission, and reception of energies
and their transmutation into forces by the receiving entity.
... it is all a question of developed reception and sensitivity."

– The Tibetan

The Earth is on a journey of becoming a 'sacred planet', that is one that carries a higher vibration of light, and where fear-based energies have been transcended and transmuted into higher light. This is not a question of the Earth 'ascending' to heaven, but rather one of 'heavenly light' descending into physical form. This is the process that is symbolized by the Soul's journey in Capricorn.

Of all twelve signs Capricorn is most associated with both the 'best' and the 'worst' of human character and to understand this, we need higher consciousness and an understanding of energy. Capricorn is said to rule governments, politics and banking. The current sorry state of the world's banks, greed, avarice, corrupt politicians greedy for power, global inequalities in wealth, health and resources, all have been attributed to the 'negative' or fear-based expressions of Capricorn. Yet esoterically this is the sign of the initiate and the disciple! How can this be?

The Soul in Capricorn is learning 'right use of resources', including our inner resources: our physical, emotional, mental and spiritual energy. We cannot learn the power of our own energies, and become skilled in their use, from books. We can only do so through experience, practical application and diligent practice, all Capricorn qualities.

Through this we develop the consciousness that results from deep self-observation where we become skilled at watching our own energies play out. Eventually we then begin to see energetic patterns, connections and deepen our understanding of the nature of energy, and the laws of cause and effect.

In spiritual traditions where deep self-observation is part of the practice, students are encouraged to examine their own motivation. This means deeply observing the energies in you that 'move you into action' and motivate your thoughts, words and actions, so that you come to know and understand your own driving forces. In this way practitioners eventually begin to see important connections between seemingly different energies.

For example it is said that anger and love are on the same energetic spectrum and that anger is simply a lower fear-based, or distorted, expression of love. Likewise greed and avarice are distorted expressions of compassion. With consciousness, greed transmutes into compassion. If this is so, then it makes perfect sense that the most avaricious of signs has the potential to also be the most compassionate. We can only come to know this for ourselves through diligent application, experience and awareness.

"our anger obscures our capacity to love,
our sadness obscures our joy,
our prejudice obscures our equanimity, and
our greed obscures our compassion"

- Tenzin Wangyal Rinpoche

The current state of affairs in the world is a catalyst for human compassion to flower on a scale the like of which has never before been known. This is the lesson and the gift of Capricorn. In order to fully understand this, we need experience of how these energy dynamics work within our own energy field, which is why Capricorn is also the sign for skillful method, initiation and discipleship.

The word 'initiate' means to begin something or to be introduced to something. Without an introduction from skilled and experienced teachers we are unlikely to see these energy dynamics for ourselves. Even Christ and the Buddha had teachers in their youth to point out the path.

Next comes the 'discipleship', or discipline of applied practice. This means keeping our attention on the path. If we follow the energy of our greed, it takes us outside of ourselves, pursuing the object(s) of our desire and trying to fill a bottomless pit inside. It is this fear-based expression of Capricorn that leads to Capricorn's worst reputation.

If we really observe ourselves deeply when we are experiencing greed, we can see that underneath it there is anxiety, fear and maybe even terror. When we experience fear and terror we naturally want to gather as many resources as we can to take care of ourselves and our own families. When our Capricorn friends succumb to fear they may mistakenly chase after more and more worldly wealth and power, naturally trying to acquire and ring-fence resources for their own use, which gives them a false sense of security and short-lived peace of mind.

Once they become well-versed and skilled in the art of energy dynamics we will see that our Capricorn friends are transformed into the most generous and compassionate people on the planet! The Capricorn Soul realizes that greed and compassion are but two expressions of the same energy and has the skill to transmute greed, avarice and the base emotions of desire into compassion, love and the highest qualities of humanity.

If you have Capricorn Rising you can consider yourself to be a Capricorn Soul. Your true skill and power lies in your innate focus, intelligence, and diligent method, which gives you the ability to trace the energy of your emotions and desires back to their source. Rather than following the outward acquisitive direction of greed, by turning your attention inwards, observing your energy, and tracing it back to it's inner root, you will see it transform into the highest compassion. First for yourself and then for others. From this connection to your innate compassion comes a deep and lasting sense of achievement, fulfillment and spiritual nourishment. You then have an endless resource from which to practically and realistically build heaven on earth.

Key Points:

- If you have Capricorn Rising you can consider yourself to be a Capricorn Soul.
- The highest Soul purpose of Capricorn is to create heaven on earth.
- When you succumb to fear you may resort to grasping, greed and avarice to try and ensure you and your family are well provided for.
- The solution is to turn your attention inwards, follow the energy back to it's source, and transmute greed into compassion.
- From there you realize your true power and discover your limitless resources of inner wealth.

Aquarius Rising - The Aquarius Soul

If you have Aquarius Rising you can consider Aquarius to be your 'Soul Sign' and consider yourself to be an Aquarius Soul. Simply put, if you have Aquarius Rising you are here to express the highest 'octave', the highest spiritual potential of Aquarius that you possibly can in this lifetime.

The sign of Aquarius is associated with science, technology, innovations, gadgets, individuality, uniqueness, the new age, humanitarian ideals and group consciousness. As the sign of the water carrier many people mistakenly believe that Aquarius is a water sign, yet if this were the case we would see much more emotion from our often cool, aloof and detached Aquarian friends.

While water signs are about mastering emotions, air signs are about mastering the mind, and as the fixed air sign Aquarius is all about the mind. Aquarius' concern about humanitarian ideals and their apparent coolness on a personal level can seem like a contradiction until we understand the nature of air and fixed energy.

How can one be concerned for the whole of humanity and be apparently uncaring or 'unfeeling' on a personal level? We might question their integrity and wonder whether they actually care or not. This is because Aquarius' 'humanitarian concerns' come from the head rather than the heart. It is an intellectual ideal born from intelligence and cold reason, rather than heartfelt compassion, "We are civilized people so we should be concerned for one another's welfare". This is one of the keys to understanding both the fear based reactions and love based expressions of Aquarius.

To really understand both the fear based reactions and love-based expressions of this enigmatic sign, we need to briefly review the nature of fixed energy. Remember, in astrology we speak of energy as having three 'modalities' or modes of expression[24]. Sometimes these are called 'qualities' because they describe the *quality of the*

---

[24] See Chapter 1

energy being expressed. These three modalities are *cardinal, fixed*, and *mutable*.

To understand how they work in harmony think of a tree. The first green shoot that fights it's way purposefully through the rocks and the earth towards the light of day, is driven by cardinal energy: the energy of creation, evolution and new beginnings. Cardinal energy is a driving force that pushes life onwards and upwards.

Now think of the trunk of the tree. That is fixed energy: the energy of a placeholder, containing and holding the energy within a fixed form or structure. Wherever there is structure – the structure of the trunk, the branches, the leaves, the cells within the leaves and even the DNA structure within those cells - we have fixed energy at work. It is fixed energy that will stabilize the tree within a structure for the duration of its life so it can fulfill its purpose.

Now think of the end of the life cycle when the tree dies. The leaves die and drop off, the trunk will eventually break down, and the matter will decompose and transform into compost. This breaking down, changing and dissolving of form is mutable energy. The energy can then be re-used (in the form of cardinal energy) once again at the beginning of a new life cycle. So in the modalities we see the three essential energies that comprise the *cycle of life*: cardinal (creation), fixed (stability) and mutable (destruction).

Now think of the octaves of the musical scale and you'll begin to understand the biggest challenge for fixed signs, and especially Aquarius. Fixed energy wants to 'fixate' on something. So the only question becomes whether you 'lock and hold' on the lowest octaves on the scale, or the highest ones. In terms of your spiritual journey, this refers to your level or state of consciousness.

As the fixed air sign, Aquarius is all about mastering the mind. The intellect. This is what makes Aquarius one of the most challenging signs for those on the spiritual path because changing course (by changing your mind) once you have locked in on your target like a heat-seeking missile, is one of the most difficult things for you to do.

This is why our Aquarian friends (and indeed all fixed signs) have a reputation for stubbornness.

On the spiritual journey, the activity of the intellect is actually considered an obstacle to spiritual awakening. If we are to fully awaken we need to be able to go beyond intellect (beyond our brain wiring) in order to perceive spiritual truth directly. This is where Aquarius often gets caught. Contrary to our contemporary Western view (where intellect is held in the highest esteem), in terms of spiritual development, attachment to intellectual ideas without the experience of direct perception is actually considered a form of ignorance[25].

> *"Ignorant people get stuck in words*
> *like an elephant on the mud."*

- Lankavatara sutra translated by Walpola Sri Rahula

The term ignorance in this context is not meant to be offensive, but refers to people who are not yet spiritually awake. We are all 'ignorant' as long as our perception of spiritual truth is obscured, and it is the intellect that can be one of our biggest obstacles. In *"Esoteric Astrology"* the Tibetan explains that we are evolving from instinct, through intellect, to intuition. In other words, intellect is a developmental stage that we are passing through. So when our Aquarian friends get 'stuck' in intellect, their spiritual development has reached a hiatus! The above quote is speaking of the problem of being stuck at the intellectual level.

Having said that, it is important to remember that we have now reached the 11th sign in our spiritual journey and the Aquarian Soul is carrying all the experience of up to eight lifetimes in each of the

---

[25] Ignorant in the simple sense of not knowing, or being *unaware*. See http://www.thefreedictionary.com/ignorant Everyone who is unaware of their true spiritual nature is, in a sense, 'ignorant'.

previous ten signs. So in spite of the challenge of getting caught at the level of intellect, the Aquarian Soul is actually carrying a deep reserve of spiritual energy accumulated over many lifetimes, only waiting for the individual to awaken their consciousness and direct it where it is needed most in the world.

Spiritual teachers and yogis speak of three levels of consciousness: gross, subtle and extremely subtle. Gross consciousness is tangible and most related to our senses: we can see a rock, we can pick it up and feel it. We can hear running water. Subtle consciousness is the realm of thoughts. We are aware of thinking but we cannot see our thoughts or touch them. This is where we experience the intellect.

Extremely subtle consciousness lies in the stillness and silence beyond thoughts, and this is where we experience intuition. It is the consciousness of the Universe and once we are able to abide at this level for prolonged periods of time, like great masters and yogis do, it is said that we have access to the wisdom of the Universe.

The 'musical scale' of our spiritual journey is leading us to the ability to reach the 'high note' of extremely subtle consciousness and remain there. While it is difficult for our Aquarian friends to navigate their way up the scale, and they may become stuck at the level of intellect for long periods, once they do reach the level of extremely subtle consciousness, their fixed nature gives them the advantage of being able to hold their attention there for long periods of time.

Fixed signs can be great meditators if they have chosen well and fixed on the right level of consciousness! This is where we see the highest octave of Aquarius. Esoterically Aquarius is the sign of 'group consciousness'. This is not the tribal consciousness that is so often associated with Cancer, but refers to the highest unity consciousness that is accessible only at the level of extremely subtle consciousness.

As we follow the Soul's journey through the twelve signs of the Zodiac, after the Soul in the Cardinal Earth sign of Capricorn has learned how to methodically take the steps up the mountain (in other words to navigate the 'musical scale' of consciousness and reach the high note of unity consciousness) *Aquarius is able to hold the tone and allow the spiritual waters of love and life to flow for the benefit of humanity.*

At this extremely subtle level of consciousness, it is not holding in the sense of grasping, but rather it is a soft focus on subtle energies that accepts the flow of the 'dual waters of Aquarius': love and life. This is why, although Aquarius is the sign of the water carrier and has the symbolism of being a 'vessel' to bring forth spiritual energy, we can also see that the water is always flowing. This is a vessel through which spiritual energy flows, and is not contained.

"You cannot understand life and its mysteries
as long as you try to grasp it.
Indeed, you cannot grasp it,
just as you cannot walk off with a river in a bucket.

If you try to capture running water in a bucket,
it is clear that you do not understand it
and that you will always be disappointed,
for in the bucket the water does not run.
To 'have' running water you must
let go of it and let it run."

- Alan Wilson Watts

At this higher level of consciousness the energy of Aquarius is one with his polar opposite, heart-centered Leo[26], and the united sign of Aquarius-Leo is flowing the energy of love and life through a pure and open heart. Once we balance the Aquarius-Leo polarity, we are centered in our hearts yet connected to the collective consciousness

---

[26] We will say more about the integration process, the six polarities, and the blending of opposite signs in the next chapter.

of humanity at one and the same time.

There is a great warmth and love here, and not the cool, uncaring, aloofness that is often associated with the intellectual Aquarian. This is also why, esoterically, at its highest spiritual expression Aquarius is the sign of the collective consciousness of humanity and the flowering of human consciousness. Once we have completed our Soul's passage through Aquarius then we are ready for the sacred heart opening that happens on the last stage of our journey, in Pisces!

If you have Aquarius Rising you can consider yourself to be an Aquarian Soul and your highest purpose is to flow the *"dual waters of love and life for the benefit of thirsty humanity"* (The Tibetan, *"Esoteric Astrology"*). The only question is whether you will fix your attention on lower consciousness by getting caught in your own mental activity, or whether you will be able to go beyond your own thoughts and focus your attention on the peace and stillness that lies within. Then you will reach your highest Soul purpose, access the flowering collective consciousness of humanity, and love and life will pour through you for the benefit of all.

Key Points:

- If you have Aquarius Rising you can consider yourself to be an Aquarian Soul.
- The highest Soul purpose of Aquarius is to dedicate one's personal energies to the collective.
- Your biggest challenge is getting caught in the intellectual realm which can become an obstacle to your spiritual growth.
- The solution is to turn your attention to the subtle consciousness that lies beyond mental concepts and focus your attention there.
- From there you'll access the subtle energy of your heart and realize from your own experience how love and life can pour through you for the benefit of all humanity .

Pisces Rising - The Pisces Soul

If you have Pisces Rising you can consider Pisces to be your 'Soul Sign' and consider yourself to be a Pisces Soul. Simply put, if you have Pisces Rising you are here to express the highest 'octave', the highest spiritual potential of Pisces that you possibly can in this lifetime.

As we complete this first round of our journey through the Zodiac exploring the love-based expressions and fear-based reactions of the twelve signs, we finally arrive at the magnificent and mysterious twelfth sign of Pisces: the sign of the Sacred Heart. The sign of Pisces is associated with escapism, suffering, retreats, religious orders, prisons, everything illusory and glamorous: photography, the movie industry, and... oceanic consciousness, devotion, and Universal Love.

To understand the mysteries of this seemingly contradictory sign, we need to understand what is sometimes known as the 'veil' of our illusion: how it is our illusion that causes suffering, and how 'disillusionment' or 'seeing reality as it truly is' can be an end to suffering and lead to the Sacred Heart opening of Humanity. Our Soul's journey through the previous eleven signs has finally prepared us for the ultimate experience in Pisces.

> *"All know that the drop merges into the ocean*
> *but few know that the ocean merges into the drop."*
>
> - Ramana Maharshi

The sign of Pisces is associated with oceanic consciousness and it is because of this oceanic awareness that Pisces is also the most sensitive sign of the Zodiac. This deep sensitivity means that our Piscean friends are keenly aware of the suffering of others, so much so that it can often feel just too much. Feeling overwhelmed by the suffering in the world can prompt our Piscean friends to withdraw.

All forms of escapism ranging from lying low with a movie and a tub of ice-cream, to full-blown alcohol, drug, gambling and gaming addictions, are the fear-based reactions and personality-based pitfalls of this beautiful and mysterious sign.

Although Pisces is a water sign, and water signs are about mastery of emotions, no-where is it more important to understand the nature of the mind than in the sign of Pisces. Especially the connection between heart and mind. It is the mind that creates all our projections and illusions[27], and it is the power of the heart that sees through all illusion. It is our mind that separates us, and our heart that returns us to wholeness. It is our illusions that generate suffering, yet on an everyday basis we do not examine how our mind creates illusion. We just accept everything at face value, and believe in the appearance of things.

This gives rise to the two Pisces 'fish', the fish who swims in the shallow waters, never questioning appearances, and accepting everything at face value, and the fish who dives to the depths to understand our deeper, spiritual nature. There are many different spiritual traditions, each having different 'methods' for revealing spiritual truth and one method is called the path of devotion. Devotional practices involve surrendering to a deeper experience of love, so that one comes to experience a greater love than that which we normally experience in our everyday lives. An example is Bhakti Yoga in India.

"Call it by any name, God, Self, the Heart or the seat of consciousness, it is all the same. The point to be grasped is this, that Heart means the very core of one's being, the centre, without which there is nothing whatever."

– Ramana Maharshi

---

[27] See Chapter 1.

Devotional practices are often misunderstood in the West. Their purpose is not (as is often believed) to encourage 'blind' devotion to a particular guru, group or cult, but rather through devotional practices it is possible to experience a higher or transcendent love: the love of God, or what may be called Universal Love. This was the original purpose behind monasteries and religious devotional orders, and it is the highest spiritual path of Pisces (although one doesn't need to enter a monastery to pursue a devotional spiritual practice).

Without a personal direct experience of Universal Love, we are stuck with ordinary life as it appears to be, and may never go beyond the illusions created by our own mind. Most of us are unaware of the mechanism through which our mind creates and sustains this illusion. In Chapter 1 and in the earlier section in this Chapter, "*Leo Rising: The Leo Soul*", we looked at how the illusion of 'me' gets created and maintained throughout our lives. If we never challenge it, then we find ourselves thirty or forty years later still trying to be a false 'me' that is purely a construct of the mind – it doesn't really exist! The biggest illusion, is YOU!

> *"Drop the idea of becoming someone,*
> *because you are already a masterpiece.*
> *You cannot be improved.*
> *You have only to come to it,*
> *to know it, to realize it.*
> *God himself has created you;*
> *you cannot be improved."*

> - OSHO

This is such an important point, and is fundamental to the understanding of Soul Astrology, that it is worth re-iterating here: as a young baby we were a pure bundle of awareness. We were aware of everything, but without mental concepts. We didn't have the ability to think "I am this" or "I am that". We just were. Then somebody told us "that is you", and the seed of an idea was planted, "Me".

This idea has continued to grow within us. It overlays and obscures the fact of the underlying reality that existed before we created our 'me' label. Just like when watching a movie we lose sight of the screen and the movie theater, and get totally lost in the story, in our own lives we get so entangled in the 'story of me' that we lose sight of our deeper reality as spiritual beings. We are like spiders caught in our own webs.

"Wakefulness passes off, I am;
the dream state passes off, I am;
the sleep state passes off, I am.
They repeat themselves, and yet I am.
They are like pictures moving
on the screen in a cinema show.
They do not affect the screen.
Similarly also, I remain unaffected
although these states pass off."

– Ramana Maharshi

According to many spiritual traditions it is this constant inner monologue of self-concern that keeps us from seeing ourselves as we truly are, and the purpose of devotional practices are to simply divert our attention away from mental activity and bring our awareness back to our heart.

Recent studies[28] into meditative practices have noticed that when we learn to shift our attention away from mental activity, there is a marked reduction in suffering. Indeed current research shows that not all mental activity leads to suffering but in particular a specific 'self-referential' type of thinking, which creates and maintains this illusion of a 'false self' (our ego-personality or 'story of me').

---

[28] See *"The Neuroscience of Suffering - And It's End"* by Jeff Warren. Online document at: http://psychologytomorrowmagazine.com/jeff-warren-neuroscience-suffering-end/

"the mind thinks of the self as separate,
the heart knows better."

- Jack Kornfield

When we believe in this 'illusory self' created by our mind, we experience a deep sense of separation, and that is suffering. Even the idea that mind and heart are separate is part of this illusion. In Universal Love there is no such separation. In *"Esoteric Astrology"* the Tibetan explains that all sickness and suffering is caused by separation.

We are all suffering from a kind of separation anxiety, caused by a false belief in our separateness from our human family, Nature, and our Divinity. Once we drop this illusion and rest in our natural self, we experience the truth of connection for ourselves. This is the true meaning of 'healing'[29].

"You are not accidental. Existence needs you.
Without you something will be missing in existence
and nobody can replace it. That's what gives you dignity,
that the whole existence will miss you. The stars and sun
and moon, the trees and birds and earth - everything in the
universe will feel a small place is vacant
which cannot be filled by anybody except you.

This gives you a tremendous joy, a fulfillment
that you are related to existence, and existence cares for you.
Once you are clean and clear,
you can see tremendous love falling on you
from all dimensions."

- OSHO

---

[29] Remember the word whole and the word heal both have their origin in the old English word 'haelan' which means "to make whole". (Chapter 1)

The truth is we never really 'leave' our heart center but we do 'forget' about it, and this is the nature of 'the veil'. Our separation is just an illusion. When we remember how to live from our hearts we realize, through our own direct experience, the true meaning of oneness with God and the whole of creation. When we learn to abide permanently in our hearts, this is true healing. The Sacred Heart of Humanity is the sacred core of our being, and it is known through the devotional path of Pisces. When we remember our true nature and drop all illusion, our hearts beat as one and true peace and Universal Love prevail. This is the Sacred Heart of Humanity.

> *"Only by doing nothing will you accomplish*
> *all there is to be done"*
>
> - Patrul Rinpoche

If you have Pisces Rising you can consider yourself to be a Pisces Soul. You are not here to do anything other than realize your own true nature. The most important thing you can do is to learn to drop all illusions and self-concern, and simply rest in the truth of your own being.

When you learn to live from your heart, your heart center opens wider, you emanate Universal Love, and you become a pacemaker for other human hearts to follow. You are simply here to remember who you are and live it fully, so others may see your light and follow your example.

> *"What I am is good enough*
> *if I would only be it openly."*
>
> - Carl Rogers

According to *"Esoteric Astrology"*, the journey of our Soul began as '*a point of light in the mind of God*' in Aries. That point of light left 'the Father's house' and experienced a fantastic journey of existence, experience, individuation and maturation in which awareness became aware of itself. Finally our journey through the Zodiac culminates here in Pisces where we remember our oneness and return 'home' bearing the gifts of awareness, wisdom, power, compassion, consciousness and Universal Love.

Through *"Esoteric Astrology"* and *"The Twelve Labors of Hercules: An Astrological Interpretation"* the Tibetan is describing the creation and development of our Soul, or light body, in 'stages' from instinct, intellect, intuition and illumination to enlightenment. It is through this greatest journey of all, our Soul's journey of consciousness, that we are able to experience and become aware of our own Divinity, and fully realize our true nature as Divine beings of love and light.

Key Points:

- If you have Pisces Rising you can consider yourself to be a Pisces Soul.
- The highest Soul purpose of Pisces is to flow Universal Love into the world through the Sacred Heart of humanity.
- Your biggest challenge is getting overwhelmed by suffering, which may cause you to want to withdraw from the world in avoidance and escapism.
- The solution is to turn your attention to your own heart and stay there.
- From there you'll not only realize that all suffering was created by the illusion of separation, but also you will return to wholeness, access the powerful energy of the Sacred Heart and emanate Universal Love into the world.

In the next Chapter we will follow the Soul's journey through the Zodiac once again, from Aries through to Pisces. This time we'll be looking at the integration process of personality-Soul fusion, from the perspective of the six polarities (or pairs of opposite signs): how they integrate into what the Tibetan Master calls 'the blended six', and the implications for our Soul's journey.

4. The Integration Process

In Chapter 1 we talked about how your brain and social conditioning keep you in an illusion of separation, and that your spiritual journey is really a process of perceiving your true nature as it is: wholeness. In *"Esoteric Astrology"* this process is referred to as *personality-Soul fusion*.

To briefly recap: your social conditioning and brain wiring lead you to experience reality *through your lower mind as dualistic thinking*: this and that, either/or, him/her, black/white and so forth. In other words *thinking (and experiencing life) in terms of opposites*.

The Zodiac[30] is made up of twelve signs arranged in a circle. Each sign therefore has it's *polar opposite* on the other side of the circle. So although we have twelve signs, they are grouped into *six pairs of opposites*. These are called the *six polarities*.

---

[30] Late 14c., from Old French *zodiaque,* from Latin *zodiacus* "zodiac," from Greek *zodiakos* (*kyklos*) "zodiac (circle)," literally "circle of little animals," from *zodiaion,* diminutive of *zoion* "animal". From http://www.etymonline.com/index.php?term=zodiac

The six polarities are:
- Aries-Libra
- Taurus-Scorpio
- Gemini-Sagittarius
- Cancer-Capricorn
- Leo-Aquarius
- Virgo-Pisces

Because of the illusion of separation, we tend to *think* of them as separate, but it is important to remember that *they are inherently connected.* In Soul Astrology, not only are they connected but *they are an important key to unlocking your spiritual journey: your healing journey to wholeness and personality-Soul fusion.*

"We may break a piece of magnetized steel as often as we like, we shall never be able to separate the positive from the negative pole; each fragment will always have both. This shows that polarity is an aspect of unity, not an arbitrary duality but an inseparable whole"

– Lama Anagarika Govinda

Opposite signs can be thought of as two 'poles' (two ends) of one continuous energetic spectrum. Understanding the totality of this spectrum can lead us out of a sense of duality into a more complete experience. The opposite pole of any sign can therefore be considered as a spiritual "gateway" in the sense that it opens us up to the higher spiritual potential of our own sign. By embracing the energy and character of the opposite sign, we energetically create an evolutionary loop (like the figure-eight infinity symbol) that enables a quantum leap to a higher Soul vibration.

To understand this we have to remember that in Soul Astrology we are always talking about energy and the movement of energy. Studies in quantum physics have shown that *matter can act as a particle or a wave* depending upon how it is observed[31]. In other words it can appear like a solid object or it can be more like a fluid wave of energy. Essentially there is no separation. There is only a difference of experience based on frequency or vibration. At the denser end of the spectrum light is matter, while at the lighter (finer) end of the spectrum, matter is light:

> *"there is no difference between energy and matter*
> *except for the rate of motion …*
> *matter is spirit vibrating at it's slowest*
> *and spirit is matter vibrating at it's fastest"*

> \- H.P. Blavatsky

Because we are creatures of habit, we tend to 'solidify' at one end of a polarity. Through our social conditioning and brain wiring we will tend to have a default set of behaviors and psychological patterns. Our default patterns are reflected in our Zodiac signs. We are born under our particular Zodiac signs because that is the energetic patterning that we are already resonating with as our default way of being. We become 'polarized' and our behavior tends to 'solidify' at our preferred end of the pole.

We can be so identified with our end of the 'pole' that we fail to recognize the qualities of the opposite sign in ourselves. We may even be attracted to someone with Sun, Moon or Rising Sign in our opposite sign because they appear to possess qualities we think we lack. Although this can be a very comfortable relationship it can also keep us stuck in terms of our own spiritual growth. The 'honey trap' is that we might always rely on the other person to provide those qualities in the relationship and fail to develop them in ourselves.

For example if we are a practical, methodical Capricorn, and our partner is a loving, nurturing Cancerian, we might always rely on

---

[31] See the double-slit experiment at
https://en.wikipedia.org/wiki/Double-slit_experiment

them to provide the emotional strength and they might always rely on us to be practical, down-to-earth, and resourceful. So we remain polarized and never recognize or develop these qualities within ourselves. If we don't develop the qualities of our opposite sign, we miss an important opportunity to move towards wholeness.

When we develop the qualities of our opposite sign in ourselves, we *move toward the center* and bring ourselves to harmony and balance. This breaks our habit of 'solidifying' at one end of the spectrum and elevates our consciousness to a new level. It's not that one end of a polarity is dense and the other more light: at the level of ego-personality both can be equally dense, but once we begin to move toward the other pole, we *generate movement* which naturally elevates our consciousness. Thus in moving toward the center we arrive at a lighter level of consciousness than is experienced at either pole.

Dr. Noel Huntly PhD explains how this happens in terms of quantum theory and vibration. At lower levels of consciousness we are vibrating at a slower rate and matter is denser. Matter therefore appears as particles that can appear to oppose one another. As we *generate movement* we increase the vibration and the particles *can begin to aid one another rather than opposing*. They can move to a harmonious state where they begin to synchronize and harmonize:

"the opposite nature of this oscillation on the lower levels gradually converts to a cyclic 'oscillation' in which the two poles are assimilated, unified, and in effect rotate around in a vortex action ... now 'aiding' one another rather than opposing ... In addition, in this ascension process, separate vortices become more in phase with one another. Undivided wholeness (for example, a quantum state) is created by putting its parts into phase (into harmony, resonance, 'on the same wave length')."

- Dr. Noel Huntly Ph.D[32]

---

[32] "*The Meaning of Beyond Duality*" online document at http://www.users.globalnet.co.uk/~noelh/Duality.htm

We can use this information to consciously accelerate our spiritual growth in two important ways:

- *by embracing the polar opposites of our personality signs*[33] (predominantly our Sun and Moon signs) we expand our perception, which then enables us to detect and perceive our more subtle Soul-sign qualities more easily.

- *by embracing the polar opposite of our Soul Sign* we raise our frequency, elevate our consciousness, become aware of more subtle energies, and can therefore express the lighter, more subtle, frequencies of our Soul in our everyday life.

Consciously embracing the qualities of our opposite signs moves us toward greater degrees of synthesis and wholeness and thereby accelerates our spiritual journey, our individual process of personality-Soul fusion. Ultimately we become a fully integrated individual: in other words we are fully Soul-Centered and we experience no separation between personality and Soul.

A fully Soul Centered individual is one who is fully integrated. This means they have integrated their Soul and personality and can access and fully express the highest octave of each sign. They will no longer experience polarity, so they can express the highest octave of Aries-Libra, Taurus-Scorpio, Gemini-Sagittarius, and so forth.

As we journey through this process together, eventually the whole of humanity will collectively shift towards wholeness. The twelve Zodiac signs as we currently experience them will then become what the Tibetan refers to as the *blended six:*

For students of Esoteric Astrology this article is highly recommended for further reading and contemplation. In particular in relation to Ray 4 and the principle and process of *harmony and beauty through conflict.*

[33] Read more about your personality signs in *"Your Essential Guide To Soul Astrology"* free with Ruth's newsletter at RuthHadikin.com

*"The 12 opposites must become the blended six,
this is brought about by the fusion in consciousness of the polar
opposites. Pause and consider this phrasing.*

*The opposites eternally remain from the point of view of human
reason, but to the initiate who's intuition is functioning they
constitute but six great potencies, because he has achieved "the
freedom of the two"³⁴ as is sometimes called.*

*For instance, the Leo subject who has an initiated consciousness
preserves the individuality developed in Leo, as well as the
universality of Aquarius; he can function, if he so chooses, as a
fully self-identified individual, yet possess simultaneously a fully
awakened universal awareness; the same thing can be said of
balanced activity and consequent fusion in all the signs.*

*This analysis constitutes in itself an interesting
and far reaching field of speculation."*

- The Tibetan, *"Esoteric Astrology"*

As we evolve in consciousness we move from a sense of separation
to an increasing sense of wholeness. In separation we experience
fear, in wholeness we experience love. Because the lower octave of
any sign is fear-based and the higher octave is love-based, it is
important for you to understand the lower fear-based vibrations of
your personality signs, and to know that the key to moving into the
higher octave of each lies in accessing the energy of their opposite
signs and then fully integrating these energies. This then creates a
clear 'lens' through which the light of your Soul Sign can shine
brightly into the world, through you.

---

³⁴ The *freedom of the two* may refer to a higher sate of consciousness
where one is no longer caught in the conditioning of either sign, but has
liberated one's mind to the point where the qualities of either one can be
accessed and utilized without one's consciousness being identified with the
lower thought-forms of either sign.

Next we'll look at the six polarities from the perspective of each of the twelve signs. So we begin with Aries-Libra: viewing the polarity through the lens of Aries and later we will again explore Libra-Aries, looking at the same polarity through from the Libra end of the spectrum. For each one it is the integration process that is paramount as we work towards 'the blended two'.

Aries-Libra
From Creation To Humanity…. With Love

The spiritual path of Aries-Libra speaks of a magical journey from Heaven to Earth and back. So is it a beautiful magical mystery tour filled with heavenly voices and Divine Love? No. Well, at least, not yet.

The Aries Soul is carrying the higher vibration of Aries (albeit unconsciously for the most part[35]) or the original "song," whereas the Aries personality is working on the egoic level of that sign. It's a bit like waking from a dream in which you understand everything and all is clear. However, upon waking the details become blurred and you lack the language to express what you just experienced. Just as we go through our day without really knowing how we are breathing or digesting our food, in this way most of us are still largely unaware of the energies that are an inherent part of us at Soul level, and we are therefore personality-centered and personality-driven.

There are two points of balance in the year, when the day and night, the polarities of dark and light, are of equal length. This happens when the Sun enters Aries, at the Spring Equinox, and again when the Sun enters Libra, at the Autumn Equinox. The Aries-Libra polarity is therefore concerned at the highest level with the energies of Divine Will, Balance, Equanimity and Divine Harmony.

---

[35] For more on Personality-Soul Fusion and The Three Crosses, see Chapter 1

Aries is the energy of Creation in its purest form. It is the spark of Divine Will that initiates all Life. In *"Esoteric Astrology"* it is said that the Soul begins its journey in Aries as a *"point of light in the mind of God."* As the first Zodiac sign, Aries is often said to be the sign that is "closest to God," because the "point of light" (which is the newly-conceived Soul) has not left God's 'mind' yet. This also possibly explains why Aries is one of the most intuitive signs. It's as though Aries has an "access-all-areas" pass into the mind of God! This is often felt by the Aries subject as an urge, an impulse, or a spontaneous movement into action.

The Aries individual just "knows" things, without knowing how they know, which can really spook their friends! Aries-type intuition can be described as "spontaneous knowing." You don't know how you know, you just do. We might describe Aries as pure intuition-in-action.

These spontaneous urges are what probably gets the Aries personality into the most trouble and brings on accusations of "arrogance" from others around them. In fact, it is often not arrogance but this inner knowing that moves Aries into action. Arians often make extremely good leaders for this very reason, if they allow themselves to move with their inner knowing and lead people. There is, however, one type of Aries who doesn't ever take the lead but prefers to take a back seat and just complain that, *"nobody around here knows what they are doing. Can't they see that if they just do so and so, that is the solution?"*

This is because what seems so obvious to Aries cannot be seen by everyone, leading some Arians to erroneously conclude that everybody else must be stupid. They cannot believe that others cannot see the solutions as obviously as they do.

It is important for the Aries personality to realize that other people aren't stupid, just because they cannot see what you can see! If you are the only one who can see, then you have a responsibility to take the lead. This is the first key to the Soul path of Aries. Aries energy is somewhat *pre-egoic* in the sense that it is a Divine spark. Ego arises when the human mind steps in and takes the credit.

This is not making ego "wrong." Our ego is necessary, but it is important that we fully understand what it is. In this context we are not talking about 'ego' in the commonly held view of someone who has a high opinion of him or herself. In fact we could have low self-esteem and still be caught in our ego. *Simply put, ego is when our mind is thinking about itself*[36].

So our Aries friend receives a God-given impulse and acts on it. This solves a problem and/or brings some kind of benefit. Nothing wrong in that. Then our friend has the thought, "I did that." That thought would be ego. So this brings us to the second important understanding about the Soul path of Aries: "Who is doing the doing?"

In *"The Labours of Hercules: An Astrological Interpretation"*, the first labor in Aries requires Hercules to capture and corral a herd of flesh-eating horses that have been ravaging the land and terrorizing the people! Full of joy and enthusiasm, Hercules quickly manages to round up the horses thinking "well that was easy." He hands over the horses to his friend, telling him to put them in the corral, while he returns to his teacher to find out what his next challenge will be.

The horses escape, ravage the local villages, and kill his friend. Filled with sadness for the loss of his friend, Hercules re-captures the horses and completes the task himself.

This illustrates some important lessons for the Aries Soul:

- To recognize that Divine gifts come from the Divine, not the personality. They are not "ours" but come through us, to benefit all.

- That if we have a Divine gift, it is our own responsibility to use it, since it may not be available to others.

---

[36] For more on the ego-personality see Chapter 1.

- That impulse alone is rarely beneficial, unless we skillfully follow our impulses through to completion.

This story also illustrates the naiveté of Aries. As mentioned earlier, Aries is the sometimes called the "child" of the Zodiac, for he has yet to develop wisdom and skill. Because Hercules found it easy to round up the horses, he thought it would be equally easy for his friend to herd them into the corral. He failed to anticipate what challenges could arise, and whether his friend had the necessary skill-set to meet those challenges. Having never left God, Aries has no worldly experience, has never experienced challenges, and therefore cannot anticipate the obstacles that can arise. This is where the ethical thinking of Aries' polar opposite, Libra, is needed.

At its highest Soul vibration, Libra is about ethics, justice and Divine harmony. This is where the personality-centered Libra has a tendency to develop rose-tinted spectacles. The desire for harmony can sometimes lead a Libra personality to appear to be a bit of a Pollyanna[37], avoiding conflict and real challenges by trying to "keep the peace," come what may.

Nevertheless, the Libra individual does have an innate understanding of harmonics. This leads Libra into ethical questioning. Often it is said that Libra individuals are indecisive (in contrast to the apparent decisiveness of their polar opposite Aries) but this is an over-simplification of what is really happening. For Libra, it is important to understand the *process* of decision-making. How can we know when a decision is the correct one?

This is the purpose of ethics[38] – the process whereby we can make "right" decisions. The Soul purpose of Libra is "right human

---

[37] Pollyanna: *"an excessively or blindly optimistic person"* from http://www.dictionary.com/browse/pollyanna

[38] *"Ethics or moral philosophy is the branch of philosophy that involves systematizing, defending, and recommending concepts of right and wrong conduct."* - from https://en.wikipedia.org/wiki/Ethics

relations," and the essence of Libra carries the very wisdom that Aries needs. Aries will develop wisdom by being more Libra-like and thinking about why a certain decision is the "right" one. What makes it "right?"

Before charging into an impulse, Aries is always wise to ask, "What makes this right?" This allows Aries to explore whether his impulse is of Divine origin or a personality-driven impulse. In this way, Aries will be able to see when his or her decisions will be most beneficial and when, like Hercules, they may be impulsive and/or incomplete.

Libra invites Aries, through ethical questioning, to become aware of *harmonics[39]*. Libra answers a very important question for Aries. The highest vibration of Libra innately knows that what makes a decision right is harmonics. The right decision is the one that is harmonious, because it is in alignment with the whole of Creation. Eventually, the influence of Libra brings truth, beauty and harmony to Aries. This is when the higher vibration of Aries will awaken and Aries will finally understand how it is that he knows what he knows. However, before Aries can access the wisdom of Libra, he has to exercise discipline to control his impulsiveness.

Mercury is the Soul-ruler of Aries[40], whereas Mars is the personality ruler. Mars can be seen to rule the responses and reactions of our lower animal-urges, whereas a Mercurial influence on Aries encourages development of the Higher Mind. The Soul path of Aries speaks of the journey from lower mind to Higher Mind, through discipline and the development of wisdom. It really is a Divine, magical mystery tour that takes us from the Divine to Earth, through

---

[39] See *"Libra Rising - The Libra Soul"* in Chapter 3.

[40] Aries is associated with the development of the mind. The wild horses can be seen as a metaphor for taming our unruly mind. Mercury, Soul ruler of Aries, is also associated with the development of the *Antahkarana* or "Rainbow Bridge" which, once fully formed, allows access to Higher Consciousness and Higher Mind.

Right Human Relations in Libra and then back to Heaven again, with greater wisdom.

Once Aries accesses Higher Mind, he or she becomes a clear channel for Divine light and wisdom and the higher Soul purpose of Aries (which is to inspire others with ideas) unfolds. With the balanced harmony of Libra, Aries (the sign of the Ram) is able to fulfill his own highest potential and lead his flock, through Divine Light, Wisdom, and Inspiration.

Taurus-Scorpio
The Desire To Know And The Path of Illumination

It is said that the Buddha had six planets (plus Chiron) in Taurus[41]. In the previous chapter we saw that he was born under Taurus, passed in Taurus, and became enlightened in Taurus. Many important Buddhist festivals are celebrated during the time of Taurus. The highest vibration of Taurus is about revelation, illumination and enlightenment. It is a very mysterious sign, associated with the opening of the third eye.

Esoterically, the ruling planet of Taurus is Vulcan, which itself is hidden (a hypothetical planet once believed to be orbiting between the Sun and Mercury, Vulcan is used only in *"Esoteric Astrology".*) Vulcan is the blacksmith of the Zodiac. In *"Esoteric Astrology"* The Tibetan Master DK says that Vulcan either forges "the chains that bind us" or "the key that sets us free." The choice between imprisonment in the material realm of *samsara*[42] (the cycle of death

---

[41] *"Buddhist Astrology"*, by Jhampa Shaneman & Jan V. Angel.

[42] *"Samsara is a Sanskrit word that means "wandering" or "world", with the connotation of cyclic, circuitous change. It also refers to the theory of rebirth and "cyclicality of all life, matter, existence", a fundamental assumption of all Indian religions. Samsara is sometimes referred to with terms or phrases such as transmigration, karmic cycle, reincarnation, and 'cycle of aimless drifting, wandering or mundane existence'".* - from https://en.wikipedia.org/wiki/Samsara

and rebirth) or liberation lies in the mysteries of Taurus.

At the personality level, Taurus has a tendency toward stubbornness. This is natural; as the fixed-earth sign, its purpose is to create stability. Anyone with a Taurean friend or relative will know the reassuring sense of stability we feel around our Taurean friends. The purpose of all "fixed" energy is to stabilize; however, the Soul purpose of Taurus relates to the deeper mysteries of "stabilizing" spirit in matter.

The vibration of Venus comes through Taurus at the personality level, which means that most Taurean individuals are seen to be placid, peaceful and only stubborn if you try to push them in a direction they don't want to go. As an earth sign, they are very much focused on the practicalities of life, so most Taureans are happy as long as the family is OK, everybody has enough food to eat and a roof over their heads, and the bills are paid. "Lazy" is not a word we would usually associate with Taurus – they can be very hard workers. Like the Bull, they plod and plod and plod, because they understand how to work steadily, make money, and cover the basics: to make sure their family's basic needs are met. Then they are happy.

If you have Taurus Sun, Moon or Rising Sign (Ascendant), this Venusian effect means you need to have beauty in your surroundings. A beautiful home, beautiful garden and/or somewhere peaceful is more than just personal preference. For you, it is vital for your well-being. To be able to sit in a peaceful environment is very important, because you are affected by your physical surroundings. Anything disharmonious disturbs you, while beauty and harmony are therapeutic for you. This is because, like Libra, you also have an innate knowing of harmony and a strong affinity for beauty. Beautiful surroundings are very healing for you.

Beauty is simply harmony expressed in form (whereas Libra is concerned with harmony in all systems, Taurus's knowledge of and concern with harmony is in its application to physical forms). You may also have an artistic streak, a beautiful voice, or at least a love and appreciation of music, because you understand harmonics. Some of my Taurean friends laugh at this (yes, you also have a great sense of humor) yet you decorate your homes and gardens with as much skill, care, attention, harmony and balance as any interior designer.

Where you can become lazy is intellectually and/or spiritually. The halls of academia are hardly filled with Taureans. You have a tendency to become content too easily, once your physical and comfort needs are met. Once you have material security and beautiful surroundings, you tend to relax and not go any further. While the Scorpios are busy packing their backpacks for the great spiritual adventure, you would rather stay home with the family in the garden with your feet up and a cocktail by the pool.

Taurus, like its polar opposite Scorpio, is on the path of Mastering Desire. But whereas Scorpio's challenge is to tame their multiple desires, you have to cultivate the "Desire to Know." Whereas Scorpio desires to dive deeply and intensely into the depths of the human psyche, your energy is the energy of primordial desire, desire for sense pleasures: beauty, harmony, comfort. This has to be cultivated into the 'desire to know', so that you can aspire to the highest vibration of enlightenment and illumination. The

inquisitiveness and deep inner probing of Scorpio is needed for Taurus to realize that there is something inside worth aspiring to. This then turns your attention away from the material world and toward a deeper exploration of your inner world and, eventually, your own true nature. There are inner mysteries awaiting your discovery!

Whereas Taurus' opposite sign Scorpio is the first to dive headlong into confrontation, Taurus can dig in their heels and actively avoid confrontation to 'keep the peace'. (Or just present a wall of stubborn silence). Contentment and preserving the status-quo are the ego-traps of Taurus: the tendency to be content with material gain and/or sense pleasures, and to avoid making waves, prevents you from asking the bigger questions, exploring your inner nature, and seeking higher knowledge. This keeps you stuck in 'spiritual ignorance', focused purely on conventional matters and not recognizing your own inner awareness. The higher Divine vibration and illuminatory nature of your Taurus Soul cannot be accessed from such a limited perspective. The deeper mystery of Taurus' esoteric ruler Vulcan is hinting that we have the key to our own destiny: we really are forging our own path. The inner mysteries of Taurus are strongly connected to the development of the three 'kayas' (three bodies of a buddha) or, in other words, the light body.

As a Taurean Soul you have an inner understanding of the process of 'involution' (a necessary precursor to evolution) whereby Spirit incarnates into matter to have a physical experience. We are spiritual beings having a human experience because of the energies of Taurus. They are the most mystical of energies. At it's highest level of illumination it is the sign of omniscience (all-knowing) and clairvoyance (clear seeing), so it is ironic that at the personality level many Taureans keep yourselves spiritually limited, by not aspiring to spiritual truth. This is the Soul-path of Taurus in a nutshell: the transformation of desire into aspiration. To transform the desire for conventional sense-pleasures into the aspiration for spiritual truth. Yes folks it's time to put down the chocolate and go meditate!

When you allow yourselves to simply 'be' in meditation, for example with the radiance of a flower, a deep inner-knowing begins to dawn upon you. More than anyone your Taurean Soul knows that your own physical body is both a Temple, and a Universe. You know the beauty and radiance of the flower, felt at a very deep level, that connects with your own inner beauty and radiance until eventually there comes a recognition of the Divine within. As a Taurean Soul you are learning to use your exquisite sensing capability to sense Divinity in all physical forms. This is how you sense and know beauty.

By being more inquisitive about the nature of your own inner world, you start moving towards Taurus' opposite pole of Scorpio. This lifts you out of your comfort zone, beyond the doldrums of contentment and cultivates your desire to know. The knowledge gained in Scorpio awakens and enlivens the higher vibration of Taurus. The full implications of your Taurean Soul Journey are hinted at in the Soul Keynote for Taurus:

"I see and when the Eye is opened, all is light"

- The Tibetan

This refers to the opening of the inner eye, following which you see and understand the workings of the Universe. The Soul path of Taurus is to know and understand all the mysteries of the workings of the Universe by recognizing and directing your own inner light. This illuminatory power of Taurus was well-known in Ancient times. The brightest star in the constellation of Taurus, "Aldebaran"[43] is commonly called the 'eye of the Bull' but it was also known in Ancient Mystery schools to be the "Eye Of Illumination".

Taurus' Soul ruler Vulcan shapes and forges primordial awareness into physical matter. This accounts for the dualistic inclinations of Taurean energy: will you direct your power and stamina outwards toward the conventional, or inwards toward the spiritual?

When the pristine primordial immature awareness of Aries (the 'point of light in the mind of God') first moves towards form in Taurus, as a result of desire, it is not yet known whether it will incline towards the conventional, become embroiled in the materialistic world and contribute to the 'great illusion' or whether it will incline towards a spiritual path and move to illumination. It could go either way. Will your journey be of benefit to all, or just benefit for yourself?

If you have Taurus strongly placed, it is very important for you to stay alert, aware, recognize your inner senses and make conscious choices to move toward the light moment by moment. During the

---

[43] See *"Aldebaran, The Eye of Illumination"* at:
http://www.Souledout.org/cosmology/highlights/aldebaran.html

time of the great spiritual festival of Wesak[44], this not only applies to those with Taurus in their natal chart, but to the rest of us as well. During the time of these three great festivals there is a powerful influx of Divine consciousness onto the planet, and we all get to bask in the energies of potential illumination. Each one of us has the potential to become a 'buddha' (enlightened one). What we make of it, is up to us. The spiritual path of Taurus is one from ignorance to illumination through a deep recognition of spiritual truth gained through the experience in Scorpio, which leads to the power to cultivate and direct spiritual energy into form.

Gemini-Sagittarius
The Sacred Marriage of Love and Wisdom

"In the beginning was the Word ..." Gemini rules the breath, speech, languages, writing, communication, networks, and communion on all levels. Hidden within Gemini are the deepest mysteries of creation and destruction. The energy of Gemini both creates and dissolves polarities, in the Universal dance of Creation, which was known, to the Ancient Rishis of India as the "breathing in and out of Brahma." Welcome to one of the most complex and contradictory signs of the Zodiac.

We mentioned above how the twelve Zodiac signs make up the six

---

[44] To support the collective evolution of human consciousness, and our individual process of personality-Soul integration, The Tibetan emphasized the benefit of meditating at the time of the Full Moon, when Sun and Moon are in opposite signs. These are called Full Sun-Moon meditations. Of these, three major spiritual festivals are considered most important: Easter (Sun in Aries - Full Moon in Libra), Wesak (Sun in Taurus - Full Moon in Scorpio) and the festival of Goodwill (Sun in Gemini - Full Moon in Sagittarius). It is also important to note that in many buddhist traditions Wesak (otherwise known as Saka Dawa or the festival of Buddha) is most often celebrated at the Full Moon in May which may or may not coincide with the Taurus-Scorpio Full Moon. See: https://www.lucistrust.org/meetings_and_events/three_major_spiritual_festivals

polarities. Gemini has a vital role to play in the process of resolving these polarities in human consciousness. One mystery of Gemini – and there are many – is the resolution of polarities into Divine Union. Because of this unique function, Gemini is the only sign that has an esoteric connection with all the other signs of the Zodiac. Just like spinning an enormous web (or story), it is through Gemini that all will be woven together at the end.

Whatever sign you are, your Gemini friend will be able to relate with you on some level. Gemini has the ability to visit every sign in order to experience and understand the energies involved. Ultimately, it is in the sign of Gemini that we realize the multi-dimensional aspects of our whole being.

By the time the Divine Intelligence of Gemini has filtered through a human mind, it becomes one of the most complex, restless and difficult to handle energies of the Zodiac. You could be forgiven for thinking your Gemini friend has ADHD or is just crazy! As the mutable (changeable) air sign, the nature of Gemini is one of constant movement. Gemini has to touch everything and hold onto nothing. Freedom to move is essential.

Gemini is associated with the lungs, and we can use the analogy of breath to understand what is going on with Gemini. In breathing, there are two stages, breathing in and breathing out. This explains the two (apparent) sides of Gemini. Gemini has a need to first gather information – this is breathing in. Our Gemini friend may be very silent and contemplative during this stage. Information is being received and processed. Then comes the breathing out ... hold onto your hat!

Depending upon the level of consciousness of our particular Gemini, this is where we may experience a profoundly inspired message or, at worst, simply gossip. Their innate compulsion to share information has no built-in quality control. The information you get seems to be whatever happens to be flitting through their head in any given moment. For this reason, Geminis have an unfair reputation for being empty-headed and superficial, yet this in itself shows a lack of understanding of the importance of Gemini.

To avoid being distracted by trivia, Gemini needs the determined focus and follow-through of its polar opposite, Sagittarius. Only then will you be able to sustain your inner journey and recognize your "twin self" – your Soul. This recognition is referred to in the Soul keynote for Gemini:

"I recognize my other self and
in the waning of that self I grow and glow".

The Twins represent the dualistic aspects of Self: our personality and our Soul. In the myth of the two brothers, Castor and Pollux (which comprise the constellation of Gemini), Castor is mortal (personality) while Pollux is immortal (Soul). Another duality is that of "two minds," the head and the heart.

At the personality level, Gemini is ruled by Mercury, which has an important role to play in the development of the antahkarana (or Rainbow Bridge). This is the mysterious "bridge'" between lower and Higher Mind, that develops once humanity has evolved to a certain point in consciousness, whereby we can fully live from Higher Mind.

At the level of our lower mind, it is the influence of Mercury that creates polarities, by focusing on our differences and creating the illusion of separation. At one stage of our development this is a necessary precursor to the process of individuation – development of the individual. If it were not for our ability to separate for example, we'd never cut the umbilical cord and stride out on our own, separate from our mothers!

Once we begin our inner journey toward Soul identification however, it is also the influence of Mercury, which bridges the (illusory) gap, connects us with our Higher Self, and brings us home to wholeness. This dual role of division and reunion contributes to the seemingly contradictory nature of Gemini. But seen from a higher perspective, it is just one road; we travel out on the road and then we use the same road to travel back home.

At Soul level, Gemini is ruled by the sacred planet Venus. Venus' higher octave awakens us to truth, beauty, harmony and the highest unconditional love. The Gemini Soul is here to unite the head and the heart, creating a bridge to Higher Mind and Higher Love.

The fully integrated Gemini resolves polarity at every level. All opposites merge in Gemini: self-others, personality-Soul; Higher Self-lower self; mind-heart, etc. This happens through a deep understanding of energetic relationships. Through Mercurial connection to Higher Mind, consciousness, and Venus, Gemini governs the Breath of Life, the movement of Spirit in Form. This awakens us to conscious relationship on all levels.

The Gemini personality, lacking the wisdom to comprehend the complexity of these relationships, has a tendency to become scattered, distracted by an array of duality. The deep, truth-seeking focus of Sagittarius is needed for Gemini to find (and stay on) the path leading to its higher Soul purpose:

> *"To teach Right Human Relations,*
> *between self and others,*
> *personality and Soul,*
> *anima and animus,*
> *higher mind and lower mind."*

> - The Tibetan, *"Esoteric Astrology"*

In its exploration of energetic relationships *"Esoteric Astrology"* discusses the subject of the Seven Rays, explaining that Earth is on the evolutionary path of the second ray of Love-Wisdom, otherwise known as the "path of love. In Buddhism, the ultimate wisdom is the "wisdom realizing emptiness" and is written in a text called "The

Heart Sutra." The ultimate wisdom is therefore considered to be "heart" wisdom or "Love-Wisdom." Thus the spiritual path of Gemini-Sagittarius is inherently linked to the spiritual evolution of the Earth and of human consciousness[45].

The spiritual path of Gemini-Sagittarius is the path of heart-wisdom leading to the realization of ultimate truth. It is the spiritual path of realizing Love-Wisdom through the revelation of truth. However, where Sagittarius is seeking truth, Gemini is asking, "What is truth?" To fully understand Gemini's Soul Path, we need to understand the concept of "two truths."

The "two truths" refers to both conventional truth, as we experience it in our everyday lives, and the ultimate truth of reality. This can be explained by the following paradox:

I'm sitting on a chair.
The chair does not exist.

Both statements are true. On a conventional, everyday, level the chair definitely exists. We can see it. Yet on the subatomic, quantum, level there is nothing. There is no thing that can be defined. There is certainly no chair and indeed there is more space than there is solidity at that level. So it is also completely true to say that the chair really does not exist.

Because of a deep realization of the relationship between energies and an ability to experience many dimensions of Being, the Gemini Soul realizes that all "conventional" truth is relative and depends upon both our perspective and our capacity for perception.

The integrated Gemini teaches others through the creation of wonderful 'stories', weaving thought, information and ideas into

---

[45] In Esoteric Astrology, the Earth is the Soul Ruler of Sagittarius and the Hierarchical ruler of Gemini. This shows the importance of the Earth for individuals under these signs and the importance of the Divine Intelligence of Gemini-Sagittarius, in the evolutionary process on Earth.

magnificent concepts, mental 'structures' that point towards ultimate truth, and by creating new systems of thought, or sciences.

Our problems arise when we confuse those mental concepts with ultimate truth. Ultimate truth can never be put into words, for it is beyond words. As soon as we put truth into words, it is no longer *ultimate* truth, but merely *one expression* of it – which reduces it to the level of *conventional* truth. In ultimate reality there is no chair, and it does not become one just because we label it as such!

> *"He who talks about truth injures it thereby;*
> *He who tries to prove it thereby maims and distorts it;*
> *He who gives it a label and a school of thought kills it;*
> *And He who declares himself a believer buries it."*

> - Lin Yutang

When we start believing our own stories, it confines us to a narrow and limited experience of truth. This is the ego-trap of Gemini: over-identification with thinking, and the mistaken belief that we are what we think. If we believe the philosopher Descartes who said, "*I think, therefore I am*," then who are you when you are not thinking? The integrated Gemini is aware of many multi-dimensional aspects of our Selves as Spiritual Beings, way beyond thinking.

If you have Sun, Moon, or Ascendant in Gemini, the challenge for you is to experience your Self beyond your thoughts. There is literally more to you than what you think! This world is very distracting for a Gemini, and it is all too easy for you to get lost in trivia, missing the magnificence of your inner being. With the sustained focus of Sagittarius, you are capable of traveling beyond your thoughts into multiple inner dimensions to the very depths of your Soul.

Will you use the extensive power of Gemini to divide, or unite? To build walls or bridges? Or will you apply the sustained focus of Sagittarius to scratch beneath the surface, discover worlds within worlds, and realize the deepest truths of your Soul and the ultimate relationship of Love-Wisdom? It all depends upon your ability to choose where you place your attention and maintain your focus.

Cancer-Capricorn
The Conscious Journey Home

Where is my Home? Who is my Family? The sign of Cancer is associated with home, family, the womb, birth, the Mother, the Moon, water, tides, feelings, emotions, emotional intelligence, empathy, Love and ultimately the highest Love of all: Compassion.

In our Soul's journey through the 12 zodiac signs, Leo rules the center of the heart but to reach the heart-center first we must pass through mysterious, watery, Cancer and the minefield of human emotions. After the 'interplay of light' in Gemini, the Divine Light in form begins to stir in the minds of humanity, and ripple throughout the masses, in Cancer:

"the Spirit of God moved upon the face of the waters"

- The Tibetan, *"Esoteric Astrology"*

Cancerians are tuned into the masses in a way that makes them great nurses and/or sales people because they usually know what people need even before they know they need it! They are the consumate 'people person'. Wherever there are people, you will find Cancer: people matter more to them, than anything else.

Cancer is motivated primarily by human need. In addition to sales, you will find Cancerians busy at work as counselors and nurses (especially ER managers where 'needs' are prioritized!), midwives, chefs, construction workers and home-builders. Wherever there is human need, you will find Cancerians quietly meeting it. They are able to send their Cancerian radar deep into the mass consciousness, take a measurement, and sense what is needed next for the benefit of all. The answer... is usually Love. When they put their mind to it, Cancerians know how to consciously flow Love. In a Cancerian kitchen you will usually find that the biggest ingredient is Love.

This is one of the keys to understanding the deeper esoteric significance of Cancer. At it's highest vibration Cancer is about meeting the deepest human need of all: our need for Divine Love and spiritual fulfillment. So does every Cancerian we meet flow unconditional love and compassion onto the planet? Not exactly, well at least, not yet.

Because of their connectedness with mass consciousness, the prevailing fear, tribalism, and mob-consciousness can dominate the Cancer personality. Until she begins to awaken to her higher nature, Cancer can too easily become overwhelmed by fear, get lost in the crowd and end up 'going with the flow' of lower consciousness.

This is because Cancer hasn't yet cultivated the strong, healthy, ego-definition of Leo. A well-defined ego and a strong sense of one's own individuality are needed to resist the tidal magnetic pull of the waters of lower mass consciousness. Cancer acquires this by moving towards her opposite sign Capricorn, which leads her away from the crowd and onto her own solitary path. Only then will she discover her inner voice, her intuition, and learn to listen to the 'one voice among the many', her own. This eventually brings her to the reality of her inner journey: her conscious journey to her real home.

As a Cancer personality you may tend to be a bit of a homebody: staying 'home' where you feel safe, prioritizing the needs of your home and close family, seeking refuge in your little world (your shell) and not venturing out into the big, scary, outside world. If this becomes a habit there is the danger of being stuck in your comfort zone and not exploring your true nature. If you have a strong Cancer influence in your chart, you need to take care not to succumb to irrational fears that could debilitate you.

Your ultimate 'refuge' is spiritual awareness and the recognition of your spiritual 'home', but you will not know this until you turn your attention to your Self and have the courage to embark upon your inner journey of spiritual awakening. Keeping busy meeting the physical needs of others, being 'Mother' to all, is indeed a Cancerian ego trap. There comes a time when you must allow others to fend for themselves so you can walk your own path.

The Cancerian Soul knows that the whole world is home and everyone you meet is your family: The Human Family. In order to realize this deeper spiritual truth, Cancer needs the ambition and persistence of her opposite sign Capricorn. Capricorn is the sign of ambition and at its highest vibration it is the sign of the 'disciple' (meaning one who unwaveringly follows a spiritual path), showing us that the highest 'ambition' of all, is spiritual ambition. The highest vibration of Capricorn, the goat, teaches us how to steadily walk the path until we reach that mountain-top.

At the personality level, your phenomenal Cancerian ability to sense and meet the needs of others can distract you from your own spiritual journey. This is where the spiritual ambition, solitude, and methodical application of your opposite sign Capricorn is vital. If Cancer is to discover deeper mysteries she has to venture out of her shell and cultivate the spiritual ambition of her opposite sign Capricorn.

In *"Esoteric Astrology"*, the Tibetan explains that hidden within the Cancer-Capricorn polarity is one of the deepest mysteries of all: *the mystery of the great cycle of death and re-birth (samsara)*. There are two "Great Gateways" in the Zodiac: one is in Cancer, the other is in Capricorn. This hints at the deeper significance, and mystery, of the Cancer-Capricorn polarity.

Cancer is known as 'the gate in' and Capricorn is known as 'the gate out'. The Tibetan explains that all Souls take incarnation into human form, in Cancer. Cancer is the gateway into human form, and the human experience, which is why this sign is associated with birth. Capricorn is the gateway into Spirit, and Spiritual experience, which is why this sign is associated with discipleship. Both are needed.

It is only after our incarnation into human form, and our human experience, that we return to Spirit with the wisdom that comes from our experience. This is not to say that every Cancerian Soul has never had a previous incarnation, but that we begin one cycle of unfoldment (or purpose) in Cancer.

Cancer is associated with form and feeling. According to Soul Astrologer Alan Oken[46] it is therefore the role of the Cancer Soul to *ground Spirit into physical form* to create an anchor point on the Earth plane for the subsequent development of the antahkarana or Rainbow Bridge. This searching for an 'anchor point' drives the Cancerian to continuously seek for a home. At the lowest vibration of Cancer this can lead the Cancer personality to wander aimlessly never feeling settled or content, unsure of where 'home' really is.

At it's highest vibration, once the individual has begun their inner journey (by embracing the spiritual ambition of Capricorn) this home-seeking leads to the discovery of a deeper truth - your inner light. This is your true home: the point of light, which is the real 'anchor point'. This therefore relates to the highest, Soul Purpose of Cancer, which is:

"to build a spiritual home and selflessly nourish others"

- Candy Hillenbrand[47]

There is great mystery in this statement, which is not to be misunderstood. The home is not a physical building, and the 'selfless nourishing' is not referring to physically cooking and catering for

---

[46] Alan Oken (2008) *"Soul Centered Astrology: A Key To Your Expanding Self."* Florida, IBIS Press.

[47] *"Esoteric Astrology: The Journey Of The Soul"* by Candy Hillenbrand - Online document at
http://www.aplaceinspace.net/Pages/CandyJourneyoftheSoul.html

others: that would be the lower personality interpretation of Cancer. In the spiritual sense, rather, it means finding the spiritual home within: one's own Soul light. Then cultivating that light until it grows to the point whereby its' very radiance is that which nourishes others.

"[The integrated Cancer Soul] is only aware of the Universal Love which underlies the Soul's expression in Life, and is thereby a server of that Love in conscious devotion to humanity"

- Alan Oken

There is a very real, deep, satisfying feeling to be had when you connect to your true 'home', your Soul. From there you truly have the capacity to serve and nourish the whole of humanity, but to get there you need to follow the example of your polar opposite Capricorn, and 'follow the path'. That path leads home, to YOU. This may mean releasing your attachment to the tribe, or your family, and following your own path. This doesn't mean physically leaving and going on a trip, but may mean setting boundaries and changing your whole approach to home and family.

Cardinal signs initiate change and Water signs are about Mastery of Emotions. So as the Cardinal Water sign this would mean Cancer takes the lead in changing old limiting patterns of attachment, and initiating new enlightened ways of relating to your home and family. This also means relieving yourself of certain duties and of old, limiting, familial patterns and obligations, which you may have consciously or unconsciously taken on board, and which are no longer serving you. So that you give yourself the freedom and space to go within, on your own conscious journey.

Your real home is nourishing, safe and very beautiful Cancer. It awaits your return, but to find it you have to take your attention off others, go within, apply Capricorn-like self-discipline, and begin your own conscious journey home.

Leo-Aquarius
Power, Purpose, and The Path of Self-Realization

"Hi diddly-dee, an actors life for me..." Thus sang "Honest John" The Fox, and his accomplice The Cat, in Disney's movie as Pinnochio sets off on his epic journey to become a real boy. As the Soul continues it's journey through the 12 Zodiac signs, the story of Pinnochio is symbolic of the Soul's experience in Leo and the higher purpose of Leo: the search for the Real Self.

The sign of Leo is associated with acting, drama, theater, creativity, children, warmth, humor, the heart, generosity, play, parties, entertainment, performing, kings, queens, royalty, nobility and ...ego. Leo is associated with the ego more than any other sign of the Zodiac, and that is understandable given the significance of Leo's journey. Understanding ego[48] is key to understanding the spiritual path of Leo-Aquarius.

Fire signs are about Mastery of Action, and Fixed signs are all about stability, so as the Fixed Fire sign we look to Leo to bring *stability in action*. Your Leo friend is nothing if not reliable: integrity and loyalty are among their highest values. If a Leo has got your back you know you're covered. Welcome to the noble and regal sign of Leo, symbolically represented by the Lion.

The brightest star in the constellation of Leo is *regulus*[49] known to the ancients as the ruler, regulator or 'lawgiver,' and 'The Heart of the Lion'. The Leo Soul understands the deepest mysteries of the human heart; the significance of Universal Law; the important role that humanity plays as a 'pacemaker' in the Heart of our Solar System and, more importantly, that Divine Law is very different from man-made law. The fully-integrated Leo 'rules' through heart-centered leadership, and their ability to be a 'regulator' of Divine

---

[48] Read more about ego under the heading "Separation" in Chapter 1

[49] An interesting article on Regulus "The Lawgiver" can be found here: http://www.Souledout.org/cosmology/highlights/regulushighlights/regulus highlights.html

Law: right expression of Divine Will and Purpose.

Does that mean that every Leo we meet nobly speaks in accord with Divine Law? Alas, no! Before Leo becomes truly regal we must meet and transcend the 'actor': the Leo personality.

Understanding Ego

Deepak Chopra once described ego as "the mask we wear to meet the outside world". As we saw in Chapter 1, our ego is not who we really are, but is an illusion created by our personality and character traits. It is a composite of all the learned behaviors, mannerisms, skills, customs, beliefs and values that we have accumulated in this and countless past lives.

The term *socialization*[50] refers to the process by which we learn the values, norms and beliefs of the group or society to which we belong. It is a process of conditioning, and we internalize it to such a degree that we 'become' it. Unwittingly, we get 'lost' behind the masks we wear, and in the roles we play, truly believing that is who we are. In this way our man-made society defines us, and we become 'typecast' (a theatrical term for being identified with, and lost in, the role you are playing). As a result of this process we each have an *idea* about who we are. This *idea* of our self is our ego.

Noblesse Oblige

Noblesse oblige is a French term originally used to describe the

---

[50] "Socialization, also spelled socialisation, is a term used by sociologists, social psychologists, anthropologists, political scientists, and educationalists to refer to the lifelong process of inheriting and disseminating norms, customs, values and ideologies, providing an individual with the skills and habits necessary for participating within their own society." - from https://en.wikipedia.org/wiki/Socialization Simply put it can be thought of as the process by which we learn 'how we do things around here'.

obligations of nobility. Figuratively speaking this is the concept that:

> **"One must act in a fashion that conforms to one's position, and with the reputation that one has earned".**

> - Wikipedia

In other words, now that society has given us an idea of who we are, there are obligations and duties that come as part of the role. Therein lies the ego-trap of Leo. Leo tends to become identified with the action, believing he *is* what he does. At this level Leo is self-conscious: pre-occupied with his role, actions, reputation and behavior. He becomes so lost in the many masks he has to wear, each with their own particular set of duties and responsibilities, that he loses sight of his true Self. A King is not free to do as he pleases: he is imprisoned in his role, bound by obligation and duty. This Lion is in a cage.

A very strong sense of duty, obligation and loyalty can imprison Leo in a pattern of continuously meeting man-made obligations which distract him from seeking out and discovering the inner truth of his Being. Unlike Pinnochio, many worldly Leo's become so lost in the unending obligations of their roles, that life passes them by until there is no time left for them to go on their own Great Adventure: the inner journey to your Real Self.

Who Am I, Really?

Whether your role is manager, CEO, unemployed, driver, fire officer, coach, pilot, teacher, actor, soldier, mother, father, friend, gang member, brother, sister, husband, wife, writer, editor, son, daughter, prisoner, homeless, junkie, dealer, addict, doctor, nurse etc., sooner or later you will lose it – because all roles are temporary. They are not who you are.

Losing your role, or position in society, can bring a feeling of being insignificant: a sense that you have lost your 'self' and don't know 'who you are anymore'. This 'existential neurosis', in which you question your self and the purpose of your existence, is your wake-up call to set off like Pinnochio to search for that which is real within you. To discover who you really are, when you are not in a role, you need the group consciousness of your opposite sign Aquarius.

There is a real Self and a false self, and it is Leo's job to discover which is which. The false self is the ego. It is a social construction formed by the various masks you wear, whereas the real Self is your true spiritual nature which can only be experienced and not spoken about.

Once you have discovered the reality of your authentic Self for yourself, your power and purpose becomes clear.

> *"...like a sudden clash of thunder.*
> *Suddenly you are together,*
> *suddenly you have a direction,*
> *suddenly you know where your gold is."*

- OSHO

To arrive at this realization of authentic Self, ironically, Leo needs the group awareness of his polar opposite Aquarius. The humanitarian group consciousness of Aquarius recognizes the whole of humanity as a single living entity: a connectedness, which is comprised of unique fully-realized individuals.

This higher realization of group awareness is very distinct from the tribalism of lower mass-consciousness - which is divisive in its attempt to separate humanity into tribes and nations. Tribalism is where the personality-centered Leo gets caught: whether playing the role of the Chief or the pauper, he is still adhering to a man-made view that has been imposed upon the existing reality, and him. It is 'false'. It is social conditioning. His struggle lies in trying to make that 'real'.

The realization that the Human Spirit really is 'as one' ignites the Leo Soul with a renewed sense of power and purpose. The inner fire burns brightly. You rise above the limited view of societal expectations and recognize your inner truth as a unique individual with an important role to play. The higher purpose of Leo is the expression of Divine Will, rather than egoic will.

"There is a reality, a life force, an energy,
a quickening that is translated through you into action,
and because there is only one of you in all of time,
this expression is unique.

And if you block it, it will never exist through any other medium
and it will be lost. The world will not have it.

It is not your business to determine how good it is
nor how valuable nor how it compares with other expressions.
It is your business to keep it yours clearly and directly,
to keep the channel open."

- Martha Graham

Whereas the personality-focused Leo erroneously thinks they are important because of what they 'do' (and/or how the society rewards that) the fully Soul-integrated Leo knows their true value lies in who they are: their Being. It is your Heart-Light that is really important.

We said earlier that the Soul 'does battle' in two signs: Leo and Scorpio. The first battle in Leo is the battle to individuate. After the Soul's journey through mass consciousness in Cancer, Leo asks "What about Me?" The sense of "Me" as an individual arises, and it is time to battle for one's individuality.

To win this battle, the Lion must walk alone, free from the masses.

This is a necessary step in the evolution of human consciousness, for it allows us to break free from the herd in order to rise above the social conditioning that creates the delusions of tribal and mob consciousness. Only through your unique inner journey can you realize the true importance of your Self.

This doesn't mean leaving the group: for how is it possible to leave something you are inherently part of? It means not allowing your sense of Self to be defined by the society, but rather acknowledging the sovereignty of your inner Self, and Divine Law. In the highest group awareness of Aquarius, Leo is able to blossom in his unique creative expression. From there he recognizes the true meaning of individual, as *one Being indivisible from the whole*.

"All the World's a stage, and all the Men and Women merely players"

- William Shakespeare

This whole world really is a stage for the unfoldment of Divine Purpose. With this realization you bring the magnificence of your essence into any role you choose, for the benefit of all humanity. The spiritual path of Leo rises above identification with the lower self, so your life becomes a creative expression of Divine Will.

This is 'right use' of ego: freely and consciously participating in roles for the expression of Divine Will and Purpose. You know your Self to be an expression of Love in action, and you are not identified with the action. Dropping all that is false, and keeping your attention on that which is real, you fulfill your role with Divine Grace and Purpose.

Pinnochio was a real boy after all, because he had Love and that is real. The enlightened Leo, shows us that we are all so much more important than the roles we play, yet play them we do... for the show must go on, for the good of the whole. As long as we realize they are only roles, we can fulfill our purpose here on Earth with all the grace, dignity and courage of a Lion.

Will you continue to be a puppet who dances to another's tune? Or will you use the universal group consciousness of Aquarius to elevate yourself above societal conditioning, set off on your own search for a star... and discover that the star is really you?

Virgo-Pisces
Returning

As the sixth sign, the Soul in Virgo has reached the mid-point of its journey through the developmental stages of the Zodiac. This is the point where the journey home, the returning, begins. The essence of the Virgo Soul is the Divine Feminine, Mother Earth, purity, one's vocation, spiritual calling, and Divine Purpose.

From it's starting point as a 'point of light in the mind of God' in Aries, the Soul has now reached the farthest point of it's journey – the deepest level of immersion in the material world. This is evident in the characteristics and concerns of the personality-oriented Virgo: work, discernment, precision, perfection, health, the physical body. Yet the true purpose of the Soul in Virgo is not to become overly concerned with conventional affairs but rather to bring spiritual energy into physical matter. To imbue our conventional world with spiritual energy through sacred action. To the Virgo Soul, work is sacred action, and its purpose is to elevate our world: to literally bring heaven to Earth by making the World sacred.

So does this mean that all Virgos embody the qualities of an Earth Goddess? Well, not exactly. Earth signs are concerned with Mastery of the Physical, and as the Mutable Earth sign, Virgo is concerned with change. Changes in the physical. In the case of the Virgo personality this often means concern with the physical body and physical health. The personality ruler of Virgo is Mercury which means Virgo has the unenviable task of trying to ground Mercurial energy into a physical body. This relates to the deeper spiritual significance of Virgo. The Virgo Soul is somewhat like a Cosmic lightening conductor: here to ground higher spiritual energies into the planetary body.

This Mercurial effect can lead to some of the so-called negative qualities of Virgo. Mercury's stimulation of the 'mental' or cognitive aspect of mind can lead to restlessness, nervousness, worry, criticism, and obsessive-compulsive tendencies, especially in relation to health and/or sickness. It is no accident that Virgo became known as the 'sign of the stomach ulcer'! At the personality level this can also lead Virgo to 'nag' their friends and family about health and wellness issues.

For any of us, one way to distinguish if we are personality-oriented or Soul-oriented, is to check whether we are internally or externally focused. When we are internally focused, we align with our Soul path and have an inner focus. We are conscious of our thoughts words and actions, our inner motivations and drives, and we follow our inner wisdom. When we are externally focused we are like a leaf blowing in the wind. We are driven by external motivators, seek external validation and externally-conferred status, and are motivated by acquiring wealth and position in the external society.

This external focus, keeps the Virgo personality entangled in the outer world: in the world of work, the affairs of others, the health and well being of others, and this can lead to criticism of others' choices and behavior, especially with regard to health, wellness, nutrition and fitness. This also leads Virgo down the fruitless path of seeking perfection in the outer world. Virgo's Soul journey is to discover spiritual perfection by becoming internally focused and for this Virgo needs to experience the oneness of her opposite sign Pisces.

The Virgo personality may be very much concerned with work, and may even have workaholic tendencies, however, this is a mis-application of the highest vibration of Virgo. The higher purpose of Virgo is concerned with vocation rather than just 'work'. It is important to have a spiritual motivation and purpose, rather than merely a conventional or ego-serving purpose. The word *vocation* comes from the Latin verb *vocare* meaning *to call*. The Virgo Soul hears her spiritual calling, and is ready, able, and willing to serve. She knows her spiritual power and purpose and is willing to pour forth her energy in the service of the Light. However, in order to hear your spiritual calling, you have to listen to your true inner guidance, and that is where the higher vibration of Pisces is needed.

The highest octave of Pisces resonates with Universal Mind, Christ Consciousness and Oneness. Virgo needs to lift her head above the parapet and re-connect with her Spiritual origin. Then she can align with her true purpose and power, and flow that energy into her everyday life. This is how the lower personality-focused Virgo vibration becomes transformed through her opposite sign Pisces, and reaches the peaks of the higher octave of Virgo who knows how to flow "Love in Action".

Yet there is even more to this mysterious sign of Virgo. The Soul Keynote for Virgo is:

"I am the Mother and the child. I, God, I, matter am."

This speaks to Virgo's vital role in the reintegration of the Divine Feminine into the planet at this time, yet one could be forgiven for thinking Virgo is a masculine sign. This is because, at the personality level, Virgo's urge to serve can become distorted if her energy is inappropriately channeled into enterprises that serve the collective ego, and support conventional structures that no longer serve humanity's highest good, rather than her highest octave of bringing sacred energy down to Earth. Bringing the sacred into the everyday is Virgo's real work.

The Mother and the Child may also refer to our dualistic nature: if we think of the Mother being our highest Divine Wisdom and the Child being our lower self, or ego. The challenge is to integrate these two – bringing Divine Wisdom to bear on the affairs of the conventional world. Imagine a world where our politicians and corporate leaders were required to have spiritual intelligence on their person specification, and to demonstrate practical skill in emotional intelligence and the ways of peace. What a different world that would be!

The Virgo Soul brings the spiritual into the physical through Higher Mind. Mercury is the personality ruler of Virgo, but also plays a key role in the development of Higher Mind. This is another clue to Virgo's higher role. Like a lightening conductor the Virgo Soul brings higher mind down to earth in very practical ways: imbuing all physical matter with enlightened wisdom, compassion and power.

If you have Sun, Moon and/or Rising Sign (Ascendant) in Virgo your challenge is to still your busy mind enough to hear the soft voice that arises in the stillness: therein lies your own inner wisdom, indeed it is the Wisdom of The Ages.

Will you hear your spiritual calling in the stillness, "return" to your true vocation, access the Universal Love of Pisces and devote your energy to the creation of Heaven on Earth? Or will you worry yourself (and possibly your friends!) into an early grave? The potential, and the choice, is all yours.

Libra-Aries
Think About It... There Must Be Higher Love

The words of that Steve Winwood song (Higher Love) echo through my mind as I write. Libra is the sign of beauty, truth, harmony, ethics and justice. Represented by the scales of Justice herself, Libra is also associated with Law. Welcome to the beautiful sign of Higher Love.

The fully integrated Libra Soul is here to administer Divine Law, Ultimate Truth and Harmony, and restore peace on Earth. No pressure there then! What does Law have to do with Love, we might ask? They are intimately connected through Libra, as we shall see. Libra is concerned with all the laws of existence: the law of attraction and the law of harmonics.

Divine Law requires the balancing of energies within any system, to maintain harmony. Existence depends upon it. In the natural world we can see this fine balancing of energies within an ecosystem. Everything is very finely and delicately dependent upon everything else. Modern science is only just beginning to realize how delicately balanced and inter-dependent the natural world (including us) really is.

Within a human system, the fully integrated[51] Libra Soul has the capacity and power to fine-tune and balance these energies through *right relations*. This includes an ability to sense any imbalance, and bring it back into alignment. Restoring balance and a harmonious existence with 'all that is'. You will often find such individuals playing an active role in the eco-movement: restoring balance through right relationship between humanity and our earth Mother.

So does this mean that every Libra we meet exudes Divine Love, Peace, and Harmony? Not quite yet. Cardinal energy is about creating new pathways, and Air signs are about Mastery of the Mind. As the Cardinal Air sign Libra does have a vital role to play in carving out new pathways of thought for creating our future: a peaceful, beautifully balanced, and harmonious future. But before this can happen Libra has to recognize and fully embrace the sheer life-force energy of her opposite sign: Aries.

All Librans resonate with peace. However, at the personality level

---

[51] A fully integrated individual is one who has completed the personality-Soul fusion process, is Soul-centered and therefore expresses the higher octaves of their Soul Sign and their personality Signs (Sun/Moon). In contrast to someone who is still very personality oriented: identifying with the lower aspects of their personality signs, (Sun/Moon) are personality-driven, and are not living their highest expression.

this innate desire for peace can lead our Libra friend to avoid difficult issues in the name of seeking 'a quiet life': avoidance is the ego-trap of Libra. Libra is known as the sign of the diplomat: our charismatic, peace-loving Libran has a tendency to wear rose-tinted glasses and a strong desire to avoid discomfort. Whereas Aries has the first awareness of 'self', Libra becomes, sometimes painfully, aware of others and of their dependence upon others for getting their needs met. This realization can lead our Libra friend into some very unhealthy, manipulative and possibly co-dependent, relationship behaviors. Here we have the keys to the main issues for Libra: balance and relationships.

Avoidance of the deeper issues in life, is not the true path of peace. Think of Libran John Lennon who used music to work towards world peace. Like John Lennon, each Libra personality has to awaken and use their own power. Living on the surface keeps them from an awareness of their real underlying energy: the very forces of nature that they came here to balance! In order to do the very work she came here to do, Libra needs to feel the 'life-force energy' of her polar opposite Aries. Libra is a Cardinal sign, and Cardinal signs are here to take the lead.

Once Libra has embraced the energy of Aries, she will realize the power of thought, and the reality of thought-forms: this awakens Libra to the natural law of harmonics. The law of inter-related energies, that results in physical manifestation. The truth that our existence is created by thought is a high-octave Libra understanding that explains Libra's affinity for beauty and harmony. That which we perceive as beauty is merely *harmony in physical form*. Our fully integrated Libra administers harmony throughout all the elements and multiple dimensions of Being.

> *"Think about it... there must be Higher Love,*
> *Down in the heart or hidden in the stars above,*
> *Without it, Life is wasted time,*
> *Look inside your heart, I'll look inside mine"*

> \- Steve Winwood

The complex and beautiful sign of Libra works with harmonics: the sheer forces of nature self-organized in a precise and balanced way. It involves a deep understanding of harmony, right relationship and a capacity to recognize and use octaves of energy in creating the 'music' of existence. It is all about the law, science, and application, of Higher Love.

As the Soul travels deeper on it's journey through the Zodiac, the higher octaves of the signs become ever more esoteric, mysterious and difficult for us to comprehend with our limited intellect.

> *"Reason, the highest property of the intellect, is what guides purposive thought. Purposes, however, are limited; and therefore reason can operate only in what is limited.*
>
> *Wisdom alone can accept and intuitively realize the unlimited, the timeless and the infinite, by renouncing explanations and by recognizing the mystery, which can only be felt, experienced, and finally realized in life - and which can never be defined."*

> - Lama Anagarika Govinda[52]

To discern the higher octaves of the signs we need to go beyond the limitations of our intellect and enter the Aries realm of intuition, which, in itself, is part of our evolutionary journey. The higher octave of Libra brings us higher knowledge of the interrelatedness of all things. Whereas the initial impulse for existence begins with Libra's polar opposite Aries, who declares "I exist'! The higher octave of Libra acknowledges that all existence is dependent upon relationship. Things exist in relation to other things. You exist because I exist. I exist because you exist.

That the whole of existence is dependent upon relationship, is key to

---

[52] *"Creative Meditation and Multi-Dimensional Consciousness"* by Lama Anagarika Govinda. Quest Books, Illinois.

the deeper mysteries of Libra. Once we reach our highest iteration, our highest evolved state, we will reach for the next. There will always be a higher octave. There is no end goal. Once we have transcended all traces of our personality vibration, and are resonating with our Soul vibration, there will be another higher octave that our expanded consciousness will aspire to, at the Hierarchical and Cosmic levels, and beyond.

We can relate to octaves best through the musical scale: do, ray, me, fah, so, la, tee, do. The space between the lowest 'do' to the higher 'do' is one octave. Once we reach the highest note in this octave, we can move to the next. There is no end to the potential octaves. The only limitation is human capacity and perception. For example when we strike a single note on a bell, the sound appears to fade away. Where does it go? In fact the sound wave continues without end. It only appears to us to 'end' because the sound wave has travelled beyond the range of human perception.

It is possible to expand our perception, as mystics have done in times gone by, until we can hear the 'music of the spheres'. This is one of the mysteries of Libra: the precise relationship between notes within octaves, between octaves themselves, and our capacity to perceive them, all come under the law of *right relations*.

Libra Souls often have the feeling of being caught between worlds. With such deep esoteric knowledge at their fingertips, they can feel like they are neither here nor there, with one foot on Earth and the other in Heaven. No wonder the Libra personality has a reputation for being indecisive! But this is not a case of choosing between camps, rather it is exactly where Libra is supposed to be. Bridging the gap between Heaven and Earth by spanning the Universe.

Before Libra can reach her highest octaves however, she first has to transcend the Libra personality: and to do this she needs the self-orientation, courage, intuition and energy of her polar opposite Aries. Ironically Libra you have to take your attention off others, and focus more on your Self, to restore balance!

There isn't just 'other' in relationship, there is you, too. The only way you can access your innate esoteric knowledge, and even begin to touch upon understanding the laws of harmonics is through your own inner journey, which opens the gateway to your intuitive Self. It is through knowing yourself that you truly come to know others. It is through healing your own system that you come to understand healing of all systems.

One of my mentors, Anya Sophia Mann, is a Libra Soul. She has a working definition for healing that reflects her experience of the higher octaves of Libra:

"Healing is the balancing of a system,
whether it be a human body,
a family, a corporation, or a country."

-Anya Sophia Mann

For a 'case-study' of Libra Soul-light expressing itself through (in this case) a Cancer/Aries personality, you may like to visit her blog, "A New World" at AnyaSophiaMann.com and take a few moments to read two or three of her posts. Notice in particular how the Libra themes of beauty, harmony, love of music, and a powerful desire to balance the human system through compassion and right relations, shine out as a common thread throughout her work.

"Love is higher thought about somebody or something"

-Anya Sophia Mann

If you have Libra Rising (Ascendant) it is your challenge in this lifetime to access the highest octave of Libra energy that you possibly can, and express this through the talents of your personality signs (mainly the Sun and Moon) for the purpose of healing (balancing) systems.

So Libra, will you use Aries-like courage to face your fears and undertake the courageous inner journey to your Self? Will you elevate your relationship dynamics and travel among the stars on heart-waves of Higher Love, until you resonate with the Music of The Spheres? As Steve Winwood reminds us, the answer lies '*deep in your heart and hidden in the stars above...*'

Scorpio-Taurus
The Sacred Path of The Spiritual Warrior

The enigmatic sign of Scorpio is associated with sex, death, rebirth, power and the deepest, darkest mysteries of the human psyche. Entering the world of Scorpio is not for the feint-hearted. It demands depth of focus, a sense of adventure, and great courage. Welcome to the Soul journey of Scorpio: the sacred path of the Spiritual Warrior.

Scorpio must do battle: simply because it is time. Just like a chick has to peck it's way out of the egg, because it is ready to be 'reborn' into the next stage of it's journey, so Scorpio must release herself from the trappings of the personality and be 'reborn' to stand fully in her Soul-Light. Earlier we noted how in *"Esoteric Astrology"* the Tibetan explains that the Soul does battle in two signs: the first is Leo and the second is Scorpio. In Leo we battled for our individuality. In Scorpio we experience the final battle: for our very Soul. There is no going back.

Scorpio is here to find the point of light in the darkness, to challenge the negativities of human ego and finally transform darkness into light. So is every Scorpio we meet an enlightened being? Not quite. Scorpio has a deep fascination with the darkest side of human nature – necessarily so for it is her job to transform this very darkness into light, but before she can do this she needs the illumination of her opposite sign Taurus.

Scorpio is nothing if not courageous, and she really does dare to go where Angels fear to tread. Your Scorpio friend may well have a fascination with sex, death, power and/or money for she is here to deeply and thoroughly explore the path of desire so that she can understand and transcend it. The Scorpio Soul knows that we must fully embrace all aspects of our nature if we are to integrate Soul and personality. Unfortunately the realm of desire is where humanity can so often fall by the wayside.

Resist Temptation and Be Fearless

Christ's teachings encouraged us to 'resist temptation'. There is a reason for this. When we give in to temptation it causes us to continue 'feeding' habits that reinforce our egoic behavior patterns and keep us trapped in the illusion of ego. Traditionally these common habit-forming behaviors were described within the concept of the 'seven deadly sins': wrath (anger), greed , sloth (laziness), envy, pride, lust and gluttony. These traits are called by many names in different spiritual traditions, for example buddhist teachings refer to *five hindrances*[53], and they are the well-recognized obstacles to our spiritual progress. They distract us from discovering our Souls' living presence by keeping our attention on something outside of ourselves.

In *"The Labours of Hercules An Astrological Interpretation"* Hercules' eighth labor represents the Soul path of Scorpio. In this labor Hercules is challenged to battle with the Lernean Hydra. The nine-headed Hydra represents nine faces of desire that we can meet (and be tempted by) on our spiritual journey. They are described as: sex, comfort, money, fear, hatred, desire for power, pride, separativeness and cruelty.

---

[53] Descriptions vary between systems, but human nature is the same everywhere. The point is to caution us about certain habits which can pull us so far off our spiritual path that we 'sin' (in the original sense of the word of 'missing the mark') and miss the whole point of our existence. Taken to extremes these are the very traits which can lead us into addiction and cause us to miss our spiritual purpose altogether.

This is why our Scorpio friend can be fascinated with (and sometimes express) these tendencies, but to suggest that Scorpio is only concerned with the seedy, sordid side of life is a gross misunderstanding of the vital and very sacred Soul path of Scorpio. It is in having the courage to face these darker aspects that Scorpio becomes fearless. No sweeping anything under the carpet when Scorpio is around! It is Scorpio's job to look these issues squarely in the eye, so we can learn how to transform the darkest aspects of our human personality into light. It is no accident that the courageous and noble sign of Scorpio is associated with both priests and psychologists.

Aside from the Scorpion, the sign of Scorpio is also represented by the animal symbol of the Eagle, which, in many Native American traditions, is a symbol of Great Spirit. Indeed it is Scorpio's destiny to plummet to the depths and then soar to the heights, bringing the darkness to the light. Revealing that which is hidden, so it may be transformed.

> *"Keep your eye on the eagle; call down the fire;*
> *do not look at the ground; be centered in divinity."*

- The Tibetan

Now we have some keys to understanding the Soul-path of Scorpio: the need to do battle, and the nature of 'the enemy'. The fully integrated Scorpio has Mastery over the Kundalini energy - the spiritual fire that burns off all illusion: illuminating and clearing the pathway to our spiritual goal.

It is Scorpio's job to transform desire into tangible spiritual energy, but before she can do this, she must have the illuminating wisdom of her opposite sign Taurus. Earlier we discussed how the sign of Taurus is associated with the opening of the third eye and spiritual illumination. The Buddha became enlightened under the sign of Taurus. Without illumination Scorpio becomes lost in a quagmire of confusion and ignorance. She is aware of desire and temptation but is lost in the darkness, without her light. Her light comes in the form of awareness, which she can only find, by going within: entering into her own inner world.

> *"Desire in Taurus becomes spiritual aspiration in Scorpio.*
> *The darkness of the experience in Scorpio*
> *becomes illumination in Taurus."*

– The Tibetan

Scorpio's compulsive urge towards conflict (remember the pecking chick?) needs to be directed towards her spiritual goals. It is Scorpio's job to challenge everything in order to reveal the underlying truth of our spiritual nature, but for those on the receiving end of Scorpio's intense questioning it can feel like the Spanish Inquisition has just interrogated you! This is because the personality-centered Scorpio erroneously directs her energies outward: toward others. The journey is within. The conflict is not with others, and they are not your enemy. The enemy is within, and it is in the nature of desire.

To embark upon the Soul path of Scorpio you need to turn your attention inwards and begin the real battle: the battle with your own desire-nature, your ego. Although Scorpio does need to battle, the focus is really on the victory. The experience in Scorpio is one of test, trial and triumph. It is not an easy path[54]. It is as though sometimes your life seems to be nothing but struggle, yet that is exactly how the chick frees itself from the egg: by constantly chipping away at it.

The noble and courageous path of Scorpio is one fraught with

---

[54] In Esoteric Astrology Scorpio is also called the sign of crucifixion, because it is in this sign that the personality is finally 'crucified' and the individual becomes fully Soul-centered.

psychological and emotional challenges. At any time, without her light, the Scorpio personality can become trapped in the illusions of her own subconscious. We can see how 'hatred' for example, has lead to Scorpio's reputation for revenge, and no imagination is needed to see what can happen when the desire for power, money or lust, gets out of control. This happens when Scorpio misdirects her energy outward, towards others.

What other's think and do is not your business Scorpio – you are here to literally 'mind your own business', in a very focused and directed way. And your 'business' is to develop your own mind to the highest degree: to discover your own Soul-light and soar like the Eagle that you are. Challenging they may be, but the trials and tribulations in Scorpio are a necessary part of our evolution, in our journey to becoming Soul-centered beings.

> *"Scorpio is the great constellation which influences*
> *the turning point both in the life of humanity*
> *and the life of the individual human being"*
>
> - The Tibetan, *"Esoteric Astrology"*

Transforming desire is not about suppressing it. Desire is not wrong in itself: it becomes a hindrance through our attachment, ignorance and lack of skill. For example when our desires are uncontrolled we can experience addictions. When we Master desire, by appropriately channeling our passion, it is a vital tool for spiritual growth and evolution. Our passion then becomes a vehicle that carries our spiritual energy out into the world in meaningful ways.

Suppressing desire would be a suppression of your life force and spiritual energy: a hindrance to your spiritual growth. The Buddha recognized this when he turned away from the ascetic lifestyle and advocated the middle way. Suppressing desire is a denial of who you are and why you are here.

Water signs are about Mastery of emotions, and Fixed energy brings
stability so, as the Fixed Water sign we can see that Scorpio is all
about stabilizing emotions. We cannot Master our emotions by
suppressing them. The key to Mastering emotions is to allow
ourselves to feel. In order to Master the energy of desire so it can be
transformed, Scorpio has to first experience each 'face' of desire for
herself, each 'head' of the Hydra.

The ability to 'fixate' on an emotional state is a dual-edged sword.
When used with skill and Mastery it gives you the ability to abide in
higher states of consciousness for prolonged periods of time, as
Master meditators do. For the Scorpio personality it can manifest as
brooding and even depression. If you have Sun, Moon or Rising
Sign in Scorpio remember you are here to Master your emotions by
shedding light on your emotional world.

It is worth noting that people with Moon in Scorpio may have a
particularly hard time facing their emotions, which can then be
mirrored in those around you. It is in the nature of fixed energy to try
and 'stabilize' or contain things. The Moon reflects our emotional
world, and all water signs in themselves are somewhere on the path
of mastering emotions. So as the fixed water sign Scorpio has a
tendency to try and master emotions initially by suppressing or
containing them.

With awareness they will eventually learn how to be a stable channel
for emotions rather than trying to stem the flow, but this takes a
willingness on their part to work with their emotional energy, which
then leads to awareness and consciousness. Until then someone with
Moon in Scorpio may have difficulty even acknowledging their own
emotions. If you have Moon in Scorpio, and you find that people
around you often 'explode' emotionally (particularly if they are very
empathic like Cancerians), consider that maybe you need to look at
where you are not facing your own suppressed emotions.

Emotional energy needs to release. If it is being suppressed ('held' in
place by one person) it will often find an outlet in the system through
another (because energy is dynamic and has to move – it cannot truly

be 'held'). It is vital for your well-being and spiritual growth that you allow yourself to feel and express your own feelings. Allowing yourself to fully experience and recognize your different emotional states is the first step towards this Mastery. Emotions need to flow.

You can't learn to drive without getting behind the wheel. Through practical experience, the fully integrated Scorpio Soul learns to stabilize the emotions of desire and channel their energy for spiritual purposes. According to the Tibetan, *points of crisis* and *moments of reorientation* are necessary experiences on Scorpio's journey, as the Scorpio Soul learns to focus and channel her energy in the right direction: firmly directed towards spiritual goals.

"Awakened heart comes from being willing
to face your state of mind"

- Chogyam Trungpa[55]

Scorpio's saving grace is courage. She usually has courage by the bucketful and as we said earlier, is often notorious for going where angels fear to tread. When Scorpio applies this courage to her own inner journey, facing her own mind, that is where she will discover her own light and access the illumination of Taurus. By keeping her attention on her own light, she discovers the secret of Taurus: the higher light of awareness that dissolves all the 'heads of the Hydra', save for the so-called 'immortal' head[56], which is awareness itself.

The 'destiny' of Scorpio is somewhat fixed, in the sense of Scorpio's role in these changing times. Scorpio has mysterious esoteric connections with Sirius; Antares (one of the four Royal Stars of

---

[55] *"Shambhala: The Sacred Path of The Warrior"* by Chogyam Trungpa

[56] In the myth of Hercules and the Hydra, one of the Hydra's heads was said to be immortal and cannot be 'killed'. See *"The Labours of Hercules: An Astrological Interpretation"* by Alice Bailey.

Persia[57]) and is one of the four signs of the Fixed Cross[58]. The Divine Energy currently pouring through Scorpio is vital for our collective transformation: without the fearless courage of Scorpio in facing our darkest fears, we can never experience a full and complete heart awakening. When we bury and suppress any aspect of our own true nature, we close off a part of our heart at the same time.

The Soul's journey through the sign of Scorpio is indeed a 'rite of passage' for our collective spiritual evolution. The Scorpio group of Souls play a vital role in the evolution of human consciousness by freeing the energy that humanity has tied up in negative and self-serving emotional states, so it can be reused for spiritual transformation.

Scorpio your path is not meant to be easy. Will you allow your precious life-force energy to be wasted in conflict with your human family? Or will you turn your attention inwards, arm yourself with the higher light of your opposite sign Taurus and, like the Spiritual Warrior that you are, Master your emotions so that your inner Eagle

---

[57] Read about Antares in Scorpio and the role of the four 'Royal' stars in this online article:
http://Souledout.org/cosmology/highlights/antares/antares.html

[58] See Chapter1. Briefly, the three crosses in *"Esoteric Astrology"* refer to stages in the development of human consciousness and not aspect patterns in an individual's horoscope. The first stage, the mutable cross, is where we are fully personality identified and personality-driven. This currently refers to most of humanity. The Fixed Cross refers to those who are awakening. There is awareness of Soul as well as personality, but they are experienced as separate and so there is still duality there. A growing minority of spiritually-inclined people on the planet are beginning this 'awakening' process. The Cardinal Cross refers to full Soul-personality integration. Very few people on the planet are at this fully awakened state. They would be the enlightened beings, advanced spiritual teachers, and avatars, who come to lead us into the next stage of our development. Divine Energy is focused through the fixed signs (Taurus, Leo, Scorpio and Aquarius) to stabilize and anchor this awakening process into the planet.

can soar? By entering this inner battle with courage, deep reverence, and the light of awareness, you will fulfill your spiritual mission: transforming the darkness within our human hearts into warm, radiant, light. All this is accomplished by finding your own true heart's desire. Step up Scorpio, your time is now.

Sagittarius-Gemini
Silence... and The Love of Wisdom

The sign of Sagittarius is associated with fun, gregariousness, optimism, friendliness, generosity, teaching, knowledge, philosophy and spiritual seeking. Welcome to the sign of great sages, wise-men (and women), and spiritual teachers. So does every Sagittarian we meet carry the wisdom of Solomon? Not exactly or, at least, not yet. Let's just say they are on their way!

Known as the great philosophers of the Zodiac, our Sagittarian friends have a thirst for knowledge. They may not necessarily be hanging out in the halls of academia (although many are!) but nevertheless they are driven by a need to understand the Universe and everything in it. The thirst for wisdom is innate in every Sagittarian. Indeed the term philosopher comes from the ancient Greek words philos (love of) and sophia (wisdom).

Esoterically Sagittarius is the first of the *signs of service*[59] and the fully integrated Sagittarian is here to *"uplift humanity through the revelation of truth and wisdom"*[60]. The highest octave of Sagittarius resonates with ultimate truth, freedom, and our highest spiritual goals, but before he can reach them our Sagittarian friend needs to transcend the ego-traps of the Sagittarian personality, and to do that he needs the eclectic, all-embracing wisdom of his polar opposite Gemini.

---

[59] See Chapter 2

[60] *"Esoteric Astrology: The Journey Of The Soul"* by Candy Hillenbrand - Online document at
http://www.aplaceinspace.net/Pages/CandyJourneyoftheSoul.html

Mutable energy is all about change, and Fire signs are all about 'Mastery of Action' so, as the Mutable Fire sign, Sagittarius is here to 'change the way we do things'. We can see how the word philosophy becomes distorted at the personality level so that, rather than simply being a love of wisdom, having 'a philosophy' becomes about having a 'prescription' for how we 'should' live our lives. This is a clue to the lower ego-trap of Sagittarius.

Spain is ruled by Sagittarius, and it is likely that the Spanish Inquisition[61] was a manifestation of lower octave Sagittarius. At it's lowest octave Sagittarius can erroneously create 'belief systems' and impose them on others.

It is indeed a Sagittarian ego-trap to fervently pursue one mental concept to the exclusion of all others, in the mistaken belief that he has found a 'truth'. This then becomes dogma. At it's highest octave Sagittarius brings us truth, freedom and sets us on our true spiritual path, but before he can reach higher truth and wisdom he needs to release himself from the exclusivity and separation of dogma, by accessing the *inclusivity and connectedness* of his opposite sign Gemini.

The term 'philosophy' has been attributed to Pythagoras who, it is said, could hear the music of the spheres. In the Pythagorean school students were required to undertake daily 'self-examination'. This meant a process of 'going within' and observing the esoteric processes within one's own body, speech and mind. Pythagoras knew that real wisdom is to be found by going within, rather than studying things outside of ourselves. As we mentioned earlier (see Gemini-Sagittarius), true wisdom is to be found beyond words:

> *"He who talks about truth injures it thereby;*
> *He who tries to prove it thereby maims and distorts it;*

---

[61] In medieval Europe religious tribunals were held where many people were tortured and executed to 'test' their affiliation to the Catholic Church. Of these the Spanish Inquisition had a particularly notorious reputation. See https://en.wikipedia.org/wiki/Spanish_Inquisition

He who gives it a label and a school of thought kills it;
And He who declares himself a believer buries it."

-Lin Yutang

The true Mastery that is required of Sagittarius is to turn his attention inwards and master his own thoughts, words and deeds. Symbolized by the Archer, or Hunter, it is quite typical of Sagittarian energy to latch onto one goal, purpose, or idea, and get totally lost down the rabbit hole, tracking down his target while being blinded to all that is around him. By accessing the diffuse, eclectic, energy of his opposite sign Gemini, Sagittarius learns to lift his head above the parapet and consider all the options, be less one-sided, and become aware of the multi-dimensional facets of Life. By going within, and realizing the multi-dimensional aspect of his true nature, Sagittarius eventually learns to discern truth from opinion, and finds that which he is seeking: true love-wisdom.

In *"Esoteric Astrology"* the Tibetan describes how humanity is currently evolving in conscious awareness from instinct, through intellect, to intuition. The intellect is a necessary part of our evolution. It allowed us to transcend instinct, or our animal 'urges' and create civilizations, yet following intellectual pursuits keeps our attention outside of ourselves[62].

Now that Sagittarius has used his intellect to free himself from the everyday burden of instinct (physically hunting for food), his next step is to go beyond his intellect, by accessing the inclusivity of Gemini, to discover higher mind and explore his intuitive realm.

Part of the Sagittarius ego-trap, is to become 'lost' in the intellectual realm, and fail to realize the next stage of his evolution: accessing Intuition through his Higher Mind. Too much intellectual processing leads to 'analysis paralysis'. Mentally going around in circles can be

---

[62] See *"Aquarius Rising: The Aquarius Soul"* in Chapter 3 for more about how the intellect can be an obstacle to our spiritual awakening.

very deceptive. In the illusion that one is 'getting somewhere' or resolving a problem, one may simply be unproductively wasting time and energy.

"The centipede was happy quite,
Until a toad in fun
Said: "Pray, which leg goes after which?"
This worked his mind to such a pitch,
He lay distracted in a ditch,
Considering how to run."

- Ogden Nash

Using his intellect as a launching pad, using Gemini-like inclusivity to release dogma, accessing his intuition, and then translating all that into wise action, is the healthiest way forward for Sagittarius if he is to avoid 'falling by the wayside', being distracted by things outside of himself, and getting stuck in an endless intellectual 'loop' like the centipede in the above rhyme!

One of the most important lessons Sagittarius will learn, is that he will never find Wisdom outside of himself. His true Soul journey is one of going within, but this is often difficult for our lovely fun-loving, gregarious, affable and sociable friend. He is such a lover of Life that there are many things outside of himself, to distract him from his journey. The symbolism of the Archer pointing his arrow at the target, is symbolic of Sagittarius' search for the 'real' goal: the search for his Soul wherein he will find his highest truth and wisdom.

"Everything we hear is an opinion, not a fact.
Everything we see is a perspective, not the truth."

- Marcus Aurelius

The above profound quote from Marcus Aurelius reflects the realization that wisdom and truth can not be found outside of ourselves. The need for silence, both internally and externally, which enables us to go within and identify the subtle pathways that lead to this inner wisdom, is emphasized under the sign of Sagittarius.

"Sagittarius is the sign preparatory to Capricorn and it is called in some ancient books "the sign of silence".
In ancient mysteries the newly admitted brother had to sit in silence, he was not allowed to walk or speak;
he had to be, to work and to watch, because one cannot enter the fifth kingdom in nature, the spiritual kingdom, or climb the mountain of Capricorn, until there has been restraint of speech and control of thought. That is the lesson of Sagittarius: restraint of speech through control of thought."

- The Tibetan,
The Labours of Hercules: an astrological interpretation

The fully integrated Sagittarius knows that true wisdom is to be found in silence. If Sagittarius is to become Master of his Actions, he needs to realize the wisdom that lies beyond words, beyond mental concepts, and beyond his own intellect. He needs to go within and access the silent wisdom of his heart and Soul that whispers to him through the language of intuition. In order to do this he needs to release dogma by accessing the all-inclusive wisdom of his opposite pole Gemini, which will allow him to consider alternate perspectives, prevent him from getting lost down a rabbit hole and, most importantly, give him the skill of placing his attention on his inner world.

Once he has turned his attention within, accessing the multi-faceted awareness of Gemini, Sagittarius will recognize his own multi-dimensional nature, access the higher wisdom of multiple intelligences (beyond intellectual, emotional and spiritual intelligence!) and find his Truth.

"The flame that gleams beyond the mind reveals direction sure."

- The Tibetan,
The Labours of Hercules: an astrological interpretation

In terms of the Soul's journey through the Zodiac, Sagittarius has been described as a 'chrysalis' stage[63]. Once a caterpillar turns into a chrysalis, everything inside dissolves into fluid, and is reconstructed into a butterfly. Contrary to popular myth this is not a 'latent' phase of development but indeed a very clear, powerful and active stage. After all is broken down and turned to fluid in Scorpio, the "three aspects of Divinity"[64] become visible, and the way forward is known.

In *"The Labours of Hercules: an astrological interpretation"* it is also said that there are 'gifts' in the three Fire signs of the Zodiac: the gift of *existence* in Aries, the gift of *opportunity through individuality* in Leo, and the gift of *power* in Sagittarius. Although Scorpio is indeed a powerful sign, it is actually in Sagittarius that this power becomes potent through 'right direction'. This is a vital stage in our Soul's development, which eventually leads to the birth of Christ Consciousness in Capricorn.

There are magical Universes to explore Sagittarius. Will you become a prisoner of your own philosophy and, like the Spanish Inquisition, limit yourself with dogmatic mental concepts? Or will your love of Wisdom permit you to turn your attention inwards, apply the inclusivity of Gemini, and give yourself the highest freedom: the freedom to broaden your horizons and explore every facet of your multi-dimensional Being beyond your own mind? Pick up your bow and arrow and set your sights on your inner goal. Sagittarius, the

---

[63] See *"The Labours of Hercules: an astrological interpretation"* by Alice Bailey

[64] "The Chrysalis Symbol" p. 163 in *"The Labours of Hercules: an astrological interpretation"* by Alice Bailey

adventure of your Lifetime begins here!

Capricorn-Cancer
The Creation of Heaven on Earth

Capricorn is the great resource manager of the Zodiac. The sign of Capricorn is associated with business, accounting, banking, finance, governance, authority, ambition, and achievement through practical, diligent, precise and methodical application of one's energy. Symbolized by the sure-footed mountain-goat, securely placing one foot in front of another until she reaches her mountain-top, one could be forgiven for thinking that the sign of Capricorn is the most practical, down-to-Earth sign of them all. This is quite true and, at one and the same time, it is also the most mysterious and Esoteric sign because the true mysteries of Capricorn remain deeply hidden. Welcome to the enigmatic world of Capricorn.

"The light of life must now shine forth within a world of dark"

- The Tibetan,
The Labours of Hercules: an astrological interpretation

In *"Esoteric Astrology"* the Tibetan tells us that Capricorn is the least understood of all the Zodiac signs because humanity does not yet have the consciousness to comprehend it's true meaning at this stage of our evolution. He also explains how the true symbol for Capricorn has never been drawn because of its power: it is said to be the signature of God. According to the Tibetan, Capricorn is the sign of Christ Consciousness.

Does this mean that every Capricorn we meet has the spiritual awareness of Christ? Of course not, however there is a clue to the deeper mysteries of Capricorn in the idea that Capricorn is at the same time associated with both the Consciousness of Christ and the material world. In our spiritual development Capricorn is where we learn to use spiritual resources and deeply imbue physical matter with spiritual energy.

Capricorn season is the time of year when the Northern hemisphere of Earth is farthest from the Sun. Winter Solstice is a time when Northern cultures would traditionally hold major festivals to celebrate the 'return of the light'. It is no accident that the birth of Christ is also celebrated at this time, and was heralded by a bright star.

Capricorn is the farthest point into matter that light has travelled thus far. So our Capricorn friends can be forgiven if they seem deeply rooted in the concrete material world - they are – and yet they have whole Universes to bridge with their light.

Hidden deep within the mysteries of Capricorn are vast undiscovered metaphysical sciences. Sacred arts, including sacred geometry and alchemy are just the 'tip of the iceberg'. Capricorn is the sign of precision engineering, and while many Capricorns do indeed use their innate knowledge of physical matter to engineer the physical realm, the highest octave of Capricorn involves engineering light. Capricorn is here to utilize spiritual resources to build heaven on Earth, and beyond! But Capricorn can never access this highest potential with her nose stuck in an accounting book.

Many spiritual traditions consider those who only believe what their eyes can see to have limited capacity for spiritual development[65]. This is the ego trap of Capricorn: becoming so deeply focused on concrete, tangible results, that she forgets to acknowledge the deepest wisdom of her other senses. Capricorn needs to acknowledge all her sense perceptions if she is to awaken not only to higher awareness, but to higher skill and capacity as an engineer of light, masterfully utilizing spiritual resources for the benefit of all sentient beings. In order to realize her higher mind, potential and greatest capacity Capricorn needs the multi-sensory capability of her polar opposite Cancer.

---

[65] *"Creative Meditation and Multi-Dimensional Consciousness"* by Lama Anagarika Govinda.

Whereas Cancer embodies empathy and emotional intelligence, at the personality level, our Capricorn friend has the unfortunate reputation of sometimes being the most ruthless sign of all. It is as though, in her diligent focus on getting through the business of the day, she is able to take into account and audit all the tangibles of a situation, while forgetting the very reason why resources need to be managed in the first place: to ensure that all creatures have opportunities for growth. A fully integrated Capricorn senses what will be needed by all, takes everything into account, and with great care, respect and Cancerian-like compassion can move mountains to make sure all needs are covered.

Cardinal energy is the pioneering energy of creation that initiates change and ushers in new ways of being and doing. Earth signs are all about mastery of the physical. So, as the Cardinal Earth sign, Capricorn is all about creating new ways of mastering our physical realm: how we utilize our energy and physical resources for the highest good. It is no accident that the Cardinal Earth sign is associated with governance and authority.

At the time of writing we are experiencing a transit of Pluto through Capricorn which began in November 2008 and lasts until 2023. These are very important times we are living through. Many of the political and Governmental upheavals that we are experiencing are as a result of the transformational energy of Pluto being in the sign of Capricorn. Pluto is the great revealer. It breaks down old systems that are no longer working, and reveals that which is hidden by bringing it to the light for healing.

Pluto is revealing to us where we have created governmental and financial systems from a low vibration Capricorn perspective, which was so off balance that it became possible for us to 'use' and 'abuse' Earth's resources ruthlessly for personal gain. During this transit we have the opportunity to transform by accessing the highest octave of Capricorn, which pioneers new ways of sharing and relating to Earth's resources, by bringing in the compassionate energy of her polar opposite Cancer.

Collectively (at the time of writing) we are currently experiencing the healing and balancing of the Capricorn-Cancer polarity. The Pluto-Capricorn transit is calling us up to heighten our awareness and access the highest octave of Capricorn for the good of all. At the end of this transit, Capricorn-Cancer will have created new ways of being in the world that honor, respect, and nurture all sentient beings, ensuring everything is taken into account (including the needs of the Earth herself) to build healthy, harmonious, sustainable futures for Mother Earth and all her creatures.

Acknowledgement of the oneness of all beings, is an essential stage in our spiritual development. It will heal the unhealthy split that separates humanity from the rest of Nature, and restore our true place in creation. Understanding the importance of our role in the whole of creation, and in particular as custodians of the Earth and our environment, is an important part of the higher wisdom of Capricorn.

In deepening our understanding of the underlying energy involved, we can think about the relationship between the three modalities[66]: cardinal, mutable and fixed. Cardinal energy is the energy of Spring. It is the driving force of creation that brings new life. Fixed energy brings stability. For the entire lifespan of a tree, the trunk represents the fixed energy that stabilizes the form in existence. Mutable energy is the energy of dissolution. It breaks down forms and boundaries, as in the Autumn (Fall) when the leaves and dead wood de-compose, so the energy can be freed up and used again.

Then it is again the role of Cardinal energy to direct the released energy into new forms. This describes the cycle of life, and the unique role of each Zodiac sign as one unfolds into another throughout the year. So it is the highest Soul purpose of Capricorn to take the lead in *directing light into form*. In this critical time of the Pluto transit, the old structures are dissolving while the higher octave of Cardinal Earth sign Capricorn, is directing us in creating new structures that more appropriately serve our future selves as spiritual,

---

[66] See *"The Three Modalities"* in Chapter 1

Soul-centered Beings.

In a sense this is a kind of homecoming. It is an awakening to the truth of who we really are as spiritual beings having a human experience. This oft-quoted statement is, for most of us at this stage in our evolution, just a nice idea. We hear the words, but is it really the truth of our experience? Do we really experience ourselves as a spiritual being in a physical body, as our everyday reality? This is where we begin to enter the deeper mysteries of Capricorn.

In *"Esoteric Astrology"* Capricorn is said to be the sign of the disciple or initiate, which indicates Capricorn's significant role in our spiritual awakening or ascension. Three animal symbols: the goat, crocodile and unicorn, are sometimes used to depict the stages of our spiritual ascent through Capricorn:

"At the foot of the mountain the goat, the materialist, seeks for nourishment in arid places. The scapegoat on the way up finds the flowers of attained desire, each with its own thorn of satiety and disillusionment. At the top of the mountain the sacred goat sees the vision and the initiate appears. In other writings the symbols are the goat, the crocodile and the unicorn."

- The Tibetan,
The Labours of Hercules: an astrological interpretation

Earlier, in the section on Cancer-Capricorn, we mentioned the two *great gateways* in the Zodiac. Cancer is the gateway into the physical and Capricorn is the gateway into the spiritual. As we evolve spiritually, and resolve the Capricorn-Cancer polarity into one, we fully experience spirit as physical matter. We will experience and know physical matter to be light: the light of God.

At the moment we can consider the idea of physical matter as light, but at this stage of our evolution it really is just that - an idea. We cannot really see physical matter and light as anything other than separate. Yet scientists are beginning to create physical matter from light[67], so we are beginning to touch upon the true mysteries of Capricorn: the process of creation, and the true alchemy of light that is hidden deep within this mysterious sign!

Our current so-called 'real-world' (the man-made world that imposes upon, pollutes and drains the natural world) is an expression of lower Capricorn consciousness, exploiting natural resources for personal gain. The highest vibration of Capricorn will urge us to honor and acknowledge Mother Earth, recognizing humanity's true role as sacred custodians of our planetary home. To reach this highest octave Capricorn needs to fully integrate the highest compassionate consciousness of Cancer.

At the moment, while the world is self-serving, greedy, and politically unstable, it would be dangerous for us to have the full power of Capricorn in our hands. We would be like children playing with matches, causing unimaginable devastation. So we can see how the integration of Capricorn-Cancer, and a wise spiritual maturity is needed before we can fully realize the power and purpose of Capricorn's highest octave.

It is time for us to grow up and care for our environment: putting systems into place that will preserve the life and health of this planet and its inhabitants for future generations. This is the purpose behind the healing Pluto-Capricorn transit.

"Unto Prometheus, O Hercules, you are asked to be a savior. Go down into the depths, and there upon the outer planes release him from his suffering. Having heard and understood, the son of man who was also a son of God, embarked upon this quest..."

- The Tibetan,
The Labours of Hercules: an astrological interpretation

---

[67] *"Scientists Use Light To Create Particles"* online document at http://www.slac.stanford.edu/exp/e144/nytimes.html

There is much hidden meaning in the above quote from Hercules' tenth labor in Capricorn. In mythology Prometheus was banished to Hades for stealing 'the fire of the Gods'. This could be an analogy for our sacred Kundalini energy, and the mis-use of our sacred life-force energy for worldly (outer) gain. Capricorn realizes her true power when she turns her attention inwards, integrates compassionate Cancerian energy, and redirects her powerful light into the world meaningfully, for the good of all.

If you have Capricorn Sun, Moon or Rising Sign, you are here to shine your light through the darkness during these vital times. Will you lose yourself in the concrete man-made material realm, believing only what your eyes see? Or will you expand your Cancerian-like perception to worlds within worlds, shine your light, and build a healthy future that heals our Earth Mother by re-uniting her with the people? Capricorn, you are an engineer of light ...and it is time to shine.

Aquarius-Leo
The Flow of Love and The Flowering of Human Consciousness

The sign of Aquarius is associated with humanitarianism, science, individuality, uniqueness, technology, the future and groups. Gather a group of Aquarians together and the one thing that they will all have in common is their desire to be unique: to be different from each other, and everyone else. Yet, somewhat ironically, the highest octave of Aquarius is group consciousness and the highest purpose of the integrated Aquarian Soul is that of World Server. The secret to the future of humanity lies hidden deep within the mysteries of Aquarius, but before he can unlock them Aquarius has to access the heart-centered energy of his opposite sign Leo. Welcome once again to the mysterious and complex sign of the water carrier.

Aquarius is often commonly mistaken for a water sign because of its symbolism of the water carrier – but the key here is in the word 'carrier'. The key to the deeper secrets of Aquarius lies in his ability to be a vessel – a vehicle for the 'dual waters' of Love and Life.

Does this mean every Aquarian we meet continuously flows love and life? Not quite yet. It is Aquarius' job to channel these vital life force energies for the good of the whole: to dedicate personal energy for the benefit of the collective, but before he can do this he must have a storehouse of spiritual energy, and must become a Master at flowing it.

"The single flame must light the other forty-nine"

- The Tibetan,
The Labours of Hercules: an astrological interpretation

As we continue our Soul's Journey around the Zodiac: having tamed the mind in Sagittarius, then cultivated and focused our Soul-Light in Capricorn, the mature Soul is ready to flow a steady stream of Love and Life in Aquarius. With the possible exception of Pisces, the Aquarian individual just might have the biggest challenge of all. It is as though the further we travel in our Soul Journey around the Zodiac, the bigger the gap between personality and Soul. To cross this great divide Aquarius needs to have the courage of his opposite sign Leo, to navigate the unfamiliar and unpredictable terrain of the human heart.

Air signs are all about Mastery of the Mind, and Fixed energy is all about stability. So, as the Fixed Air sign, Aquarius brings structure and stability not only to our mental processes, but also to the whole experience of our heart-mind. Only in the West do we think of heart and mind as separate: as if our mental processes were something distinct and separate from our heart and feelings. The true path of Aquarius depends upon fusion and stability in the use of heart-mind energy. The fully integrated Aquarian Soul knows that the way to flow the energy of Love and Life is through skillful use of the mind: that mental energy is not meant to be 'wasted' as we currently do in petty conflicts or the pursuit of 'mental games' to amuse the ego, but that our mind is meant to be a focused 'vehicle' for the influx of spiritual energy.

Once Mutable Air sign Gemini dissolves old, outmoded heart-mind patterns that are no longer working, Cardinal Air sign Libra restores right relationship between thought and feeling, thus bringing coherent harmony. Then it is the job of Fixed Air sign Aquarius to stabilize heart-mind patterns, building etheric structures and neural pathways for the transmission of vital energies as we enter the new Age of Aquarius.

These are indeed challenging energies to Master, and it is why Aquarius has the often unfair reputation of being aloof, emotionally cool, detached and distant, for the first thing the Aquarian personality has to Master is the use of mental energy. We noted earlier in Chapter 3 how the intellect can be an obstacle in terms of our spiritual progress. With his brilliant and innovative laser-like mind, combined with the mental dexterity of a brain surgeon, Aquarius has a tendency to divide and separate.

The ability to label all incoming information and place it into categories earns Aquarius the distinction of scientist, and many distinguished medical doctors are born under this sign because it allows them to 'marry' their humanitarian ideals with a love of science. Unfortunately it can also make our Aquarian friend the ultimate materialist, reducing the value of everything to that which can be seen, observed, studied, researched, dissected, ...and labeled!

One of the ego traps for Aquarius lies in believing his own labels. Such divisions may help us when communicating and learning, but we would be wise to remember they have no basis in reality. Nature has only one season: the eternal NOW. It is the human mind that divides it into Spring, Summer, Autumn and Winter, purely for descriptive purposes. Our Aquarian friends would be wise to remember this point.

The urge towards humanitarianism, and the tendency to have their attention on group activities, can also lead the Aquarian personality to miss the point of their own existence altogether: their own inner journey. The Aquarian personality can fall into the trap of busybody – telling others how they 'should' be living their lives, keeping themselves focused on the group agenda, while overruling the needs of the individual and conveniently neglecting to attend to their own back yard, in terms of their own personal and spiritual development. Before he can ignite others, Aquarius must first ensure his own flame is burning brightly.

Although Aquarius has a great love of, and respect for, individuality it is actually in his opposite sign of Leo that he finds the gift of *"opportunity through individuality"*[68] and finally manages to experience this for himself. The Aquarian personality, in his desire to please and remain loyal to his group, may actually keep himself stuck in group conformity. He will only access the highest octave of Aquarius (and thus Master the powerful spiritual energies that he is here to channel) when he allows himself to follow his heart, stand alone, and find his true individuality.

"The undeveloped Aquarian upon the Mutable Cross manifests through a superficial self-awareness. This matures in Leo and becomes a deep seated self-consciousness and a profound interest in self and its need and wishes. As the interplay goes on between Leo and Aquarius (for they are polar opposites) there comes a deepening of all qualities and the superficialities disappear until - upon the reversed wheel - the intensive self-consciousness of Leo expands into the group awareness of Aquarius. The individual becomes the universal."

- The Tibetan, *"Esoteric Astrology"*

The group consciousness that is the highest octave of Aquarius is difficult to comprehend from our current level of consciousness. It is not misplaced loyalty to one's own group or tribe, nor is it being swept along in mob consciousness. Rather it is a higher perception that comes from inner connection to one's own Higher Mind.

[68] *"The Labours of Hercules: an astrological interpretation"* by Alice Bailey

It is a true realization, firmly rooted in personal experience, that Humanity is One Being. This dual awareness of ones own individuality while at the same time being attuned to the larger group awareness of Humanity, is the highest octave of Aquarius. The humanitarianism of Aquarius refers to a higher state of awareness: not as an idealized philosophy but as a realization of spiritual truth rooted in personal experience.

> *"Esoteric Astrology concerns itself primarily*
> *with the unfoldment of consciousness"*
>
> - The Tibetan, *"Esoteric Astrology"*

At this level, specific attributes of Higher Mind begin to unfold: clairvoyance, clairaudience, omniscience and telepathy. It is a higher vibration, a higher frequency, than we can currently comprehend from this stage of our evolution. In *"Esoteric Astrology"* six 'stages' of consciousness are outlined:

> *"Aries: subjective latent consciousness*
> *Gemini: the consciousness of duality*
> *Cancer: mass consciousness*
> *Leo: individual self-consciousness*
> *Libra: equilibrised consciousness and*
> *Aquarius: group consciousness"*
>
> - The Tibetan, *"Esoteric Astrology"*

When we see mass riots and mob consciousness, that is clearly the influence of mass consciousness in Cancer. There is a clear distinction between this and the higher group consciousness that we are talking about in Aquarius. There is still an 'us and them' mentality in Cancer, whereas in the highest octave of Aquarius all polarity has resolved leaving only 'us' as one Humanity.

The individual has 'broken away from the herd' in Leo, cultivated equanimity for all living things in Libra, and (as a fully realized individual) becomes aware of the group mind in Aquarius. The fully integrated Aquarian Soul is no longer personality-driven, yet still has an individual spiritual identity, which has integrated Christ Consciousness and is ready to be of service. The personality is now in full service to the Soul.

The Soul Journey through Aquarius mirrors the unfoldment of Human Consciousness at this current point of our evolution as we enter the Aquarian Age. Over a period of time, roughly spanning the next 140 years, the whole of Humanity will undergo a 'rite of passage' akin to the Soul's Journey through Aquarius. As we shift from unconscious reacting to our external environment (impulsiveness in Aries), we pass through Self Awareness (in Leo) and eventually become conscious co-creators of our reality, powerful Masters of our own energy flow, in Aquarius.

How many of us are consciously able to choose a specific emotional energy wavelength, for example Love? Or Appreciation? And then consciously flow that energy for a prolonged period of time without any interruption or distraction? The ability to become a continuous outpouring of Love and Life without interruption from our 'monkey mind' is the hallmark of the fully integrated Aquarian Soul.

There are some key distinctions that will help us to understand the progression from the lower Aquarian vibration to the higher Aquarian octaves. As we collectively journey through the Age of Aquarius, these shifts in consciousness are some of the signposts we may see along the way:

From Indifference to Compassion

The urge to be of service to the group can lead the Aquarian personality to adopt an aloof air of indifference, for fear of being subsumed by the needs of others. This indifference becomes transformed into detached compassion and true equanimity in the fully integrated Aquarian Soul as deep empathy and the importance of each individual within the group is recognized.

From Powerlessness to Empowerment

In spite of an 'urge to serve' the Aquarian personality often feels powerless in the face of all the problems in the world, and can often be found in political activist groups, protesting the perceived 'enemy'. The fully integrated Aquarian Soul has built up powerful spiritual energies over many lifetimes that radiate from him like the Sun - transforming all around him. He combines this with a capacity to direct the flow of this energy wherever it is needed. He knows it is not what he says or does that matters as much as his presence and how he is flowing his energy. This is Christ Consciousness.

From "Us and Them" to We (There is no separation)

The Aquarian personality has a tendency to divide and separate: there is still polarity and a tendency to view the world in categories: this type of thing and/or that type of person. Supporting one group over another, or taking sides with one group against another. The fully integrated Aquarian Soul has realized true Equanimity: that there is only one Humanity, there is no separation, we are all connected, have equal needs, and we all matter. There is no Aquarius vs. Leo: it is all one energy, on a continuum.

From Emotional Coolness to Emotional Intelligence

Because of his preoccupation with mental processing the Aquarian personality can sometimes be emotionally immature, and often presents as a scientist or 'boffin' who is intellectually brilliant yet emotionally insecure, detached and socially inept. In contrast the fully integrated Aquarian Soul is highly spiritually and emotionally intelligent: utilizing all his senses including empathy, warmth, self-awareness and intuition, to discern where and how he may next be of selfless service.

"Aquarius is depicted as a man holding an inverted vase.
The man inverts the vase and out of it come two streams of water,
the river of life and the river of love,
and those two words, life and love,
are the two words that embody the technique of the Aquarian age;
not form, not mind, but life and love."

- The Tibetan,
The Labours of Hercules: an astrological interpretation

The fully integrated Aquarian Soul is the World Server: an individual expression of Christ Consciousness in service, *"pouring forth the dual waters of love and life for thirsty humanity"* (*"Esoteric Astrology"*). But before he can reach such spiritual heights the Aquarian personality has a long way to go, and his journey takes him within: discovering the unpredictable terrain of his own heart by accessing the energy of his polar opposite Leo.

This is a tricky path. Another ego trap for the Aquarian personality (and there are many!) lies in believing he is already 'there', already enlightened. Because he quickly grasps concepts mentally, he believes there is nothing more for him to do in terms of his own spiritual journey. He may make the common mistake of thinking he has 'got it' when in fact he has yet to realize the concept within his own experience, and integrate it into his physical Being.

The powerful energies of Love and Life which flow through the fully integrated Aquarian Soul, have accumulated over many lifetimes spent transforming fear and negative thought patterns, while cultivating life-force energy, unconditional love and compassion. The Buddha used the analogy of 'untying knots' to explain our spiritual process. As we re-trace our steps on our inner journey home, we undo all the 'knots' of our own pain and suffering. This experiential learning is first grasped mentally, synthesized emotionally, and then fully integrated physically. We cannot skip over it, or bypass[69] this pathway.

Aquarius can't leap to the end result, without having walked the path in Capricorn (although he may want to!). It is interesting that Saturn, the task master and Lord of Karma, is the personality ruler of Capricorn and also the old ruler of Aquarius. No Zodiac sign stands in isolation and it is important for Aquarius more than any to remember this important point. Each sign unfolds one into the other, and Aquarius needs to remember the important lessons learned in Capricorn, if he is to fully flower into Christ Consciousness.

Only by going deep within will Aquarius discover powerful energies within himself that he has the power to bring under his conscious control:

"[In Aquarius] Hercules had to aid in the cleansing of the world
by the right direction of the forces of life through it.
You appreciate that we are entering into the Aquarian age
where materialism, as we know it,
will have completely died out at the close
and when the whole life
will be interpreted in terms of energies.
We are dealing entirely with forces...
You are dealing with energies
and you are mis- using energies.
Watch yourself and begin to work
in the world of forces within yourself."

- Alice Bailey,
The Labours of Hercules: an astrological interpretation

---

[69] Spiritual bypassing is a term used to describe when we use spiritual ideals to avoid dealing with our own very real psychological and emotional development. See *"Spiritual Bypassing"* by Robert Augustus Masters and Ken Wilber online document at https://www.integrallife.com/node/85982

There are deeper mysteries hidden in Aquarius that we cannot yet begin to comprehend. Many of these will be revealed to us as we progress through the Age of Aquarius, expanding our perception and inner awareness. In *"The Labours of Hercules: an astrological interpretation"*, Hercules' eleventh labor is a metaphor for the Soul's Journey through Aquarius. After completing his task successfully, not only was his work not recognized, but the King accused Hercules of trickery and refused to pay him! This is an important key to understanding the heightened state of consciousness and advanced skill that is demonstrated by the Aquarian Soul.

At this level the flow of Love and Life continues as a steady stream, not for personal reward, payment or recognition (these are concerns of the ego, which would be a distraction from our Soul work). If the flow of Love and Life was dependent upon praise, which then never came, these vital energies would wane. This is an important point.

This point is illustrated in the story of a Tibetan Monk who was imprisoned and tortured for many years by Chinese soldiers[70]. When asked if he was ever afraid his reply was yes, he was afraid he would lose compassion. He knew that his ability to continue flowing benevolent energy was what mattered most, irrespective of the attitude and behavior of those around him, and the external circumstances. It is the same point that Jesus Christ was making when He taught about 'turning the other cheek'.

The Sun continues to shine whether we remember to appreciate it, or not. The Aquarian Soul is here to be of service to Humanity for no other reason but that (in the words of his Leo counterpart) "The show must go on!" If you have Sun, Moon or Rising Sign in Aquarius you are here to consciously flow your energy into the world in ways that make a positive difference.

You matter Aquarius. Your energy is truly vital for the good of the whole, but you will never realize this by Self-denial, and using group

---

[70] Garchen Rinpoche tells his story in the documentary *"The Yogis of Tibet"*

activism as an excuse to avoid your inner path. Your own ego is a vital foundation for the flowering of your Soul. Adopt the heart-centered courage of your opposite number Leo. With the heart of a lion look your own ego squarely in the eye, complete with all your deepest fears, failings, needs and vulnerabilities, and be prepared to walk your inner path to the very end. This way you will discover your true magnificence: your inner light that is brighter than any Sun, and the beautiful energies of Love and Life may flow through you continuously without end, for the good of the whole.

Pisces-Virgo
The Healing Heart

The sign of Pisces is associated with illusion, delusion, glamour, suffering, sensitivity, bondage, captivity, prisons, hospitals, religious orders, renunciation, detachment, self-sacrifice and death. Sound like fun? If you thought Scorpio was intense welcome to the oceanic depths of Pisces. Having journeyed through the previous 11 signs of the Zodiac, spending up to eight lifetimes in each, the Soul in Pisces has been around the block to say the least. No wonder your Piscean friends sometimes seem to be carrying the weight of the world on their shoulders.

Having learned to flow the energies of love and life consciously, accurately and consistently in Aquarius to become the World Server, the Soul in Pisces becomes a liberated, radiant, expression of Christ Consciousness: a World Savior. A developmental cycle is complete and the Soul is now fully mature and ready to fulfill Divine Purpose.

*"In Aquarius, the sign of world service,
the lesson is finally learned
that produces the world Savior in Pisces"*

- The Tibetan, *"Esoteric Astrology"*

Does this mean every Piscean we meet has the saintly qualities of a World Savior? Not quite. As we shall see, there is a big difference between the personality vibration, and the Soul expression of Pisces. The gap between the lower octaves and higher octaves of this mysterious sign is the biggest in the whole Zodiac, and the difference is one of fear and love. Bridging this gap is the longest journey humanity will ever make.

The sign of Pisces embodies oceanic consciousness. Water signs are all about Mastery of emotions and mutable signs are all about change, so that gives us a clue to the higher purpose of this sign. Collectively, under the influence of Pisces, we are here to transform through our emotions. As the sign of oceanic consciousness Pisces is aware of, and experiences, the consciousness of humanity. This is why Pisces has the reputation of being the most sensitive sign of all. It means sensitive in the sense of being aware of, and able to use, all of our senses. Not, as some people unfairly presume, in the sense of being a wimp.

Indeed our Piscean friends can really step up to the plate when the chips are down and stand their ground as good as anybody. You wouldn't want to cross a Piscean who is standing up for what they believe is right. The real sensitivity of Pisces comes from their ability to sense everything. Now think about that. Would you really want to feel everything that everyone is feeling? All of the time? Pisces does. And with that comes great sadness, and great responsibility.

Pisces feels, and lives with, the truth of suffering every moment of every day. No wonder some drink! All forms of escapism are a very real risk for our Piscean friends: Movies, TV, computer games, drugs, alcohol – anything that numbs the pain is a big temptation for them. For Pisces the suffering of humanity is a real, lived, experience. Not a mental concept or idea. Pisces feels the interconnectedness of us all, and feels your pain. In a sense they really are carrying the burden of humanity. If you have Sun, Moon or Rising Sign in Pisces you'd be wise to avoid the temptation to 'numb' yourself. Learn about the higher power and purpose of your magnificent sign, and know what you can do to ease the pain for yourself and others, by using the 'medicine' of your opposite sign Virgo.

The challenge for the Pisces personality, is one of identification. Water signs tend to become identified with their feelings, and the Pisces personality all too easily becomes identified with deep feelings of sadness, self-pity and low self-esteem. (Low self-esteem comes from the 'illusion' that negative and painful feelings ARE your Self). Blinded by glamour[71], and desperate to escape from their fears, the biggest life lesson for a Pisces personality is to learn that they are not their feelings. Your fears will dissolve like morning mist when you realize your true spiritual nature but to do this you first need the laser-like discernment of your opposite sign Virgo.

The Piscean personality often confuses 'self-sacrifice' with 'people-pleasing', which leads to the mistaken thinking that you are either a victim or a martyr who has to continually neglect your own needs and defer to the whims of others. This misguided thinking is part of what you are here to transform and transcend. At Soul level Pisces knows the deeper spiritual significance of 'self-sacrifice': in the sense that the deeper meaning of the word 'sacrifice' means 'to make sacred'. The 'sacrifice' is of your lower fear-based self, as you awaken to your Sacred Heart energy and align with the Self that knows all are one.

What do we mean by a Sacred Heart? We are not talking about the physical heart, but a very subtle and powerful energy field. The Sacred Heart is the subtle connection between us and the Divine which, when awakened, allows us to flow Divine Energy into the physical world. All you need to do to awaken it, is to continuously and consistently place your attention upon it. Before this can happen, the pure focus and discernment of Virgo is needed: first to cultivate

---

[71] Read more about glamour under *"Astrology and Healing"* in Chapter 1 and about how it particularly relates to Pisces in *"The Age of Pisces: Spiritual Redemption"* online document at
http://lifecoachingmagazine.net/age-of-pisces/

somatic (body) awareness and then to discern subtler and subtler energies within our whole Being. The word 'sacrifice' refers to the practice of bringing loving attention to the subtler aspects of our Being, so that we realize our own spiritual nature, our 'Sacred Self'. Our Sacred Heart lies at the center of our Sacred Self, and is that which connects us all.

"The fluid, sensitive, temperament in Pisces
– mediumistic and psychically polarized –
must be stabilized in Virgo,
in which sign mental introspection and critical analysis
become possible and serve to arrest the fluidity of Pisces.
These two signs balance each other."

- The Tibetan, *"Esoteric Astrology"*

When the oceanic consciousness of Pisces accesses the pristine purity and loving awareness of Virgo, something miraculous happens. Rather than being numb, the focus and precision of Virgo helps you to feel more deeply and precisely, until you identify and access your Sacred Heart. You experience the transformation of negative emotions as you breathe through your own heart. This felt experience in Virgo, brings Pisces to the realization that when you make just one small change within yourself, it changes the whole. This is the true power and mystery of Pisces, and it comes from a real lived experience, not from a belief or an idea. It is the knowledge of how one transforms the many: that one pure droplet, changes the whole ocean.

It is in the sign of Pisces that Humanity's greatest spiritual achievements are fully realized, and so it makes sense that our greatest challenges also lie in this sign. Before we can realize the spiritual heights we have to acknowledge the depths. Acknowledging the truth of the ocean of human suffering, rather than trying to escape, avoid or run from it, is the greatest challenge our Pisces friends will ever face. Yet it is only by fully examining suffering, with the critical eye of Virgo, that we begin to fully understand the cause.

Having cultivated spiritual realizations to the point of enlightenment, and with an opportunity to finally return to 'the Father's house' the Piscean Soul, now fully equipped, awake, and aware, turns back in order to save others.

> ***"I leave the Father's home***
> ***and turning back, I save"***
>
> - The Tibetan, *"Esoteric Astrology"*

The deeper mysteries of Pisces speak to the spiritual development of humanity, and the fulfillment of spiritual purpose.

The Piscean Soul doesn't turn back to save others from some glamorous idea of being a hero, but rather from a quiet and simple recognition of Divine Purpose. That the point of existence and incarnation is to be a spiritual 'pacemaker', keeping the beat of spirit in matter, so all sentient beings may do likewise through a process similar to (but subtler than) entrainment[72]. To attain this capacity is the whole purpose of incarnation in general, and human incarnation in particular.

---

[72] It is interesting to note that only one species - humans - can clap hands, tap feet, and dance in time with music. This speaks to our role as 'pacemakers' as the Divine symphony unfolds on earth. *"Entrainment in the biomusicological sense refers to the synchronization of organisms to an external rhythm, usually produced by other organisms with whom they interact socially. Examples include firefly flashing, mosquito wing clapping as well as human music and dance such as foot tapping."* From Wikipedia at
http://en.wikipedia.org/wiki/Entrainment_%28biomusicology%29

"For as long as space remains
And as long as sentient beings remain
Until then may I too remain
To dispel the suffering of all beings."

- Shantideva

The Soul's journey through the Zodiac signs is one of Human Spiritual Development. The completion of the cycle in Pisces beings resolution: the dissolution of illusory boundaries and final fusion of Soul and Personality. The fully mature Human Soul in Pisces at last has the power and capacity to be of service. According to *"Esoteric Astrology"* the true spiritual purpose of Humanity is to be a kind of conduit for spiritual energy: as spirit descends into matter through Humanity, our role is to flow and direct Divine energy for the benefit of the animal, plant and mineral kingdoms.

Pisces plays a vital role in Humanity's awakening process. As each one of us purifies our thoughts and intentions we rise up from fear, and learn to focus and direct our Sacred Heart energy like a laser-beam. Each human that awakens then becomes like a spiritual pacemaker! Each pacemaker 'cell' in the heart of humanity, works silently in service. Radiating pure Divine energy from their Sacred Heart, which invites others to fully mature, awaken, and join them in the fulfillment of Divine Purpose. In this way the fully awakened Sacred Heart acts as a pacemaker for an awakening Humanity. Many individuals are now sensing, responding to, and aligning with, this growing pulse of Sacred Heart energy as its rhythm ripples throughout Human consciousness.

In conventional Astrology the sign of Leo rules the heart, for it is in Leo that the individual first awakens to the warmth and love flowing through his own heart yet, as we shall see, it is in Pisces that we finally have the power, consciousness and capacity to emit a continuous 'pulse' of transformation!

Our current state of mind, with our focus on (man-made) war and suffering, is the result of our spiritual immaturity, which leads us to be blinded by glamour. We are so easily deceived by the appearance of things, and we do not yet have the spiritual maturity to see things as they really are. Our spiritual eyes are still closed. We believe what we see and hear, which causes fear, negative emotions and results in us continuously living in a fearful, reactive, state. Watch a TV drama, thriller, or horror movie, and notice what happens to your emotions (and especially your heart rate!) when, in truth, nothing is actually happening to you.

This problem of not perceiving reality as it is, is what creates fear and a false idea of ourselves that is rooted in our ego-personality and sustained by the illusory nature of glamour. It will change because it is only a phase we are going through. We will grow up and awaken to our Divine nature because it is part of our natural development. A child cannot remain a child. This is what was meant when Jesus Christ said *"We are as children"*. He was referring to our spiritual immaturity, and our inability to connect with, and be a channel for, Divine Love and Purpose.

In the Pisces personality there is still polarity. The personality and Soul are experienced as separate and, in a sense, the Soul is in 'bondage' to the personality as the higher vibration Piscean energy is filtered through the 'lens' of a human mind, with all it's fear and illusion. The mind creates an 'idea' of separation: an ego-personality, which sustains the veil of illusion through fear. Realizing that we create the very illusions that keep us asleep, is an important part of our awakening, and this happens in Pisces.

It is under the influence of Pisces that each 'cell' in the Sacred Heart of Humanity, each 'drop' in the ocean of consciousness, ripens, matures, and starts beating 'in synch' with the Divine. Such is the magnificence and importance of Pisces. There isn't much that can be said that offers consolation to the personality. Pisces is associated with death because there is a symbolic death. Symbolically, the personality 'dies' in this sign - it 'fuses' with the Soul as the individual becomes fully Soul-Centered.

This is not nearly so dramatic as it sounds – the truth is that because our personality is also a glamorous illusion, when we fully awaken it simply dissolves and leaves us standing in the truth of our Sacred Self. We retain our awareness of being an individual drop, and part of the Ocean, at the same time. That is the point of our Soul's Journey: to bring us into contact with important lessons and experiences that catalyze us into becoming fully awakened, conscious, individuals, in alignment with Divine Will and Purpose, and in service to all sentient beings. All hearts beating as one.

So Pisces, it's time to put down that cocktail, turn off the TV, and hear the call of your heart. Don't worry – you won't have to go anywhere, or DO anything. You are not here to take center stage. You are simply here to be awake and focus on the power of your own heart, and to do that you need to access the focus and discernment of your opposite sign Virgo. Then Mother Nature will do the rest.   You will soon realize how suffering really is transformed in your heart: through the power of your pure love.

When enough of us mature spiritually, and become heart centered, transformation naturally happens. All you need to do is silently keep focusing on your heart-center while the rest of your human family wakes up and joins you in Divine Service.

Integration and Oppositions

Integrating the energy of our opposite sign, especially the opposite sign to our Sun, Moon and Rising Sign, will accelerate our unfolding process of personality-Soul fusion, and help each of us to move closer to the experience of wholeness or oneness. For some, this integration process will be a major life theme, for example if there are 'oppositions' in your horoscope. For example Sun in Libra and Moon directly opposite in Aries, or Cancer Rising and Saturn directly opposite in Capricorn. If there are oppositions in our chart we have no choice in a sense but to address these polarities, because life will continue to place us with people and situations that bring up the characteristics of the opposite ends of the polarity, as a catalyst for us to integrate the energies.

If we do not have such oppositions in our chart we still need to integrate the energies, although we may need to make a conscious choice to connect with and become familiar with the energy of our opposite signs.

Having seen how our Soul journeys through the twelve signs of the Zodiac, and how we are each of us on a personal journey of personality-Soul fusion through the integration of opposing polarities, in the next chapter we will look at the planets themselves and how they are spaceholders in a sense, as they help to create the conditions necessary for our spiritual growth and awakening.

5. The Planetary Spaceholders

One of the things that sets Soul Astrology apart from other forms of astrology is the approach to the ruling planets. In Soul Astrology the conventional rulers of the sign are considered to be the rulers at personality level and we also have a ruling planet at Soul level.

Rulership is a very old term from the days back when the king or 'ruler' was the custodian of his land and his people. Rulership doesn't seem like a good thing to us in our modern era where we see the effects of malevolent 'rulership', dictators, war and power games every day in the news, but this is not what is meant in the astrological sense.

A planetary ruler is not something or someone that has power over us, but rather something that contributes to the conditions that support us in our growth- much like a loving gardener who knows exactly what conditions are necessary not only for plants to survive but to thrive and reach their highest potential. So in this sense the planetary 'ruler' is more like a guardian, or custodian. It is therefore more useful to think of planetary rulers as spaceholders, providing the necessary vital conditions for specific stages of our individual Soul's growth and our collective evolutionary unfoldment.

Our ruling planet is one that has a great energetic affinity with our Rising Sign and is therefore showing us the major theme of our life by helping to create the conditions for our growth. If the Earth is the

stage upon which the play of our life is being acted out, then the
ruling planet is showing us the main storyline in the script!

Zodiac Sign	Personality Ruler	Soul Ruler*
Aries	Mars	Mercury
Taurus	Venus	Vulcan
Gemini	Mercury	Venus
Cancer	Moon	Neptune
Leo	Sun	Sun
Virgo	Mercury	Moon
Libra	Venus	Uranus
Scorpio	Mars/Pluto	Mars
Sagittarius	Jupiter	Earth
Capricorn	Saturn	Saturn
Aquarius	Saturn/Uranus	Jupiter
Pisces	Neptune/Jupiter	Pluto

*Source: Esoteric Astrology by Alice Bailey.

Most signs have both a personality and a Soul ruler. How do you
know what your ruling planets are? They are the personality and
Soul rulers of your Rising Sign (see above table). So if you have
Gemini Rising, Mercury is your personality ruler and Venus is your
Soul ruler. Leo and Capricorn are the two exceptions, where the
personality and Soul Ruler are the same, however they do have a
different energetic influence.

In *"Esoteric Astrology"* the twelve signs of the Zodiac tell a story:
the magical story of consciousness incarnating[73] into matter, in the
form of a Human Being. Irrespective of different faiths, and known
by many names, all scriptures tell of Holy Beings that are here to
help. Guiding the Human Soul on its journey and ensuring we don't
stray too far from the path.

*"Every blade of grass has an Angel
that bends over it and whispers
Grow! Grow!"*

-The Talmud

---

[73] Incarnate: "in the flesh" from Ecclesiastical Latin *incarnatus*, past
participle of *incarnari* (be made flesh), from in- + caro (flesh) Definition
from http://wiktionary.com

"Esoteric Astrology" also tells us that the twelve signs of the Zodiac are Divine Intelligences, or Angelic Beings, that 'oversee' the different stages of our Soul's development. So we can think of your Rising Sign as an Angel who knows exactly what is needed for the next stage of your Soul's growth, and the planets themselves as the spaceholders or custodians, embodying the energies that create specific physical conditions until that growth stage is complete. Next we'll take a look at the specific conditions that the personality and Soul 'rulers' create for each sign.

Mars, Mercury, and The Inner Journey of Aries

As mentioned in Chapter 2, on it's journey through all twelve Zodiac signs the Soul begins in Aries as *"a point of light in the mind of God"*, and that Aries carries the initial spark of inspiration: the first impulse to exist.

So the Soul in Aries is carrying the blueprint and the potential. While we might have a map, and guides to help us keep to it, the success of our grand expedition also depends upon our own efforts and the conditions we meet along the way.

Just as the seeds of Spring have the potential to become trees, under the right conditions. They are not yet trees, and the seed is very different from the tree. It is similar with our Soul's journey. We are in the process of growth and, under the right conditions, we will realize our spiritual potential. Just as the seed needs the right mix of sunlight, warmth, water, earth and nutrients in order to grow, so a Human Soul is also 'conditioned' by a number of factors, not least of which are the planets.

The planets play a vital role in this conditioning of our Soul and three planets have an important relationship with Aries: Mars, Mercury and Uranus. At the personality level Mars is the primary energy providing the motivating, driving force. Mars is related to the 'vital body' and brings life-force energy into physical existence. It provides the motivation, power, and movement, that causes the tender shoot to break out of the dark womb-like seed, to strive against the earth and stones, against all odds, to reach the light.

Mars brings drive, *motive*[74] and motivation. It is the driving force that pushes life-force energy into the physical world. It is the energy of creation, conception and new life (think sperm)! It enlivens and 'vitalizes', brings life and vitality, and is closely related to Patanjali's 'energy' body. The driving force of Mars motivates us into action. This universal force is present throughout Nature.

Animals live, and are driven, primarily by their 'vital', or energy, bodies. Only in humans did Mars fall out of favor as its influence historically became associated with war and aggression. This is because of man's misinterpretation through his lower consciousness: the message of Mars is 'take action' or 'move'. When this pure life-giving energy is distorted through the filter of our ego-personality (see Chapter 1), it all too often becomes 'let's fight' or 'go to war'.

This is partly due to the consciousness of humanity at this current time, and the effect of Mars vitalizing our 'lower nature'. In time, as we expand our consciousness, we will experience and respond to Mars differently, and perceive it's influence as largely beneficial.

"The effect of Mars is, therefore,
largely mass effect and group results,
producing great struggles
but eventually leading to great revelation.

---

[74] Motive: the underlying energy that drives us into action - from Medieval Latin *motivus* (serving to move, motive), from Latin *motus*, past participle of *movere* (to move). Definition from http://wiktionary.com

In Aries, it is the final revelation
of the nature of knowledge
and the purpose of incarnation."

- The Tibetan, *"Esoteric Astrology"*

Mars moves us into action. Ultimately it is up to us to choose the action we take, conscious action or unconscious reaction. The outcome of our actions depends on our own motivation. It is important for anyone with planets in Aries, especially Mars, to continuously check their motives: are your actions motivated by the needs of your head (ego) or the call of your heart and Soul?

Mars rules the lower octave[75] of Aries, the personality. Empowering Aries with motive – the need to move the Self forward into life and light. For the Soul-centered individual, who has fully integrated personality and Soul, the ruler of Aries is Mercury. The hierarchical ruler[76] of Aries is Uranus. As we evolve in consciousness, our spiritual eyes are opened, and we are suddenly able to perceive that which we could not before. More subtle energies and influences become apparent to us. At this point in our evolution the hierarchical level is beyond our perception so we will focus on the personality and Soul rulers: Mars and Mercury.

In Chapter 1 we explained how *"Esoteric Astrology"* speaks of three stages of spiritual development known as the mutable, fixed and cardinal cross[77]. Those on the mutable cross are personality-centered and have little or no awareness of Soul. Those on the fixed cross

---

[75] For more about the lower and higher octaves of Aries see Chapter 4

[76] Further discussion of hierarchical rulerships is beyond the scope of this book but if you are interested you can read more about hierarchical rulership in *"Esoteric Astrology"* by Alice Bailey.

[77] This is not the same as having a Grand Square or Cosmic Cross in one's own natal chart but rather refers to the unfolding process of *personality-Soul fusion and the three crosses* as described in Chapter 1.

have some experience of Soul. They have begun awakening, but there is still duality: separation between personality and Soul. The individual on the cardinal cross has fully integrated Soul and personality. There is no separation. Such an individual would be a highly realized spiritual Being like Christ or Buddha. Most of us on the planet at this time will be on the mutable cross, while a fast-growing minority are beginning to awaken on the fixed cross.

The majority of people on the mutable cross will still relate, and be receptive, to Mars as the ruler of Aries. Those on the fixed cross who are awakening and becoming aware of their Soul Presence will begin perceiving the qualities of Mercury, and it's influence in Aries. When the Being is sensitive, and receptive enough to receive Mercurial energy, then Mercury takes over from Mars and begins the process of awakening, ripening, conditioning and developing the intuitive body.

Mercury is responsible for the development of the antahkarana, or Rainbow Bridge, by which we connect lower and Higher Mind. Aries is very much a sign of the mind, and it is through this ripening and conditioning effect of Mercury that Aries arises from his lower nature to reach his full spiritual potential. The effect of Uranus in Aries lies beyond the individual and is known only at the Hierarchical level. As we awaken spiritually, developing our senses and deepening our perceptive capacity, we become aware of the more subtle influences of these energies. In Aries it is the effects of both Mars and Mercury that are creating the perfect conditions for spiritual development.

During the early stages of our spiritual journey, like tender vulnerable seedlings, we are very susceptible to the energies that condition our growth, but there is a reciprocal effect that comes later. Just like a fully mature forest gives back and sustains the environment which nurtured the individual trees so we too, as fully flowering mature Spiritual beings, will have the capacity to emanate beneficial energies, such as compassion, to nurture and sustain all sentient beings.

Soul Astrology is the astrology of our inner world: our energy field, of growth stages and our journey through them. The natal chart is our own personal mandala, showing us the energetic patterns and dynamics that were present at the precise moment that we came into incarnation, and the planets that are co-creating the conditions for our growth. How much we grow spiritually, and increase our capacity to receive and perceive the potential influences, depends very much on us: our motives, intention, motivation and the choices we make. We must strive to expand our perception if we are to be aware of more subtle influences.

Will we recognize Mars as the benevolent Father of Life on Earth, driving us steadily towards Mercury and the revelation of our Higher Self? Or will we continue to cast him down as a God of War? The choice is ours.

Venus, Vulcan, and The Inner Journey of Taurus

We saw how the Soul begins in Aries as *"a point of light in the mind of God"*. By the time the Soul reaches Taurus that point of light begins to *extend out as a single beam of light*. After the initial pulse of Life in Aries, desire in Taurus becomes the driving force in shaping what form Life will take. Will we forge ahead driven by our egoic desires and wishes? Or will we align with Divine Will and shape our primordial Life-force energy into spiritual path and purpose?

Taurus, the sign of the bull, is associated with steadfastness, material possessions, beauty (especially in physical forms), art, stubbornness, security and even enlightenment. In previous chapters we mentioned that the Buddha himself had six planets and Chiron, in Taurus, and that the Buddha was born, passed and entered parinirvana all during the time of this auspicious sign. Esoterically Taurus is associated with illumination and the opening of the third eye.

It is under the sign of Taurus that humanity is learning the deeper spiritual lessons of desire and the transformation of the energy of desire. It is through desire that we take a physical incarnation and it is desire that also keeps us trapped in 'samsara', the cycle of death and rebirth. Taurus teaches us about the nature of desire, and what needs to happen so we can release our personal attachments and transform the energy of desire into Spiritual Realizations.

"humanity... is beginning to come under the influence of Taurus.
The great question is – Will this influence
...produce the floodlight of illumination
of which Taurus is the custodian,
or will it simply foment desire, increase selfishness
and bring humanity to the 'fiery heights of self-interest'
instead of to the mountain of vision and initiation?"

- The Tibetan, *"Esoteric Astrology"*

Taurus has two planetary rulers: Venus and Vulcan. Venus is the personality ruler and Vulcan is both the Soul ruler and the Hierarchical ruler. According to *"Esoteric Astrology"* both Venus and Vulcan are Sacred planets, while Vulcan is a 'hidden' planet. *"Esoteric Astrology"* tells us that there are 'hidden' planets that we are unaware of because we do not yet have the consciousness to perceive them or to be receptive to their energy. Once we have expanded our consciousness to the degree that we are more receptive and aware of these subtler energies we will become aware of these planets. The fact that both ruling planets are sacred (and one is hidden) hints that the inner journey of Taurus is deeply hidden, mysterious, highly significant, and sacred.

"The Soul is our individual link to
the essential substance of the Creative Source...
Astrology is a system that seeks to interpret
the nature of the Universal Life Force
as It moves, shapes, and creates human life and all events.

The planets, signs, and houses,
are not the causal elements of manifestation.
They are, rather, the reflections
of a transcendental synchronicity
manifesting through the rhythms
and timing of a cosmic clock."

-Alan Oken, *"Soul Centered Astrology"*

When considering planetary 'influences' from a Soul Astrology perspective it is more appropriate to think of the planets as lenses, or focalizers, of Divine energy rather than as causative agents. In *"Esoteric Astrology"* the basic energies of creation are referred to in terms of Seven Rays. I will say more about these in future publications but for our purposes here it is enough to know that there are Seven Great Rays, within which our Universe aligns with just one, and then within our Universe there are Seven sub-rays. Just as the sunlight contributes to the optimum conditions for Life on Earth to thrive so Divine energy, in the form of these Seven Rays working through planetary 'lenses', is contributing to the optimum conditions for the flowering of human consciousness.

Venus is the goddess of Love: the powerful energy of desire, which translates as romantic love, when filtered through a human mind! She rules both Libra and Taurus. In Libra she endows her subjects with a harmonizing aspect that manifests through the mind: in terms of conceptualizing or idealizing ideas of ethics, beauty, attractiveness and justice. Her work in Libra is more closely linked to harmony in the mental body[78]. In Taurus the loving energy of Venus has a more sensuous, earthy, influence. She works initially through the physical senses to eventually bring awareness of the bliss body.

As Venus works through desire in Taurus, she seeks to awaken the

---

[78] See *"The Dawning of Your Life"* in Chapter 2 for a reminder about Patanjali's 'five bodies'.

senses. She awakens our sense perception through the physical senses of sight, sound, taste, touch and smell. This has the potential to open us to an experience of bliss, and awareness of the bliss body. Herein lies the danger of the Taurean path. If the individual is still centered in the ego-personality the tendency can be towards grasping at more external objects to feed the bliss experience: clinging to possessions of beauty, beautiful people, music, food, a beautiful body, and losing sight of the spiritual journey. This is a symptom of the lower mind externalizing the bliss experience and projecting it onto outer worldly objects.

The ego-mind uses logic to the extreme. If one chocolate made me feel good, then ten chocolates will make me feel ten times as good, right? Yet we all know this is not so: too much of a good thing leads to lethargy, dullness, weight gain and that uncomfortable (even painful) feeling of being over-full. Then we have the addiction effect: we begin to believe we need something outside of ourselves (the chocolate, new shoes or whatever our craved substance, possession, or person may be) in order to feel good. We begin clamoring for more of the 'object' that we believe will lead to more pleasure (bliss). This leads us to pursue 'worldly concerns' (objects outside of ourselves) and the sad part is that while doing so we are neglecting our inner spiritual path, which is the true path to inner peace, bliss, and beyond.

"Desire is the force of the form in nature;
will is the energy of the Soul expressing itself as direction,
progress, and conformity to the [Divine] Plan"

- The Tibetan, *"Esoteric Astrology"*

In Patanjali's description of the five energy bodies (Chapter 2) we can see that the bliss body is the closest to our ultimate spiritual goal of "Universal Mind" and so is considered a very powerful (and dangerous) path to enlightenment. Tantric practice is based on the transformation of blissful energy into the path. But this path is fraught with danger, in the form of being 'seduced' from our path and getting lost in the realm of sensory pleasures. It is for this very reason that sense pleasures are considered 'sinful' in so many spiritual traditions (the origin of the word sin means *'to miss the mark'*)[79]. Without cast-iron will and discipline, forged in the furnaces of Vulcan, (and under the guidance of a qualified spiritual teacher) they are more likely to cause us to miss the mark, miss our spiritual purpose, and miss the point of our Life altogether. If we don't have such powerful will, we are better to steer well clear of this path.

When correctly focused and disciplined the path of bliss can lead to the higher octave of Taurus, which brings spiritual illumination, and the knowledge that bliss arises from within. It is not 'caused' by external objects but is part of our very own inner nature. Once Taurus has mastered the lower desire nature, through meditation, patient effort and discipline, she is open to receive the transformative energies of Vulcan. Whereas Venus brings the energy of desire and sensuality, Vulcan is more aligned with will. Divine Will in particular.

Once Venus has done her job of opening our senses to the presence of blissful energy within our physical form, it is Vulcan's job to guide us in the correct use of that energy. The dangers of addiction and being 'lost' in the bliss would arrest our spiritual development and bring our journey to a premature end. The path is one of transcending all five energy bodies to arrive at our true nature and Universal Mind[80]. The energy of Vulcan brings the gift of steadfast

---

[79] The English word sin is a translation of the Greek word *harmartia* which literally means *to miss the mark*. This phrase in itself is interesting in terms of the path of Taurus, because in archery to miss the mark means to miss the bullseye or the Eye of the Bull. The implication of this is that when we hit the true Eye of The Bull then we are 'on target' for our spiritual unfoldment.

[80] There may be a description of five, seven or twelve energy 'bodies', depending upon your school, tradition, and/or level of study. The anatomy of the Human energy field has been described in different ways through many different schools, too numerous to mention here.

willpower: that allows us to continue our spiritual path. Blow by blow, like Vulcan's hammer, forging the personality into something that is useful for our Soul's purpose. Driving us forward on the spiritual path, although there is always the danger that we could go either way. While the ruling planets may provide the conditions, how we react or respond to them is up to us.

The path of Taurus involves strong will, and strong choices, for desire has the habit of leading our attention outwards towards worldly concerns. It is part of the Soul's journey through Taurus to learn to focus this energy inwards toward the spiritual path.

"One reaction produces the onward rush of the materialistic systems of life, thought and desire, dashing blindly forward in the force of their own momentum and producing a stage of powerful expression and active movement;

the other demonstrates in a far vision of possibility and a steady movement forward in spite of the immediate dangers and difficulties... The question is: Will the Bull of desire or the Bull of illumined expression succeed?"

- The Tibetan, *"Esoteric Astrology"*

For example in the Tibetan tradition five major chakras are most commonly identified while the Vedic tradition describe seven. The differences in emphasis are due to the different approaches in spiritual paths, and take account of varying levels of understanding and awareness. For example to a five-year old you might describe your hand as having a palm, four fingers and a thumb; but to a medical student you would probably include skin, bone, muscle, ligaments, fascia; hormonal, endocrine, lymphatic, immune, nervous and circulatory systems, and then explain how they all relate to one another to create a functional cohesive whole. It is important to remember that, although descriptions and labels vary, the underlying reality remains the same.

In mythology Vulcan is known as the blacksmith of the Gods. His job is to shape and fashion substance: forging physical matter from light in the heat of his furnace. Once illumination in Taurus has been realized, it is also Vulcan's job to then shape that energy into some tangible practical shape, in physical form, to fulfill Divine Will, or spiritual purpose.

One thing that happens to metal, once it is melted down in the blacksmiths forge, is that it can also be purified. In a liquid state anything that is not gold, for example, can be removed so that pure gold can be poured out and fashioned into shape. This alchemical function of Vulcan gives a clue to one of the deepest mysteries of Taurus: the opening of the third eye.

There are many references in esoteric writing to the "Eye of Light", the "Eye of the Bull"[81] and even the consciousness of Buddha has been referred to as the "Diamond Eye". In nature, natural diamonds form in conditions of high pressure, and high temperature, deep within the Earth. So we have the energy of Vulcan at work: transforming ordinary rock through fire and pressure into something that is pure, clear, and revealing: it illuminates by showing us the nature of light[82]. These higher octave properties of illumination and revelation are hinted at in the esoteric keynote for Taurus that we mentioned in the previous Chapter:

"I see and when the Eye is opened, all is light"

- The Tibetan, *"Esoteric Astrology"*

Venus brings us the power of Love, and the potential for Higher Love, but if the Love of Venus is not to be degraded into worldly

---

[81] *"Esoteric Psychology, Vol I"* by Alice Bailey.

[82] A diamond shows us the nature of light by revealing the many rainbow colors present within light itself.

desire, we also need to pass through the fiery forges of Vulcan. This purification process transforms primordial love and desire, through Divine Will and revelation, into Higher Love, compassion and illumination.

As we discipline ourselves to eliminate the undesirable aspects of our lower ego-personality so we become aware of, and aligned with, our Soul. The Soul begins to take shape and becomes the true vehicle for the fulfillment of our spiritual purpose. We begin to realize, and know ourselves to be, a Soul. To recognize that our physical body is only one part of our Soul, and to recognize that all physical forms are manifestations of One Great Spirit.

Mercury, Venus, and The Inner Journey of Gemini

Gemini brings the interplay of light through form. The Soul, which began its journey in Aries as a 'point of light in the mind of God' and became a beam of light in Taurus, now divides into multiple beams of light in Gemini. Think of the quality of sunshine playing through the leaves, or the dancing sparkles of light on water and you have the light, playful, fairy-like quality of Gemini. The one becomes many, and the Divine dance has begun.

Don't misunderstand the playfulness of light, indeed a sense of play is in the nature of light and is inherent in the whole of Creation. The apparent superficial quality of Gemini belies his deepest mysteries: the mystery of Life and the mysteries of our Divine purpose as a spiritually awakened Humanity. Gemini is associated with the breath, and indeed the Divine use of the breath, through words and sound is a clue to the deepest mysteries of Gemini.

Gemini has three planetary 'rulers' each of which is important in understanding these deeper mysteries of Gemini. The personality ruler of Gemini is Mercury, the Soul ruler of Gemini is Venus and the hierarchical ruler of Gemini is the Earth herself (Esoterically Venus and Earth are said to be sister planets). Indeed it is through

Gemini that Humanity fulfills it's Divine purpose as custodian for Earth and the elemental kingdoms. Gemini connects us to the etheric and the elemental at one and the same time. This apparent sign of duality is actually a sign of multiplicity, connection and communion. Through Gemini we realize our interconnectedness with one another, Earth and her creatures, and all sentient beings.

At the personality level Gemini is ruled by Mercury, the winged messenger of the Gods. Esoterically Mercury is responsible for the Rainbow Bridge, or Antahkarana, connecting lower and Higher Mind. It is through Mercury that we learn to connect and commune with our Higher Selves and hear our spiritual calling. It is ultimately through the activity of Mercury, conditioning, expanding and awakening our perception, that we attune to higher consciousness and perceive our Divine Purpose. It is through Mercury that we realize our interconnectedness to one another, that the brotherhood (or sisterhood) of Humanity becomes the body of Humanity as we transcend separatism and realize the Divine Task of Humanity as Custodian of the Earth and her creatures.

At Soul level Gemini is ruled by Venus. Once the activity of Mercury has expanded our perception, we are open to the activity of Venus through the heart center. This brings a spiritual awakening in the form of a deep sense of communion and connectedness with all sentient beings. There is an awareness of Love, not as an idea, but as a living energy that permeates and radiates throughout all life. This shift in perception brings us to the realization of our interrelatedness with one another and all living things.

Mercury opens portals of communion between lower and Higher Self, so we connect with our inner 'guru', coach, or our own, wise Self. However, there is still a perceived duality, a separation, as experienced from the side of the personality. Earlier we looked at the harmonizing aspect of Venus, as experienced through physical matter in Taurus. Venus achieves harmony through the *law of Right Relationship*. What makes the difference between music and a collection of disharmonious sounds? It is the relationship between each note. When each note sounds in right relationship to the others, the human ear (and indeed all of existence) receives it as music: in other words, sounds that are played in harmony with one another.

As Venus begins her work Gemini moves from the lower octave to the Higher octave and begins harmonizing all perceived duality. It is the conditioning effect of Venus, and the law of Right Relationship, that allows Gemini's higher octave to resolve all duality. Gemini has a unique role in the Zodiac. In *"Esoteric Astrology"* it is said to be the only sign that is connected with each of the other 11 Zodiac signs. This is because, according to the Tibetan, Gemini plays a vital role in the future astrology, by being an active agent in the *integration process* of resolving all duality and polarities so that eventually we have the *blended six* Zodiac signs that we mentioned in the previous chapter. This synthesizing effect of Gemini is due to this unique relationship between Mercury and Venus, opening a pathway to Higher Love.

As this Mercury-Venus connection grows, clarifying and strengthening the Rainbow Bridge, the Soul presents ever more clearly and strongly to the individual. Hence the Soul keynote for Gemini:

"I recognize my other self
and in the waning of that self
I grow and glow"

- The Tibetan, *"Esoteric Astrology"*

This speaks to the individual process of Soul recognition and identification, whereby eventually the Soul experience is so strong, the connection is such, that the individual realizes: this is who I Am. At that point the grip of the personality is loosened and the individual lives freely as a fully Soul-centered being.

There are many ways to describe this long journey from the head to the heart, but the simplest way is probably to think of it as a shift from fear to love. The fear-love polarity is just one of the polarities resolved in Gemini. Gemini has a unique role to play in the spiritual awakening and evolution of planet Earth, and this happens through the conditioning effect of Mercury-Venus on an awakening Humanity, such that Humanity recognizes it's unique and vital role as *custodian of Earth*. We are here to be lovers: lovers of our Earth home. Just like nurturing Mothers or spiritual Midwives we are all here to hold our Earth-home in love as she goes through her own birthing process.

"Esoteric Astrology" tells of the unique relationship between Earth and Venus as sister planets, and the unique relationship that Gemini has with *the heart of the Sun* (Cancer is associated with the physical Sun, Aquarius with the central Spiritual Sun, and Gemini with the heart of the Sun). Of the Seven Rays Gemini is only associated with Ray Two: Love-Wisdom, otherwise known as *the path of love*. Since Gemini rules Humanity, this gives us a clear indicator of the Divine purpose of Humanity: the reason we are here.

In exoteric astrology the sign of Gemini is not usually associated with love and romance, and that is because it is not romantic love of which we speak here. It is the highest love that connects all sentient beings and that sacred connection is the highest mystery of Gemini, and the reason why Gemini is the sign that permeates and touches everything.

Gemini's highest purpose is, through the conditioning effects of Mercury and Venus, to bring real, tangible, Love into everything he touches. To Love everything in existence, through right relationship, and the dissolution of all polarity: love-hate, male-female, friend-enemy, us-them, etc. until we experience ourselves living as one body. The body of Humanity. A 'brotherhood' of individuals breathing vitality and Love into the Earth.

The symbol for Venus (and our contemporary symbol for the female), a circle above a cross, is similar to the Egyptian Ankh. The Ankh is known as the *breath of Life*, and in Ancient Egyptian tomb-paintings the deity can often be seen holding an Ankh to the nose of the deceased Pharaoh to give him the breath of Life. It is said that Midwives in Ancient Egypt would often carried an Ankh for this reason, so they always had the *breath of Life* for the newborn infant.

This is a reminder of the conditioning effect of Venus in Gemini, connecting us all with Love-Wisdom, and the breath of Life. It is also a reminder of the importance of Gemini for the spiritual awakening of Humanity, and ultimately the evolution of planet Earth as she transcends and transforms into a sacred planet like her twin sister Venus. The journey begins as Humanity bridges the gap from our heads to our hearts.

The Moon, Neptune, and the Inner Journey of Cancer

Cancer is associated with home, birth, family, and our tribe, clan or nation. It is also the sign of empathy, emotional intelligence, re-birth and mass consciousness. The mysterious sign of Cancer is one of the quietest. It is the tiniest of constellations in the Zodiac, and could easily slip by without being noticed. Yet within this tiny silent sign are held the deepest secrets of reincarnation, for Cancer is the gateway into the physical realm. The sacred marriage of matter and spirit happens through this gateway of Cancer.

In considering the planetary rulers of Cancer, it is most important to remind ourselves what we really mean by 'rulership'. At the beginning of this chapter we pointed out that, what may have been considered 'ruling' in times gone by, as in domination or holding power over us, is really referring to a kind of custodianship in which certain conditions that are necessary for growth and evolution to unfold, are held in place. It is therefore more useful to think of planetary rulers as space-holders, providing the necessary vital conditions for specific stages of evolutionary unfoldment. Once this is understood, we can then begin to understand why, according to the Tibetan, *Cancer is said to have only one true space-holder (ruler) at personality, Soul and Hierarchical level, and that is Neptune.*

However, the Moon 'veils' Neptune, at the personality level, for this stage of our evolution. In this sense it acts almost like a filter, adjusting the energy of Neptune to something that can be utilized by humanity at this time. This is why the Moon has such a powerful effect on the masses. The true spiritual energy of Neptune is too subtle to be sensed or perceived by us at this time and, once we have fully awakened our sense-perception, we will be able to sense and fully utilize Neptunian energy. It is in Cancer that we cultivate and fine-tune our sense-perception, which is why Cancerians are so empathic and in tune with their emotional world.

Just as a gardener digs, turns, prepares and softens the hardened earth to become receptive to tender seeds, so the Moon softens our hardened hearts to become more receptive to tender spiritual energies. By creating the conditions of ebb and flow in the emotional tides of humanity, the Moon provides the masses with the experiences necessary to awaken us to compassion and deeper sense-perception. We cannot continue to ignore the fact that we are feeling, sensing, sentient beings and the doorway in to this deeper knowledge is through our emotions. We begin the journey of acknowledging and cultivating our sense-awareness by first of all becoming aware of our emotions.

> *"Love and compassion are necessities, not luxuries.*
> *Without them humanity cannot survive."*
>
> - HH Tenzin Gyatso, XIV Dalai Lama
> (Sun and Rising Sign in Cancer)

The Moon 'rules' the physical form, while Neptune 'rules' spirit. In *"Esoteric Astrology"* the Tibetan tells us that the Moon is the "Mother of All Forms" while Neptune is the "God of the Waters". In Cancer we have the sacred union of the Mother of all Forms (the Moon) and the God of the Waters (Neptune), which represents spirit. This is a clue to the deepest mysteries of Cancer, which is to be a gateway for spirit in physical form, that is later consummated in Virgo.

"...in orthodox Astrology, the Moon is substituted for Neptune because it is the form nature which is dominant in the longest stage of human unfoldment."

- The Tibetan, *"Esoteric Astrology"*

More clues to the vital role of Cancer can be found if we study *"The Labours of Hercules: an astrological interpretation."* In Hercules' fourth labor, which pertains to Cancer, he rescues a Doe by taking her to his heart and carrying her to the Sun Temple, whereupon she dies of a leg wound. On returning to his teacher Hercules sees the Doe standing out in the field again on the very spot where he had first seen her.

This hints at the spiritual lessons of care, loving concern and compassion in Cancer. Having concern for all creatures by taking them to our hearts. It also symbolizes rebirth. This story is a metaphor for the spiritual truth that (under the custodianship of the Moon) physical forms are subject to the tides of change and yet (under the custodianship of Neptune) there is a continuous influx of Spirit that remains steady within and throughout the changing forms.

"The process of incarnation takes a lifetime. [It] is organic Soul movement in which the higher, finer vibrations or Soul aspects are continually radiated downward through the finer auric bodies into the more dense ones and then finally into the physical body. These successive energies are utilized by the individual in her growth throughout her life."

- Barbara A. Brennan, *"Hands of Light"*

It is Neptune that sensitizes us to spirit, conditions us to receive spirit in matter, and increases our capacity for spiritual awareness. In this sense Neptune spiritualizes whatever he touches. After the Moon has done her work, by conditioning humanity through our emotions,

Neptune increases our capacity for spiritual awareness. Neptune's reputation as an 'illusionist' in conventional astrology, stems from this role in challenging our attachment to, and identification with, appearances and form. Neptune clearly shows us how forms themselves are constantly changing and illusory in nature, so we may turn our attention inwards and discover the unchanging spiritual reality that is our true nature. Neptune invites us to go within and keep our attention on that which is steady, constant, and is in fact our true nature.

We are currently still being conditioned by the Moon to awaken to our emotions and the power of our emotions. Emotional intelligence is, at the time of writing, a hot topic and will be for many years to come, because we are all at different stages in the development of emotional intelligence and awareness. For those who may be thinking that emotional intelligence is an old topic because the term was first used back in the 1920's, be assured that the subject will be with us for many years yet to come.

At the moment humanity is able to *talk about* emotional intelligence but very few can walk the talk by translating that intellectual understanding into *emotional skill and competency*. This is why we still have war, aggression, violence and bullying rippling through the masses, and their associated behaviors tend to leak out and peak around the time of the Full Moon. If we really understood the importance of emotional intelligence, and had fully integrated compassion and heart-wisdom into our being, it would be at the core of every educational system on the planet, rather than being tagged on as an afterthought, and marginalized.

It is the conditioning effect of the Moon on the masses that leads to these tides of emotion, and it is humanity's lack of skill in the emotional realm that leads to conflict. As the Moon continues to do her work humanity will become more open to acknowledging emotions and more skillful in handling our emotional experiences. This will pave the way for us to be receptive to the energy of Neptune, which will awaken us to our true spiritual nature. It is through the gateway of our emotions that we will begin this stage of our journey. Before we can even come close to receiving the energy of Neptune, we need to become much gentler in spirit!

This brings us to the Law of Rebirth, which is the realm of Cancer. It is through a continuous experience of rebirth and suffering in this realm that we learn:

- the true meaning of compassion
- the consequences of our actions
- how to change so that we stop the many man-made causes of suffering
- how to cultivate great skill in relating
- emotional competence, and
- the truth of our inter-connectedness

This is how we will rise above our current tribal cultures, as we increasingly recognize the whole of humanity as our family.

The more we allow ourselves to feel our emotions, the more we develop sensitivity and empathy. The more empathic we become, the more we realize the deep spiritual truth that we really are all connected. The more we realize our connectedness, the more difficult it becomes to harm others, because when we feel their pain, we know from experience that we really are only ever hurting ourselves. The pain of others, is our pain too.

*"In this world period, and in a peculiar manner ...
Neptune is known esoterically as the Initiator"*

- The Tibetan, *"Esoteric Astrology"*

Cancer is a Cardinal sign and Cardinal energy has an initiating quality to it. It is a creative energy of leadership. If you have Sun, Moon or Rising Sign in Cancer a major theme in your life, and perhaps a major part of your life purpose, is to play a significant lead role in the transformation of emotions, the shift towards intuition through emotional intelligence, and the shift from tribal culture to that of one interconnected human family. It is important to take care that you don't get caught in tribal-thinking and carried away on a tide of (lower) mob consciousness. Go deep within, listen to your intuitive voice, and honor all of humanity as your true family.

> *"It is the planet Neptune which is predominantly active*
> *in bringing about such an activity in Cancer*
> *that adequate momentum can be set up to produce*
> *progress (through the intervening signs) to Aquarius."*

> - The Tibetan, *"Esoteric Astrology"*

We can see that, even though the Moon is conditioning humanity at present, she is really acting as a filter, and that the real energy behind these shifts in perception, awareness and consciousness, is Neptune. This is why the sign of Cancer is also associated with deep listening, because it is only through deep listening, intuition, and recognition of subtle energy streams, that we may begin to receive the deeper Soul impressions of Neptune.

In the Soul's journey through the Zodiac, it is in Cancer that we hear the first whispers of our intuition. One of the lessons for the Cancerian Soul is to learn to hear your own still, quiet voice, above the many voices of the crowd. Because of this dual activity of the Moon and Neptune in Cancer, we hear both the call of the tribe (the Moon) and the call of the ocean (Neptune). We will find a way to honor both by going within and listening deeply to our hearts. In this way we will be evolving both emotionally and intuitively, and walking our very own conscious journey home to the center of humanity within our own hearts.

The Sun and The Inner Journey of Leo

Leo brings an opportunity to reflect upon our own uniqueness, individuality, and purpose. The noble sign of Leo is associated with warmth, creativity, play, children, the heart, role-play, acting and royalty. It is Leo that governs the roles we play in society, throughout our lives. It is in Leo that we walk the path of Self-realization, which begins with the development of the ego. In order to fulfill Divine purpose, we need a well-defined ego. The challenge is to cultivate a mature ego that recognizes the distinction between individuality and separation.

Continuing our Soul's journey through the 12 Zodiac signs, after Cancer brings the diffuse divine light into form, the light in Leo individuates. Leo's deeper spiritual purpose is to express Divine Will through realization of Self as an individual. In Leo we individuate, but we can never separate from the rest of humanity, for that isn't possible. Each of us is an individual ray of light that, just like the rays of the Sun, is never separate from the light of the Divine.

In understanding the planetary rulership of Leo, it is important to consider the fullness of our own Being. To really comprehend the role of the Sun in relation to human evolution, we need to begin experiencing ourselves as far greater than just our physical form. In the process of the evolution of consciousness, we are really expanding our perception so that we become aware of that which already is.

"There are no levels of Reality;
only levels of experience for the individual"

- Ramana Maharshi

Esoterically Leo is said to have 'only' one planetary ruler at the personality, Soul, and hierarchical levels, and that is the Sun. In order to understand this we have to think way beyond the astronomical model of the Sun as a piece of molten rock that is burning away in space, and begin to think of the Sun as ancient people's once did: as a *conscious Divine Intelligence*. The Sun is a living Being that has a triple aspect which, in *"Esoteric Astrology"*, is called the *Solar Logos*.

This triple aspect of the Sun has custodianship over three specific areas of our spiritual development: The physical Sun (the corona that we can see) creates and sustains the conditions for the development of our outer worldly life as experienced through our ego-personality. The heart of the Sun creates and sustains the conditions for the development of our heart and Soul, and the core of the Sun (which is at one with the Central Spiritual Sun) creates and sustains the conditions for our development at hierarchical level. All three are one. Understanding how the Sun is one and yet plays three individual roles, is similar to understanding how humanity is one and yet we each play our individual roles.

The Sun epitomizes the idea of planetary rulership as custodianship or space-holding, providing the perfect conditions for evolutionary processes to unfold, in stages, with precise Divine timing. The Sun is the centre of our planetary system. We live within a Solar system, named from the Latin word 'Sol' meaning Sun. The Sun provides a constant emanation of vital life force, prana, which permeates and sustains this system. Leo is a fixed sign and here we see an example of the purpose of fixed energy for stabilization: in this case creating a *stable environment for sustaining Life*, through constancy and continuity.

> *"It is the Sun that is a great living consciousness,*
> *a great pulsating solar heart"*
>
> – Errol Weiner, *"Transpersonal Astrology"*

The Sun is more than just a symbol for humanity – he also is the epitome of the maxim 'as above, so below'. Understanding that there is a spiritual core, which emanates through the heart and then radiates through the outer corona, or personality, is a truer understanding of our own nature as Human Beings. We are, each of us, energetically like a Sun in miniature and if we only focus on our corona (personality) we will miss the true depth and nature of our being. To find the truth of our own being we also need to go within, passing through our heart center, to discover our own spiritual core. The Sun is not only a symbol of our Self-realization, but he is our guide.

The Sun invites us to go within for deeper understanding. We cannot understand the deeper spiritual mysteries of the Sun by looking at him. Indeed looking directly at the Sun would be harmful. It's as though he is saying to us *"go back, this is not the way"*! Just as the physical Sun connects to the Great Spiritual Sun through the heart of the Sun, so the Sun indicates to us that the path to our own deeper spiritual truth is *an inner journey through our hearts to our spiritual core*. We cannot know the truth of these esoteric teachings by thinking about them, but only through experience. We need to go deep into our hearts in meditation to experience the truth of our innate connection with the heart of the Sun.

> *"The Sun's heart beats at eleven-year intervals,*
> *and with this 'beat' it sends out its life-force*
> *into its entire system,*
> *just as the human heart*
> *sends out this same vital force,*
> *via the bloodstream"*
>
> – Errol Weiner, *"Transpersonal Astrology"*

Through the infusion of life-force energy the Sun illuminates the path to Self-realization, and Leo is the sign of Self-realization. There are many steps on this path and they can be put into three stages: self-consciousness, Self-awareness and Self-realization. These three stages can also be equated to the three aspects of the Sun and three stages of development on the Soul path of Leo.

The path of Self-realization in Leo is itself a vital stage in the overall evolution of human consciousness. The German philosopher Friedrich Neitzche spoke of three stages of consciousness in terms of the Camel, the Lion and the Child. The Camel represents tribal consciousness, where we follow the herd, follow the masses, and go along with the collective consciousness. This is the pre-egoic state.

The Lion represents individualization – the ability and the willingness to stand alone. Separate. Apart from the herd. In terms of our personal spiritual development this is the development of, and identification with, our ego. At the same time this is the beginning of our spiritual awakening. Just as the great river Ganges has its source in a tiny mountain stream, so our collective spiritual awakening has its origin in our currently emerging egoic state. Nietzche's 'Lion' stage includes stages one and two (self-consciousness and self-awareness) of our astrological path of Leo.

The Child represents the 'free spirit' once we are liberated from our egoic challenges and delusions. This is the post-egoic state (and the third stage of the astrological path of Leo, which is why Leo is also associated with creativity, playfulness, and children). Our spirit is 'free'. The Child is our fully awakened state of Self-Realization, or enlightenment. In this final stage we arrive at a deeper realization, through experience, that we are not separate but have an individual expression in our oneness. When we finally reach this stage we experience the truth of our connectedness with the Sun, and all living beings.

> *"Know thyself. If thou canst learn the true nature of thine own self, thou wilt know the reality of the Universe."*
>
> - Abhedananda

We can see how important the path of Leo is for the evolution of consciousness. During the first stage of the path of Leo (self-consciousness) we become aware of self vs. 'other'. This is the first stage towards individuation. The path to individuation begins with an idea. An idea of separation. We become aware of the idea that there is a 'me' in here, and there are others 'out there'. This focus on the outer world, conditioned by the corona of the Sun, is vital for the development of a sense of an individual self. The individual at this stage will (necessarily) be personality–oriented with no sense of Soul. This is the stage where we become self-ish, because our world is centered on our developing idea of 'me' and meeting the immediate needs of our personality.

In the second stage of the path (Self-awareness), we move to the heart. Conditioned by the heart of the Sun we begin asking *"Who Am I?"* We hear the call of spirit and our journey moves within. The individual at this stage is still largely personality-driven but has experienced Soul awakening. We are aware of our spiritual nature but still experience Soul and personality as separate. We become less selfish and more altruistic in our outlook.

At the final stage of the path, conditioned by the core of the Sun (the Great Spiritual Sun) the individual is fully Self-realized. We realize there is no separation and we live from unity consciousness (oneness). We are fully integrated in that there is full personality-Soul fusion and no experience of separation. We become oriented toward world-service for the benefit of all living things because we know from personal experience the deepest meaning of the Soul Keynote for Leo:

"I Am That, and That Am I"

- The Tibetan, *"Esoteric Astrology"*

It is under the warm, loving, life-giving, custodianship of the Sun in all his aspects, that we walk the path of Leo to the full realization of our true nature as spiritual beings. To fully express our Divine purpose we need a strongly defined sense of Self. From our fully integrated Self-realized state we are able to fulfill our Soul purpose, which is to be a unique individual expression of Divine Will.

Mercury, The Moon, and The Inner Journey of Virgo

Virgo brings the opportunity to focus on our true vocation, or Divine Purpose. Virgo is associated with purity, purification, health, healing, well-being, the Virgin Mother, Mother and Child, the physical human form, and Divinity in form. It is no accident that Virgo season is harvest time in the Northern hemisphere, as Virgo is also associated with the harvesting, or results, of what was sown. Virgo reminds us of the practical reality of reaping what we sow, and if we don't like what we see, it gives us an opportunity to prepare the ground to plant a different crop next year. Likewise is the Soul purpose of Virgo to purify and prepare our physical form so that it is more receptive to light and becomes a suitable vehicle for the cultivation and gestation of the Christ Consciousness that will be born in Capricorn.

Following the journey of the Soul through the 12 signs of the Zodiac, after the completion of the individuation process in Leo, the individual now prepares for service by ensuring that the physical vehicle is ready to receive the light. Virgo has two planetary spaceholders (rulers) that create the conditions necessary for this crucial stage of our Soul's development: Mercury and the Moon. We already explored Mercury's role in both Aries and Gemini, and the Moon's role in Cancer, and now here in Virgo both planets create different conditions again. Virgo is an Earth sign, so they are more practically and tangibly conditioning the physical form rather than thought and feeling.

Mercury creates connections and pathways for communication, or communion. Esoterically Mercury creates the ultimate pathway to connect us with Higher Mind, the antahkarana or 'rainbow bridge'. Although we are strictly speaking in terms of energy and energetic pathways, it is helpful to think of the analogy of mercury as liquid metal. Imagine the speed and fluidity of liquid metal as it creates tiny sparkling rivulets, which become streams, and then rivers, spreading and branching out wherever needed to create pathways of light.

At one end of the bridge Mercury connects with the light of the Divine, at the other end of the bridge Mercury is sending roots down into physical form: enlivening and stimulating the growth of neural pathways, natures own communication network for consciousness, so that conscious awareness can travel ever deeper into physical form. This is a two-way communication. Through the activity of Mercury consciousness 'communes' with form, and form becomes awakened and aware of consciousness. As a result, *somatic awareness* (the felt-sense in our body) deepens in Virgo and the fully integrated Virgo Soul can feel when they are flowing pure Love through their physical work and/or actions. Using your nervous system as a medium for communion, Mercury sensitizes you to spirit. Awakening you to subtler and subtler levels of energy and consciousness.

Whereas in Gemini (at personality level) there is still duality, a perceived separation between form and Spirit, between the Divine and the personality, Virgo is a sign of synthesis. So in Virgo, at personality level, the action of Mercury prepares the physical form to receive. The connections made by Mercury prepare for the synthesis of Spirit and form, so that ultimately there is no separation. Spirit is form and form is Spirit.

This is not an easy stage of our developmental process. Part of the process involves cognitive stimulation, the stimulation of thoughts and cognitive processing, and it is this side-effect of Mercury that leads some people with Sun, Moon or Virgo Rising to feel edgy, anxious or to worry to excess. If you are experiencing this it is because you need to ground this Mercurial energy, and that is easier said than done. Having said that, it is part of your Divine Purpose as a Virgo to be a kind of cosmic lightening conductor! Do whatever you need to do to connect with your heart center, it can be yoga, reiki, or even gardening, but do whatever you need to do *to feel the physical flow of energy through your heart center radiating throughout your body and down to Earth*. Once you have done that, your energy will become grounded into the physical, rather than having too much energy in your head!

As we saw earlier in Cancer, the Moon rules *physical form*. So it makes sense that once Mercury has created the pathways, the Moon would step into a higher role in holding the space and ensuring the conditions are ripe, for Spirit to be fully imbued into physical form. The sign of Virgo is associated with perfection. This leads the Virgo personality to misguidedly seek perfection in the outer world, whereas the Virgo Soul seeks perfection of the inner world. In Buddhist teaching the highest perfection is said to be the perfection of wisdom.

There is an ancient Buddhist scripture called the "Holy Heart Sutra of the Perfection of Wisdom" (often just called "The Heart Sutra" for short). This scripture tells of a conversation between the historical Buddha and one of his heart disciples, Sariputra. In this scripture the Buddha says to Sariputra:

> *"Form is emptiness, emptiness is form*
> *Emptiness does not differ from form,*
> *and form does not differ from emptiness."*

> - The Heart Sutra

This speaks to the deepest mysteries of Virgo, and it is important to understand what is really meant by 'emptiness' in this context. It doesn't mean 'nothing', but rather refers to space, which is 'empty' of physical forms, but is 'filled' with Spirit, filled with Love, filled with consciousness. Filled with all that we value, yet cannot see or touch. It speaks to the synthesis of Spirit and form that happens in Virgo.

In *"Esoteric Astrology"*, the Tibetan refers to the Moon as the "Mother of All Forms". In certain Buddhist traditions, reference is made to the 'Mother Void' and the 'Son awareness'. This is referring to the karmic cycle through which physical forms arise from the 'void' (or space), then awareness arises through form, and then Divine awareness (Soul) returns to the void (space) through synthesis, after the dissolution of form. Esoterically this is described as the synthesis of Father (Spirit) and Mother (Form) which gives rise to the birth of the child (Christ Consciousness). At a higher level the unified Mother-Father is simply referred to as Mother. The deeper mysteries of this Divine process lie within the Virgo-Pisces cycle of arising, awareness, synthesis and then resolution. This is how the deeper mystery of Virgo, symbolized by Mother (Spirit/Form) and child (awareness), leads to the expansion of Divine Love.

After the Moon has done her earlier work in Cancer, creating the conditions for us to transform negative emotions into positive altruistic states such as compassion, she returns in Virgo to teach us how to flow the subtle physical energies of compassion through the subtle channels that have been created by Mercury. Again this is a two-way street that speaks to the highest purpose of Virgo. Through the channels created by Mercury and under the conditions created by the Moon, we experience a greater expansion of Divinity into physical form and come one step closer to experience our Soul: that 'droplet' of Divinity which resides within each of us.

Likewise as a result of the expansion of the Human Heart and a greater flow of human compassion, there is a greater experience of human potential, within the Divine. Heaven travels to Earth, and Earth meets Heaven. Interestingly the 'ruler' of Virgo at hierarchical level is the expansive, magnifying, planet Jupiter. So we can see that the expansion of Love on many levels and throughout many realms is deeply connected with the highest Soul purpose of Virgo.

"Virgo stands for the 'womb of time' wherein God's plan (the mystery and the secret of the ages) is slowly matured and – with pain and discomfort and through struggle and conflict – brought into manifestation at the appointed time"

- The Tibetan, *"Esoteric Astrology"*

The Moon is a bit of an anomaly, an enigma, in astrology. Technically, She isn't really a planet at all (for moons are not planets). Indeed H.P. Blavatsky (Author of the earlier esoteric works The Secret Doctrine and Isis Unveiled), Alice Bailey (channel for The Tibetan, Author of *"Esoteric Astrology"*), and mystic Vera Stanley Alder, all agree that the Moon is 'dead' having no life-force (prana) or vitality of Her own. Yet the magnetic pull of the Moon affects the Earth's tides, and likewise the emotions of humanity. So here we have the esoteric symbology of the Moon: something that is 'dead', connected to the past, yet is still tugging at us. The Moon symbolizes those aspects of our past, which are no longer useful, or beneficial for our spiritual progress, yet we collectively and individually haven't released them yet.

The Moon thus creates conditions of human experience that are womb-like in the sense of being deep, dark and quiet. In Virgo she creates the conditions for:

"the valley of deep experience
wherein secrets are discovered
and eventually 'brought to light';

[Virgo] is the place of slow,
gentle and yet powerful crisis
and periodic developments

which take place in the dark
and yet which lead to light"

- The Tibetan, *"Esoteric Astrology"*

Esoterically the Moon veils Vulcan, and as we saw earlier Vulcan is known as the blacksmith of the Gods. In the alchemical fiery furnace of Vulcan physical forms are transformed like molten lead into gold. It is this alchemical action of Vulcan that conditions the physical form to be more receptive to light and thus enables the synthesis of Spirit and Matter in Virgo.

The Moon / Vulcan conditions the form while Mercury lays down a connective network of light on all levels. With this dual action of Mercury and the Moon / Vulcan the physical human form becomes a pure and suitable vehicle for light and the subsequent birth of Christ Consciousness. If you have Sun, Moon or Rising Sign in Virgo it is important that you be aware of your physical energy and stay grounded. You are here to radiate love into the world.

Venus, Uranus, and The Inner Journey of Libra

Libra brings an opportunity for balance and harmony, multi-dimensionally. The sign of Libra is associated with balance, harmony, relationship, ethics, beauty and law. These are all expressions of, and are connected through, the *principle of harmonics*, which in itself is based upon the fundamental *law of right relationship*. Therein lies the secret to the deeper mysteries of Libra, and indeed, the mysteries of existence.

The whole of existence depends upon right relationship. For example, science is only just beginning to realize how delicately balanced an ecosystem is. A disruption in one tiny area can have devastating effects throughout the whole system. The balance of our whole Universe depends upon *right relationship*, which we perceive through our senses as *harmony*.

Following the journey of the Soul through the 12 signs of the Zodiac, after the synthesis of spirit and matter in Virgo, the Light in Libra comes to rest. However it is not a peaceful rest, not yet. It is resting in the knowledge of what is to come. It is in Libra that the battleground becomes apparent, in readiness for the battle that must ensue in Scorpio. Earlier we said how we do battle in two signs: Leo and Scorpio. In Leo we battle for our individuality, in Scorpio we battle for our Soul. In Libra, we prepare by becoming increasingly aware of duality. We finally recognize the relationship between polarities. In our awareness of the separation between the opposites: self and other, yin and yang, personality and Soul, in Libra *we see what needs to be done, to restore right relationship, and resolve the duality.* The final resolution happens in Scorpio. What happens in Libra, is an expansion of perception, awareness, and an important shift in consciousness.

Libra has three planetary rulers or 'space-holders', which are important for understanding the deeper mysteries of this important sign. Venus is the 'ruler' at personality level, Uranus is the ruler at Soul level and Saturn is the ruler at hierarchical level. For the purposes of this article we are only looking at the personality and Soul rulers, Venus and Uranus, since the hierarchical level is cosmic in nature and beyond our capacity for comprehension at our current level of consciousness. Having said that, we can see that having the "Lord of Karma" Saturn, as ruler at this hierarchical level hints at the significance of Libra for the resolution of karma, the evolution of humanity, and humanity's role in the karmic balancing of our Earth home and her ecosystem.

It is also worth noting that, esoterically, all three planetary 'rulers' of Libra are considered to be sacred planets. Air signs are all about Mastery of the Mind, and Cardinal energy is all about carving out new pathways, so as the Cardinal Air sign we can only begin to imagine the deep significance of Libra's sacred role in the evolution of consciousness.

Venus brings the energy of magnetic attraction. Initially this is animal magnetism, and at the personality level she awakens desire and passion within the individual, which lays the foundation for experiences of Love. We see this Venusian influence expressed as sensuality at personality level in Taurus and as a pathway through Higher Mind to Higher Love at Soul level in Gemini. Now in Libra, as a result of the preparation in Virgo, the individual is able to conceive of Higher Love and harmony at the personality level, bring this down to Earth (thanks to Virgo) and express this into the outer world through the personality. This is done through right relationship between Self and other.

Harmony is our way of knowing when components within a system are in right relationship to one another. Think of an orchestra tuning up, before playing a symphony. During the tune-up each instrument is just making it's own sound with no regard for the other instruments. The result is just noise. We wouldn't call it music because it isn't harmonious. When we hear music, harmony is present. There is 'right' relationship between the notes. When each note is played in right relationship to the others, harmony is the result.

The whole field of ethics is dedicated to the study of 'right' decision making. How do we know when we have made a 'right' decision? Right decisions are those that are in alignment with Divine Law. They lead to greater harmony because they are in right relationship with the whole of existence. Wrong decisions are those that are out of step, out of tune, and bring disharmony. There is a lack of regard for, or relationship with, the other components within the system. The Libra personality, often unfairly, has a reputation for being indecisive, yet we can see that it is actually the process of decision-making that concerns Libra greatly. It is important that Libra understands how to arrive at the 'right' decision, so that we can increasingly move towards greater harmony.

In this context we can see that sometimes man-made 'laws' can actually be disharmonious. So when we say Libra is associated with law, we are speaking of the Divine Laws of attraction, right relationship, harmony and natural law. These are not laws like man-made laws, but rather natural principles, like the law of gravity, which guide the whole of existence. Harmony itself is a natural, balancing, principle. In *"Esoteric Astrology"* the Tibetan explains that the sign of Libra is greatly concerned with the themes of law, sex and money. Sex and money are more often associated with Scorpio in conventional astrology, yet it is actually through the sign of Libra where imbalances and abuses of power in these areas can be brought to balance, through right relationship.

To make progress on our spiritual path, we need a degree of stability in our ordinary life. If we have a chaotic life where we are constantly in turmoil meeting our daily needs, we will have no inclination to pursue a spiritual path. The action of Venus in Libra plays a vital role in balancing and stabilizing our conventional 'ordinary' lives, ensuring we live simply, in alignment with natural law, so that our energy is free for transformation, and our Being is open and receptive to our spiritual development. The action of Venus in Libra harmonizes, balances and stabilizes our personality, and thereby our conventional world. When the light in Libra has 'come to rest' we are then open to receiving the subtle energy of Uranus, which transforms consciousness.

Uranus is the energy of rebellion. Not rebellion for the sake of trouble-making, but rebellion because it is necessary to evolve and align with Divine Law. In Greek mythology Uranus is the Sky, vastness, space. The primordial Being from which all other beings arise. He is the Father of the Gods who begat all the Gods on Mount Olympus and their rivals the Titans. Primordial consciousness. Uranus is a planet of transformation who has the power to transform consciousness in particular. When we have been touched by Uranus our lives are never the same. There is no going back.

> *"He who has penetrated to the limits of thought,*
> *dares to take the leap into the Great Emptiness,*
> *the primordial ground of his own boundless being."*

- Lama Anagarika Govinda

Sometimes in conventional astrology, the energy of Uranus is referred to as rebellious. It is important at this point to make a distinction between a rebel and a revolutionary, if we are to fully understand the spiritual purpose of the rebellious energy of Uranus and it's ability to transform consciousness.

A succinct explanation of this distinction comes from the Indian mystic OSHO who says:

> *"The rebel ... brings into the world a change of consciousness –*
> *and if the consciousness changes, then the structure of the society*
> *is bound to follow it ... No revolution has yet succeeded in*
> *changing man; but it seems man is not aware of the fact. He still*
> *goes on thinking in terms of revolution, of changing society, of*
> *changing the government, of changing the bureaucracy, of*
> *changing laws, political systems. Feudalism, capitalism,*
> *communism, socialism, fascism – they are all in their own way*
> *revolutionary. They all have failed, and failed utterly, because man*
> *has remained the same ... The rebel is a spiritual phenomenon.*
> *His approach is absolutely individual.*
> *His vision is that if we want to change the society,*
> *we have to change the individual."*

> – OSHO, *"The Rebel"*

The revolutionary has the same consciousness as the society in which he arose. He may overthrow a dictator and then himself become the new dictator. He is just the other side of the same coin. There has been a change in name, but not a change of consciousness.

The energy of Uranus is therefore not revolutionary, it is rebellious because it transforms consciousness. The rebel brings inner change: a change of consciousness within the individual. The rebellion is not 'against' anything but, like a flower blossoming, is a natural unfoldment into the next stage of evolution. Where Uranus is concerned, it can be a complete quantum leap that bears no resemblance to that which has gone before.

Once Venus has done her job of opening the heart, then the individual is open to receive the touch of Uranus – to allow inspiration to move them and break free from the limitations of the lower mind. Venus initially brings desire, attraction, animal magnetism. Through the experiences of Venus the individual experiences the beginnings of love, but this lower consciousness love has a price: it comes with conditions. There is a possessiveness to it. Once Venus has softened the heart, Uranus is able to bring in expansiveness. The expansiveness of space, of Being, and the individual is never the same again. They are made 'anew'. Passion can now make a quantum leap into Higher Love and then further again, into limitless compassion.

"Love is Higher Thought about someone"

– Anya Sophia Mann

We are evolving from instinct, through intellect, to intuition. In this process Venus initially opens our hearts and minds, opening us up to shift from instinct to intellect. Then Uranus catapults us from intellect to intuition. Uranus brings inspiration, clarity, intuition and vast, clear space. Boundless Sky untouched by clouds. Initiating, catalyzing the evolution from intellect to intuition. Unexpected, because how can we know what to expect from a level of consciousness that we have not yet experienced? Under the influence of Uranus, without the limitation of intellect, Libra is capable of quantum-leaping through 'octaves' of Higher Mind to Higher Love.

"Reason, the highest property of the intellect,
is what guides purposive thought.
Purposes, however, are limited;
and therefore reason can operate only in what is limited.

Wisdom alone can accept and intuitively realize the unlimited,
the timeless and the infinite, by renouncing explanations
and by recognizing the mystery,
which can only be felt, experienced, and finally realized in life
- and which can never be defined."

– Lama Anagarika Govinda

If you have Sun, Moon and especially Rising Sign in Libra, you are here to go beyond your own limitations and become an expression of Higher Love in the world. You will do this through right relationship between yourself and other. When you lean too far toward the Aries end of the spectrum, there is too much emphasis on self; When you lean too far toward the Libra end of the spectrum, there is too much emphasis on others. When you come to rest at the center, the balance-point, you are in perfect harmony; and this creates the window through which the energy of Uranus can enter to transform consciousness.

Pluto, Mars and The Inner Journey of Scorpio

Scorpio brings an opportunity to look more deeply into our own psyche than we have ever done before. The enigmatic sign of Scorpio is associated with such intense themes as sex, death, cruelty, rebirth, power, regeneration, money and the deepest darkest depths of our own minds. Scorpio goes where angels fear to tread and for this reason is also the sign of priests and psychologists. All seven so-called 'deadly sins' can be explored in Scorpio with a couple more thrown in for good measure. So what is it all about? It is time to take courage, dive deeply, and understand the spiritual significance of this vitally important sign and the deepest mysteries of existence.

Following the journey of the Soul through the 12 signs of the Zodiac, after the point of balance between body and Soul has been reached in Libra, the final struggle takes place in Scorpio, the last of the four signs of crisis[83]. This is a kind of birthing and, just like the contractions in physical childbirth, this spiritual rebirth happens in waves. As the personality gradually comes under the command of the Soul, there are waves of 'depression' where the personality feels as though it is being 'squashed', followed by waves of rebellion where it fights back. The personality doesn't give up easily without a fight! The personality isn't being squashed however, it is being gradually assimilated, as more spiritual energy is able to enter into the being. The end result of this struggle is total fusion of Soul and

---

[83] See Chapter 2 for more on the signs of preparation, crisis and service.

personality, body and Soul. The personality is the 'interface', the meeting place between the body, with all its animal urges and instinctive impulses, and the finer energies and ethereal vibrations of the Soul.

Three planetary rulers, or space-holders, are the guardians of this birthing process, which is vital for the evolution of humanity from an animalistic being into a fully awakened Soul-centered being. Both Mars and Pluto are guardians of this process at personality level, while Mars is the guardian at Soul level. In *"Esoteric Astrology"* Mars is considered a great beneficent planet (not malefic as is thought in some Astrological systems). It is through the activity of Mars that this final struggle between personality and Soul is fought and won, with the fully integrated (fused) Soul emerging victorious. Triumph and victory are keywords with Scorpio and it is important to remember this especially when the going gets tough. Mercury is the planetary ruler at Hierarchical level which we won't explore here except to notice that this again hints at the vital importance of Scorpio for the spiritual evolution of humanity.

> *"It is in Scorpio that the preponderance of the spiritual energy is imposed upon the lower personal forces"*
>
> - The Tibetan, *"Esoteric Astrology"*

The combined effect of Mars and Pluto at personality level serve to bring awareness to the potency of desire working through the form nature and that, although we experience desire, it is not fundamental to our nature and can be brought under control through illumination. At this level Mars governs life-force energy: stirs the blood, agitates and activates our animal instinct, and arouses the passions. It is the fuel that feeds the fire of desire. Pluto, at personality level, brings somatic awareness. The instinctual felt-sense in the body. Otherwise known as the great revealer, Pluto, is able to hold our animal urges up to the light, for healing and understanding. While in the dark they have control and power over us, once they are brought to light, the

Soul has victory. It is this dual effect of Mars and Pluto that bring about both the 'tests' and the triumph in Scorpio.

"The tests in Scorpio and the activity of Mars
are potent to arouse the entire lower nature
and bring about its final rebellion
and the last stand, so to speak,
of the personality against the Soul"

- The Tibetan, *"Esoteric Astrology"*

The tests in Scorpio are the temptations of desire that keep our attention trapped in the cycles of materialistic existence. In *"Esoteric Astrology"* they are listed as nine, in three groups. The first test is appetite which relates to sex, physical comfort and money; the second is desire and relates to fear, hatred and ambition and the third test is of the lower mind and relates to pride, separativeness and cruelty.

When explored deeply with the light of awareness, these 'tests' (which Christian theologists called the 'seven deadly sins' and in Buddhism are known as the 'destructive emotions' or kleshas) can clearly be seen to be 'faults' of attention, or discipline, and are not inherent to our true nature. They are distractions that sway us from our path. We can see that it is not the activities themselves that cause problems, but the tendency within our own psyche to become attached, obsessed and addicted to them. Then we make the mistake of identifying with them, and not recognizing our true spiritual nature.

We can see how such obsessions keep us from our spiritual path, and how evident they are as dominating factors in our current world age. It is a mis-use of our Divine energy. While we are 'lost' in the pursuit of these activities we remain unaware of our spiritual nature. In *The Labours of Hercules: an astrological interpretation*, Hercules ninth labor, in which he enters a stagnant swamp to battle a nine-headed Hydra, is symbolic of this battle in Scorpio. Whenever Hercules cut off one of the heads of the Hydra, another would grow in its place.

The only way Hercules triumphed was by lifting the Hydra above ground, into the light, whereupon it withered and died[84]. This symbolizes our struggle with the desires of the personality, which have control over us for as long as they remain in the dark, unseen. The relentless activity of Mars magnifies these desires to the degree that we can no longer ignore them, and then the activity of Pluto brings them into the light of our awareness. We cannot change what we cannot see. Once we see and fully understand the nature of desire, and the source of the struggle, it is transformed. The struggle itself lies in our trying to hold onto something that needs to change.

This is similar to the symbolism of the lotus. A lotus usually grows in a filthy, stagnant, swamp. The symbology is that, just like Hercules' battle with the hydra, our own spiritual essence blossoms as a result of our inner struggles. Interestingly, in addition to being known as the 'Lord of the Underworld', the mythological figure of Pluto was also known in some traditions as a Lord of abundance, riches, or wealth. The symbolism here is the spiritual wealth that arises when we emerge victorious from our struggle with our own underworld (our lower nature).

> *"Soft conquers hard,*
> *weak conquers strong.*
> *The flexible is always superior to the immovable.*
> *This is the principle of controlling things*
> *By bringing oneself into tune with them,*
> *The principle of mastery through harmony."*
>
> - Lao Tzu

---

[84] All that remained was the so-called 'immortal' or 'eternal' head, which Hercules buried under a rock. This could be symbolic of consciousess itself, which never ides but is eternal.

Once Pluto and Mars have done their work at personality level, by revealing this darkness to not be our true nature but rather a result of the mis-direction of our mind and energy, we are now receptive to a higher octave of Mars, which transforms passion into spiritual energy, through awareness, thus revealing our true Divine nature. When Mars has conditioned the 'passions' at personality level, and Pluto has brought illumination, Mars at Soul level reveals knowledge through awareness.

At Soul level Mars brings the higher consciousness that is pure awareness beyond the five senses. From this perspective it becomes clear that all our 'darkness' is the result of our mis-interpretation of energetic influences as perceived by our five senses and mis-interpreted through our ignorant, fearful and confused lower mind. With the illumination of Pluto we are then able to use this higher wisdom of Mars to perceive through our senses our own Divine energy and that of others. Once this happens we naturally correct any excesses and mis-applications of our energy, and use the power of our mind to direct our energy to the highest good.

"The sage avoids excesses, extremes, and complacency"

- Lao Tzu

In *"Esoteric Astrology"* the Tibetan refers to Scorpio as a 'sign of discipleship'. The word disciple and discipline come from the same root, which means learning, or knowledge. With the knowledge gained through these 'tests' in Scorpio we acquire deep wisdom and understanding of our role as a spiritual being. We are ready to 'renounce' worldly pursuits, those activities that mis-use our spiritual energy, and dedicate our lives to our spiritual path and purpose. As the Soul develops through the twelve zodiac signs, the first four signs are signs of preparation, the middle four are signs of crisis and challenge (for the purpose of growth and learning), and the final four signs are the signs of service to humanity. Scorpio is the last of the signs of challenge.

*"The self-indulgence which was initiated in Taurus
gives way in Scorpio to the selfless attitude of the disciple;
ambition gives place to the executive quality of the Soul,
whilst attachment to personality desires, likes and dislikes
is transmuted into the tenacity of Soul purpose.*

*The hidden powers of the Soul nature -
misused because misunderstood
and misapplied and, therefore, misdirected –
are superseded by ...
the practical understanding of the energies."*

- The Tibetan, *"Esoteric Astrology"*

Due to the revelatory action of Mars and Pluto we will all (sooner or later) undergo these trials and tribulations in Scorpio, as we continue our Soul's journey. The Soul's purpose in Scorpio is to transform darkness into light. The activity of Mars and Pluto elevates and illuminates, lifting our collective 'hydra' to the light so we can see that we are not our darkness, and that we truly are an emanation of Divine love and light.

Jupiter, Earth and The Inner Journey of Sagittarius

Sagittarius brings an opportunity for deeper wisdom and the possibility to recognize and focus on our spiritual goals. The fun-loving gregarious sign of Sagittarius is associated with freedom, truth, optimism, travel, adventure, spirituality, religion and philosophy. What do all these have in common? The search for ultimate truth and freedom. The true freedom that Sagittarius seeks, is liberation of the mind.

Following the journey of the Soul through the 12 signs of the Zodiac, after the final struggle in Scorpio the way forward becomes clear. Scorpio brought necessary purification and transformation in preparation for the experience in Sagittarius where:

"the Archer has to acquire and hold a steady eye,
hand and stance prior to firing the arrow which,
when rightly directed and correctly followed,
will carry him through the portal of initiation [in Capricorn]"

- The Tibetan, *"Esoteric Astrology"*

Previously we saw how Scorpio was the last of the signs of crisis and here in Sagittarius we have the first of the signs of service. The Soul is now matured and ready to fulfill divine purpose with confidence. Throughout this chapter we have been looking at how specific planets provide the necessary conditions for each stage of our Soul's growth and development. Three planets are important to Sagittarius: Jupiter (at personality level), the Earth (at Soul level) and Mars (at hierarchical level). For our purposes here in understanding our journey from personality-centered beings to Soul-centered beings, we will only be looking at Jupiter and the Earth in this chapter. It is just a passing note of interest that once again we have the influence of Mars at a much higher level of consciousness than he would normally be associated with!

Scorpio is a sign of purification that finally sets the Soul on a path of discipleship (discipline), so here in Sagittarius the experience is one of discipline, focus, and direction. Jupiter is a planet of expansiveness and higher mind, so his role in conditioning us at personality level is one of expanding awareness and consciousness. It is through the influence of Jupiter, that one realizes there is something 'higher' to aim for: a bigger, larger, grander picture of ourselves beyond our small, limited, mind.

Jupiter invites us to expand our vision, our awareness and our experience of our self. Initially the earliest inkling of self-awareness, shows up as self-consciousness, as we mentioned in Leo. Jupiter's expansive influence in Sagittarius invites us to expand our experience on all levels, so we can expand our awareness. Taken to extremes at personality level this expansive tendency can lead to self-indulgence and leave our Sagittarian friends with an expanding waistline! However it is important to note that although Jupiter is the largest planet in the solar system, it is largely comprised of gas. The symbology here implies expansion beyond the density of physical matter. Jupiter encourages us to expand our minds.

Jupiter's role is to create the conditions to guide us from small mind to higher mind. When we are in small mind we are limited by mental concepts and ideals. We impose limitation on ourselves by creating mental concepts and then adhering to them as though they were truth. When we know the difference between small mind (personality level) and higher mind (Soul level), we see a distinction between religion and spirituality and begin to understand why both are associated with Sagittarius.

When we follow a religious path, at first we adhere closely to a creed or code of conduct. Although religious traditions are mental constructs, they have been created for the ultimate purpose of taking us beyond religion itself to experience higher spiritual truth. It is a path that someone created. The danger lies in mistaking the path itself for spiritual reality, and this is one of the pitfalls of Sagittarius.

Under the guardianship of Jupiter, Sagittarius resonates with the highest truth of our spiritual nature but before this is realized, the Sagittarian personality has to let go of all mental conceptions that are mistaken as truth. Sooner or later the Sagittarian personality realizes that his beloved mental concepts actually obscure his perception of truth.

"The weighing of opinions only prevents the perception of truth"

- Jiddu Krishnamurti

Following the preparation of the Soul in the preceding eight Zodiac signs, Jupiter steps in to bring a magnificent expansion of consciousness, the likes of which we have never known before. This is different than the higher consciousness that we experienced in

Libra under the influence of Uranus. The touch of Uranus is like being zapped by a lightning-bolt flash of insight, which gives us a taste, a glimpse into higher consciousness. When the lightning flashes, for an instant we can see more than usual, but when the lightning stops we are in the dark again. Jupiter is very different. As might be expected with Jupiter, our awareness is being expanded on a much grander scale. Jupiter invites us to expand our own mind to embody the highest consciousness as our own highest mind. To expand our sense of self on a Universal scale, so that we become it. From this perspective we see the Universe, as ourselves.

Once we have embodied the expanded awareness of Jupiter on a grand scale, we are ready to receive the higher teachings of Gaia, our Earth Mother, and discover our true role as custodians of this beautiful planet. We first felt Earth's influence in Gemini albeit in the form of a subtle hint to our grander purpose from the hierarchical level. Now in Gemini's opposite sign of Sagittarius, after the full expansion and embodiment of higher mind brought to us by Jupiter, we have the awareness to realize who we are and why we are here. From this higher expanded consciousness we know ourselves to be an aspect of Gaia herself. We realize the truth of no-separation, and that we are here to contribute to the evolution of Earth herself by being a conduit for Divine Love and Light.

"The result of all experience in any sign of the zodiac should work out as an expansion of consciousness"

- The Tibetan, *"Esoteric Astrology"*

With the expanded awareness that Jupiter brings, we know beyond doubt, from our own experience, that earth is a living being, as is the whole solar system, and we know our own vital role within it. Earth has always provided. Not only does she feed, nourish and sustain us, but she is also the physical field of experience through which we cultivate higher qualities. For example through our own suffering we develop compassion for the suffering of others. She provides the foundation for our spiritual evolution. Following the expansive embodiment of higher mind in Jupiter, we mature and are ready to offer service back to Earth herself. We are ready to return the love of our Mother.

In *"Esoteric Astrology"* the Tibetan talks about two stages on our spiritual journey: discipleship and initiation. We become the disciple during the experience in Scorpio, which means we have purified and transformed our lower animal urges and are ready to discipline ourselves by focusing on our spiritual goal. The experience in Sagittarius, under the guardianship of Jupiter and Earth herself, assists us in staying focused on the path (discipleship) and holding steady until we reach our goal of *initiation* in Capricorn.

"every life experience or cycle of life experiences
should work out as an initiation
into a wider field of awareness,
of expression and of resultant contact"

- The Tibetan, *"Esoteric Astrology"*

In this context we don't mean initiation as this term is most commonly used, as in a ceremonial rite of passage into a man-made group or society, but rather in the sense of starting or beginning something. In this sense we initiate a new stage of human development and evolution in which we are fully aware of ourselves as Soul-centered beings.

It is precisely the conditions provided by Jupiter and Earth that cause Sagittarius to raise his vision beyond physical goals and set his sights on goals of a more spiritual nature. This naturally leads to the initiation of the next stage of our spiritual evolution in Capricorn. The Soul purpose of Sagittarius is to uplift humanity through the revelation of truth and wisdom. If you have Sun, Moon or Rising Sign in Sagittarius, your work is to question everything. How do you know what you know? You are here to release mental conceptions, thoughts, ideas and words, and seek the highest love-wisdom of Universal Mind, beyond the limitations of the lower mind.

Saturn and The Inner Journey of Capricorn

Capricorn brings an opportunity to return to the light. While having their feet planted firmly upon the ground our Capricorn friends have clear sight of the mountaintop and a sure, steady, method that will take them there. The sign of Capricorn is associated with practical methodology, steadfastness, business, finances, resource management, ambition and spiritual aspiration. This sign of extremes is associated with both the worst excesses of materialistic egotism at personality level, and yet esoterically is associated with the heights of spiritual aspiration leading to Christ consciousness. We will understand why as we explore the planetary conditions that exist for the Soul's highest development in the mysterious sign of Capricorn.

"Esoterically, all world Saviours and Sun Gods are born in Capricorn but also the very worst type of man- hard, materialistic, cruel, proud, selfishly ambitious and egoistic. The head rules the heart in such cases, whereas in the perfect example of the influences of Capricorn , head and heart are perfectly balanced."

- The Tibetan, *"Esoteric Astrology"*

As we follow the Soul's journey through the 12 signs of the Zodiac, after the Archer clearly identified the path in Sagittarius, in Capricorn it is time to follow that path of light all the way to Christ Consciousness.

Two planets are important in creating the conditions for the Soul's experience and development in Capricorn. Saturn is the planetary space-holder (ruler) at both personality and Soul level while interestingly it is Venus that holds space at Hierarchical level. We saw earlier how, in *"Esoteric Astrology"*, the Tibetan described the evolution of consciousness in three stages, which he referred to as the three crosses.

To recap, the Mutable cross is where most of humanity currently is. This is where we are largely personality-centered, and personality-driven. The Fixed cross is where we begin to have some Soul awareness and follow a more spiritual path, yet we are still identified with personality so duality is still present. The Cardinal cross is where we are fully integrated, living and expressing our lives as fully Soul-centered Beings. According to *"Esoteric Astrology"* Saturn cannot follow mankind onto the Cardinal cross, and so only has influence at personality and Soul level:

> *"Saturn's power is completely ended*
> *and his work accomplished*
> *when man (the spiritual man)*
> *has freed himself from Karma*
> *and from the power of the two Crosses –*
> *the Common [Mutable] and the Fixed.*
> *Esoterically, Saturn cannot follow man*
> *on to the Cardinal Cross"*
>
> - The Tibetan, *"Esoteric Astrology"*

Saturn has a reputation for being a serious, strict, limiting, authoritarian, law-giving Father figure. He is known as the Lord of Karma and the Lord of Time and is known for being a very harsh taskmaster. Believe it or not, this is ultimately all for the highest good for it keeps Capricorn on the truest path towards Christ Consciousness and prevents any wayward diversions that would tempt Capricorn to stray from his path and become lost in the trappings of material existence.

To understand Saturn's role we must understand karma and natural law. If you put your hand in the fire, it will be burned. You are not being punished for putting your hand in the fire, it is simply the result of natural law. The nature of fire is heat, and so anything coming into proximity with it, will simply be burned. Although we are spiritual by nature, Saturn brings us important lessons that we must heed while we are living a material existence: namely the law of cause and effect (karma) and the realities of time and limitation. If we are to plant seeds, grow crops and harvest them effectively, to provide food for our survival, we must heed the cycles of time, plant and harvest, according to the seasons. These are the simple lessons of Saturn.

Interestingly the Romans thought of Saturn not only as a God of agriculture and time, but as a God of liberation, and there is also a key here to the higher purpose of Saturn and Capricorn. The Soul in Capricorn has to journey up the mountain from the very depths of humanity to the very heights of Christ Consciousness, and this is no small task. The higher purpose of Capricorn involves choosing a spiritual path and understanding the laws of creation so that we may create heaven on Earth.

Capricorn rules the knees and this symbology is important in understanding the Soul's journey through Capricorn. It is Saturn's job, at personality level, to bring Capricorn to his knees so he develops insight, humility, and turns his attention away from the trappings and excesses of materialism that would keep him trapped in ego.

> *"...only when the Capricornian subject learns to kneel*
> *in all humility and with his knees upon the rocky mountain top*
> *to offer his heart and life to the Soul and to human service,*
> *can he be permitted to pass through the door of initiation*
> *and be entrusted with the secrets of life.*
> *Only on his knees can he go through that door."*

- The Tibetan, *"Esoteric Astrology"*

Saturn is a wise teacher bringing important lessons and guidance to support us in making choices that align with our highest good. The word creation comes from the Latin creõ which means to create, make, produce, beget, give birth to, prepare, cause or choose. So in creating heaven on Earth, there is an element of choice: it is through our choices and actions that we create heaven on Earth, or not.

Karma can be thought of simply as the law of cause and effect, and there seems to be a common belief that it refers to the results of our actions. Yet according to some Buddhist traditions karma specifically refers to the volition, motivation, intention and action that creates the result. It is more about the action and intention, than the result. So our personal karma is our past actions and intentions that planted the seeds for the results we are currently experiencing.

Saturn is bringing us the important lesson that these seeds ripen over time, and that if we truly want to create heaven on Earth, we need to change our actions and plant different seeds! Once our intentions, motivation, thoughts and actions are fully aligned with Divine Will, we are liberated from the cyclic existence that keeps us trapped in ego and the physical realm (Samsara) and Saturn has fulfilled His role as a God of liberation.

Saturn is not only about restriction and limitation, because karma is not only about restriction and limitation. Conventionally many people feel that natal or transiting Saturn is 'blocking' them in some way. This might seem to be the case from the perspective of the ego-personality that isn't getting what it wants, but in reality Saturn brings important lessons about natural law, natures cycles, rhythms, potential, and possibility.

"from the ego's point of view
spiritual progress is 'one insult after another'"

- Chogyam Trungpa Rinpoche

At personality level, Saturn teaches important and necessary natural laws. The nature of the physical realm is one of limitation because everything works according to change and cycles of time. The limitation is not imposed by Saturn, but actually by our own mind. The lessons of Saturn are guiding us beyond our small mind, beyond the limitations of ego and the intellect, so we can see the greater reality: the truth of our own being.

"Mind gives place to intuition and reason to pure perception"

- The Tibetan, *"Esoteric Astrology"*

It is our egoic ideas that limit us and once Saturn has 'brought us to our knees' at the personality level, we are forced to accept that there is a greater reality happening outside of our small world, of which we are also a part. It is then that we align with our Soul path, and become receptive to the higher teachings of Saturn. Saturn then becomes the Lord of Liberation by showing us the true path to freedom.

If you have Sun, Moon, and especially Rising Sign in Capricorn you have an important role to play in creating heaven on earth, by paying attention to your motives and choices and ensuring they are fully aligned with Divine Will for the highest and best good of all.

Uranus, Jupiter and The Inner Journey of Aquarius

Aquarius brings an opportunity to dedicate our personal energy to the body of humanity. The sign of Aquarius is associated with individuality, uniqueness, science, technology, the future, humanitarianism, the new age and group consciousness.

We mentioned earlier that according to *"Esoteric Astrology"*, the last four signs of the Zodiac: Sagittarius, Capricorn, Aquarius and Pisces are *signs of service*. Following the Soul's journey through the 12 signs of the Zodiac, after the Soul in Capricorn has followed and completed the path of light, leading to Christ Consciousness, it is time for the Soul in Aquarius to become the World Server, flowing 'love and life for the benefit of thirsty humanity'.

Four planets are important in creating the conditions necessary for the Soul's development and experience in Aquarius: Saturn, Uranus, Jupiter and the Moon. Saturn was traditionally considered to be the planetary ruler of Aquarius, and to many people still will be. The conditions that we mentioned in last month's article pertaining to Saturn and Capricorn, also relate to Aquarius when humanity is largely personality-centered and driven by fear and attachment. Once the Soul has completed the stage of development in Capricorn, and has accessed Christ Consciousness, it no longer is limited by the constraints of Saturn and comes under the custodianship (planetary rulership) of Uranus:

"On the reversed wheel... The Saturnian influence exhausts itself in Capricorn and the man is then set free from karma and needs no presentation of opportunity for he stands a free initiate ... and can proceed with world service undeterred and held back by no thought of self or selfish desire"

- The Tibetan, *"Esoteric Astrology"*

As humanity increasingly moves onto the fixed cross where there is awareness of Soul and personality, Uranus increasingly becomes the custodian of Aquarius at personality level. Jupiter is the custodian of Aquarius at Soul level while interestingly the Moon is the custodian at hierarchical level.

Since we already explored Saturn previously under Capricorn (and the effect would be the same here in Aquarius until the individual consciousness has become receptive to the energies of Uranus), for our purposes in this article we will focus on the two major influences for this early phase of the Aquarian Age: Uranus and Jupiter.

"Uranus causes the great transference
in the human consciousness
from intellectual perception
to intuitive knowledge"

- The Tibetan, *"Esoteric Astrology"*

The subtle influence of Uranus begins in Aries at hierarchical level, continues working through Libra at Soul level, and here in Aquarius, human consciousness has evolved to the degree that the subtle energies of Uranus can be received at personality level so the individual can perceive and fully utilize the intuitive faculty. Although even talking about 'perceiving' and 'utilizing' is misleading because it sounds like there is something distinct and separate outside of ourselves to be perceived and utilized which is not the case.

By the time we have a conscious Soul in Aquarius we have gone beyond duality and the experience of the intuitive faculty is that of embodiment. We realize it is who we are. We are aware of ourselves simply as awareness, and there is no separation between experience and experiencer. This is also why Jupiter is the custodian at Soul level in Aquarius because we are experiencing our most expanded and expansive nature (without self).

The Soul in Aquarius becomes the World Server and the highest Soul purpose of Aquarius is the dedication of personal energy to the collective, because at this level it is seen that there is no separation between the individual and the collective. All are one. Once again even the term 'collective' could be misleading because our common understanding of collective is separate individuals forming a group, yet the highest Soul experience in Aquarius is that of many individuals forming one whole body of humanity. Humanity is experienced as one cohesive whole, with each individual being an integral part, just like the cells within a human body that are individual yet indivisible from the whole. Since there is no experience of a separate self, there is no question of harming 'others' as to do so would be tantamount to chopping off one's own fingers or toes! Others do not exist as such and all that is experienced is we, as one.

The symbology of Aquarius as the water carrier belies the higher purpose of Aquarius, which is to flow the dual waters of love and life for thirsty humanity like a Divine fountain or wellspring. Aquarius' role within this one body of humanity is to provide this constant source of divine energy, through the fusion of heart and mind. This is why conventionally in astrology, even though Leo rules the heart, it is Aquarius that rules the circulation and flow of blood. Esoterically Aquarius governs the distribution of the vital waters of love and life throughout both the individual human body, and the larger body of humanity!

Throughout this book we have referred to Patanjali's description of consciousness in terms of five 'bodies' or dimensions of experience: physical, energy, mental, intuitive, bliss and ultimately, universal mind. It seems that Uranus and Jupiter in Aquarius combine to create those conditions necessary for us to experience and transcend the intuitive and bliss dimensions, on our journey to universal mind.

The heightened intuition of Uranus combined with the expansiveness of Jupiter serve to expand the fullness of experience towards Universal Mind by supporting the fusion of mind energy (intuition) and heart energy (bliss). Jupiter plays a major role in the fusion of head and heart, so that the *dual waters* in Aquarius combine to form one steady stream that we may call 'heart-mind'.

"Jupiter gives an inherent tendency to fusion
which nothing can arrest.
The achievement of ultimate synthesis is inevitable,
and this Jupiter promotes"

- The Tibetan, *"Esoteric Astrology"*

The Soul experience in Aquarius can be likened to a collective awakening, of which we will have more experiential knowledge as we reach the culmination of the Aquarian Age. As a result of the conditioning effects of Uranus and Jupiter there is a flowering of human consciousness which we may think of as a collective awakening yet it is more akin to an awareness of our individual roles within the universal mind. Here there is a hint at the role of the Moon at hierarchical level in this mass awakening of humanity. The experience of universal mind is the higher group consciousness of Aquarius and is nothing like our current mental-intellectual experience. Rather it is a level of higher mind that is born within from the fusion of higher mind (intuition) and heart-wisdom.

"If an egg is broken by an outside force life ends.
If an egg is broken by an inside force, life begins."

- (Unknown)

Your vital life-force energy comes from within. While it is natural for Aquarius to circulate (Aquarians are amazing networkers) it is more important that you pay attention to how you are flowing your energy. A fully integrated Aquarius will have accessed the heart-energy of their opposite sign Leo, and be flowing vital heart-mind energy through an open heart. The Aquarian who is not yet fully attuned to their heart may just be circulating mental information at best (and misinformation at worst). If you have Sun, Moon and especially Rising Sign in Aquarius a major theme in your life is the circulation of life-force energy in the form of heart-wisdom. Be sure to access the inner dimensions of your own heart first to discover the inner fountain of life force energy and heart-wisdom, so you can then flow this energy with conscious intent for the benefit of humanity.

Jupiter, Neptune, Pluto, and The Inner Journey of Pisces

Pisces brings an opportunity to check in where we are up to on the vast continuum of human experience ranging from glamour, illusion and delusion right up to enlightenment and Universal Love! Pisces brings us full circle. Not only with the completion of one Zodiac year, but in our current journey of exploring the personality and Soul rulers of each sign.

In this book we have followed the Soul's journey three times, through the twelve signs of the Zodiac where the Soul began as *a point of light in the mind of God in Aries*, right through to the *flowering of human consciousness in Aquarius,* arriving at our third visit to the sign of the World Savior in Pisces.

The 'World Savior' referred to here is the recognition of humanity's true role in respect to our Mother Earth, when we have fully blossomed as a species and all our hearts beat as one, as the 'sacred heart' of humanity in Pisces.

"In essence the World Savior is
the incarnation of Love
within each one of us."

- Alan Oken

In this chapter we have discussed how the planetary 'rulers' are space holders or custodians maintaining the necessary conditions for specific stages of development in the evolution of human consciousness, and three planets are important when we look to the human experience in Pisces. Jupiter and Neptune are custodians at personality level while Pluto is the custodian at both Soul and hierarchical level. This speaks to the transformative potential inherent in Pisces.

In Aquarius we saw how Jupiter's role is one of expansion, fusion, and synthesis, and since there is a degree of overlap between stages (and therefore signs) this process continues as the Soul enters Pisces. Hence Pisces has two custodians at personality level. The expansive conditions of Jupiter create a greater capacity in us to perceive and respond to the subtler energies of Neptune. Neptune's influence on human development began in Cancer at Soul and Hierarchical level, and by the time the Soul has reached this stage of development in Pisces the individual is now sensitive enough to receive Neptune's energy at personality level.

"You are not a drop in the ocean;
You are the ocean in a drop"

- Rumi

For most people who are still on the mutable cross (see the Capricorn section in this chapter for a summary of consciousness described in terms of the three crosses), the experience with Neptune in Pisces can be one of being 'swept away' by the ocean, 'going with the flow' and 'falling' deeper into glamour, illusion and escapism. This is because they have not yet completed the individuation process, which begins in Leo and completes in Capricorn. The whole story of the incarnation process, in astrological terms from Aries up to this present point in Pisces, has been one of personal experience through individuation. Individuation is a vital stage in the evolution of consciousness, for without it, we cannot return to the ocean intact with the remembrance of our experience as a drop.

"The purpose of involution is to allow
Spirit to penetrate deeper into matter
so that eventually all things of matter
realize their spiritual Essence."

– Alan Oken

Neptune's job at personality level is to dissolve limiting physical and mental conditions that would impede the influx of spirit in physical matter in the form of Universal Love, so that we may once again remember the oceanic nature of our consciousness, the Divine Love within and experience this within the context of our individual physical incarnation. If the effects of Neptune are felt before we have successfully completed our individuation process, then we can experience problems with addictive and co-dependent behaviors as we will be challenged to set appropriate personal boundaries in our individual sphere of influence. Hence some of the pitfalls for Pisces at personality level.

"The Fishes in Pisces are bound together, as we have seen, and this is symbolic of the captivity of the Soul in form, prior to the experience upon the Fixed Cross."

- The Tibetan, *"Esoteric Astrology"*

How we experience and respond to Neptune's universal influence depends upon the degree of our own individual consciousness. If we are on the mutable cross where we are still identified with our ego-personality, we will experience Neptune's energy as illusion and delusion, where we can become lost in the thick fog of mass consciousness. If we are on the fixed cross, where we are beginning to awaken spiritually, we will experience Neptune as a planet of Universal Love. He shows us that our true nature is one of oceanic consciousness, that we are an aspect of Divine Love and that all separation is illusory, so we may begin to appreciate our underlying spiritual reality.

It might be helpful at this point to make a clear distinction between individuation and separation. Individuation and separation are not the same thing. The fingers on your hand are individual: they have the capacity to move independently of one another, and have individual experience. You may hurt one finger for example while the others remain unharmed. However, they are not ever, at any point, separated from you or your hand. If they become separated, they die. Likewise, while it is vital and necessary for the evolution of human consciousness that we each have the capacity to move independently from one another and have our own individual experience we are never, at any time, separated from the whole body of humanity. At the level of consciousness, we are connected and we experience one another's pain.

"This is the inner mathematics,
that the part of the whole is
not smaller than the whole.
That will be difficult to understand.
The part of the whole is equal to the whole,
because the whole cannot be divided into parts.
Division is not possible.

That's why we call the real authentic
being in you `individual'.
Individual means indivisible —
that which cannot be divided."

- OSHO

When personality and Soul fusion is complete, we are aware of both ourselves as an individual and the ocean of consciousness, at one and the same time. It is then that Pluto, the great revealer, can step in at Soul level bringing the conditions for the final transformation at Soul level in Pisces.

Esoterically it is said that the "final death" happens in Pisces. What could this mean, the final death? Possibly the end of Samsara. Samsara is the cycle of death and rebirth and many spiritual traditions, including Buddhism, teach that it is possible to become enlightened and finally be free of this cycle of continuous death and rebirth.

"Here, at the final stage,
Pisces stands for the death of the personality
and the release of the Soul from captivity
and its return into the task of the world Savior.

The great achievement is finished
and the final death is undergone."

\- The Tibetan, *"Esoteric Astrology"*

We first experienced Pluto's influence in Scorpio at personality level. Pluto is a deep and mysterious planet that was only discovered on February 18th 1930 and incorporated into astrology after that date. In *"Esoteric Astrology"* the Tibetan Master explains that until mankind has the consciousness to respond to the subtle influences of planets, they remain undiscovered and such was the case with Pluto. Pluto was discovered, and is now included in modern astrology, precisely because humanity now has the consciousness to perceive and respond appropriately to his subtle spiritual influence.

"Towards the end of the evolutionary process
the disciple begins to respond consciously
to the fourth indirect influence –that of Pluto,
producing the death of the hindering factors
and of all that prevents synthesis."

\- The Tibetan, *"Esoteric Astrology"*

Mythologically, Pluto is interesting. His journey begins in duality in Greek mythology as Hades "Lord of the Underworld" and Plouton the "giver of wealth" before myth finally unites him as Pluto. He is said to hold custodianship over all that lies beneath the surface of the Earth, which includes graves and all of the Earth's riches: the fertility of the soil and the wealth of her gems. The story of Pluto hints that there is something at our core, a jewel, an inner light that is carried over beyond death. In *"Esoteric Astrology"* the Tibetan states that:

"Pluto or death never destroys the consciousness aspect".

While Neptune sensitizes us to receive ever increasing vibrations of spirit in physical form, Pluto reduces our attachment to physical form and brings us to the light. In this way we begin to more closely identify with our inner light, or Soul: that which continues beyond death. While Pluto brings the cycle of life to an end, Neptune ensures we carry with us as much illumination as possible.

The concept of returning to the light as an individual, 'enlightened' being, seems fundamental to the whole purpose of physical incarnation. Buddhist scripture speaks of attaining the rainbow body or 'body of light', wherein we return to the ocean of consciousness from whence we came, but with our individuality intact. We return to the light, yet are not lost in that light.

**"I leave the Father's home
and turning back, I save"**

- The Tibetan, *"Esoteric Astrology"*

The combined effects of Jupiter, Neptune and Pluto in Pisces support us in 'embodying' and identifying with the Divine Light at the core of our being. As a result of our adventure into physical incarnation that began in Aries, we return to "the Father's house" fully laden with the riches of experience, within an individual Soul.

If you have Sun, Moon and especially Rising Sign in Pisces, you are here to walk your individual path while holding the awareness that, at one and the same time, you are the ocean. This awareness will strengthen the power of your heart and allow the World Savior (the essence of Universal Love) to flow freely into the world through you.

So far we have followed the Soul's journey through the signs three times: each time from a slightly different perspective, yet we have seen that there is one constant factor that remains continuous throughout our journey, and that is developing awareness, or consciousness. In the next chapter we will take a brief overview of the science of self-awareness, how it relates to Soul Astrology, and why it can be considered a holistic science for the coming age of spiritual awakening.

6. Self-Awareness: The Science of Your Soul

A Spiritual Science For An Evolving Humanity

It is beyond doubt that we are at an evolutionary point in human consciousness, one that brings understanding of our true nature and our role here, on this planet, at this time. In studying the evolution of humanity it becomes apparent that we are on the verge of what some might call a spiritual dawn. From the earliest apes that walked upright as humans, not knowing that they were 'aware' (conscious), we have evolved through stages of 'knowing', to the point where we are now 'aware that we are aware', or conscious. Awareness has become aware of itself.

We are realizing that we are not helpless victims in a Universe that does things 'to' us, but rather we are conscious co-creators of our own evolution. For the first time, the realization is dawning on us that we are co-creating the reality that we experience. Not only is our environment affecting us, but also we are having a huge effect on it. We are facing the reality that we are part of one whole system, not separate from it. This knowing brings an urgent need for us to study and understand our world from a very different perspective. A truly holistic one.

This new awareness raises many questions that traditional science doesn't readily have answers for. As we step into our role as conscious co-creators, we might wonder:

Where are we going?
What are we co-creating?
Who are we co-creating with?
Who, or what, is God?

This shift in consciousness is known by many names. It has been described as a global spiritual awakening. Certainly there is an increased awareness of, and interest in, spiritual matters. In times to come this period of human evolution may well be called the Soul-Age. It has been predicted[85] that during this period of our evolution we are to have a conscious experience of our Soul. Not just one or two isolated individuals, like the saints and avatars in ages gone by, but this time we will all experience this as one Humanity. It seems we are set for a mass quantum leap in human consciousness.

As we move forward into the Twenty-First Century, as more fully awake, aware, conscious beings, we will therefore need a different approach to science. The science of the Nineteenth and Twentieth Centuries was based on separation: dissection, categorization, classification and labeling. It was a product of the consciousness of the age, which thought the key to understanding anything was to observe it (objectively) and label it. From the newly-evolving consciousness that is emerging within the mind of humanity, we can see obvious flaws in this approach.

We cannot observe wholeness from the outside because in wholeness there is no duality, and so there is no outside (nor is there an 'inside' for that matter)! It is clear that in moving forward from here we will need a different approach to science. A holistic approach that brings us deeper understandings of unity, wholeness, the interrelatedness of all things, and oneness. We will need sciences

---

[85] In the works of seers such as HP Blavatsky, and in some Buddhist writings.

that are congruent with our spiritual being and experience. Maybe we already have in place some of the rudimentary elements for this. Maybe wisdom teachers through the ages have been guiding us, but we didn't have the consciousness to recognize what was before us, until now.

Soul Astrology has the potential to become a comprehensive applied science of energy and relationships that gives us a framework for understanding the nature of the universe, quantum physics, the mind, and healing. We just need to recognize it and learn how to use it properly, in the way it was intended. Before this can happen we need to understand what Soul Astrology and science are, and their purposes.

"At the moment I am looking into astrology, which seems indispensable for a proper understanding of mythology. There are strange and wondrous things in these lands of darkness. Please, don't worry about my wanderings in these infinitudes. I shall return laden with rich booty for our knowledge of the human psyche."

- Carl Jung

Music and Celestial Harmonics, The Origins of Soul Astrology

Soul Astrology is the name given to forms of astrology that draw upon psychological astrology, transpersonal psychology and *"Esoteric Astrology"*, to create a model of the Universe and how we fit into it. It is one thing to put forward a model, or framework, for understanding the Universe; it is quite another to suggest this can be applied as a science. So let's take a moment to understand what Soul Astrology actually is, where it originates from, and how it can be used as a practical applied science for this new age, to enable us to understand the nature of everything from the universe to the mind. Indeed the true nature of everything.

Many eminent people throughout history have also been astrologers.

Carl Jung, one of the fathers of modern psychology, and the great
mathematician Pythagoras, were also accomplished astrologers. Yet
in the Twentieth Century, astrology fell from grace and rather than
being considered a science it was relegated to the status of fortune
telling. What happened? Were Pythagoras, Carl Jung, and many
other wise teachers throughout history mistaken? Or, in our
arrogance at the height of twentieth-century materialism, was there
something about astrology that we couldn't understand because in
our ignorance we didn't yet have the consciousness to comprehend
it?

Most Westerners only know of Pythagoras as a mathematician. Few
know that he was also a mystic and scientist who ran an ancient
mystery school. His students began with the study of mathematics.
Once accomplished in mathematics, his students were required to
study music. It is said of Pythagoras that he heard the 'music of the
spheres'[86]. Certainly he held music in high regard.

Each of his students was given a 'monochord': a one-stringed
instrument, and told that once they understood the secrets of the
monochord, they would understand the secrets of the Universe. So
what could his students learn from this instrument? Well, they could
learn the relationship between notes on the musical scale. They
could also learn that a musical note never dies. Once that string is
struck, the vibration continues until infinity. It may pass beyond the
current range of human perception, but it doesn't end there.

Once we grasp this fundamental truth, we can begin to realize the
possibility of omniscience. It may be possible, just as many mystics
and yogis have told us over the ages, to expand human perception to
the place where 'all is known'. This potential lies in each of us,
because we are not separate from that place, but just 'blind' to it at
this time, by virtue of our limited perceptions.

---

[86] "Pythagoras and The Music of the Spheres" online document at
http://www.dartmouth.edu/~matc/math5.geometry/unit3/unit3.html

"There are no levels of Reality;
only levels of experience for the individual"

- Ramana Maharshi

Soul Astrology As A True Holistic Science

Astrology in its truest form is an invitation to us to expand our knowledge by expanding our perceptive abilities. We can only fully understand and comprehend this through personal experience. Twentieth-century science was limited by its own obsession with materialism: a limiting fixation with 'objective' research almost to the point of ignorance, whereby evidence had to be externally verified in order to be valid and, if it could not be, then it was rejected.

Twentieth-century scientists continued along this vein, in spite of an awareness of 'the observer effect': a well-known phenomenon in scientific research whereby 'that which is observed is changed by the observation'. Much evidence of this is found in quantum physics, whereby results often depend upon what researchers expect to see. The researcher cannot remove him or herself from the equation, and everything affects everything else, because all is inter-related.

During the latter years of the Twentieth Century a field known as 'heuristic research'[87] was developed as a tool in certain social sciences, such as psychology, which attempt to expand our understanding of the human mind. In heuristic research the researcher uses himself as the 'subject'.

At last 'self' observation has found a place in conventional scientific circles! As yogis and mystics have told us (and as modern science is now discovering), there is no way to explore the realm of human consciousness, other than from within, because our mind is creating

---

[87] "Heuristic Inquiry and Transpersonal Research" by Dave Hiles. Online document at http://www.psy.dmu.ac.uk/drhiles/HIpaper.htm

that which we observe.

What is science? The meaning of the word 'science' changed over time, deviating from its original meaning in the Latin word *scientia* meaning "knowledge" or "knowing". It was only from the Nineteenth Century onwards that the term 'science' came to be used only to denote 'knowledge obtained through a scientific method'. There was no consensus of opinion at the time as to what *scientific method* should be, which lead to a rise in popularity of objective methods while subjective methods were perceived as too 'biased' to be of value.

In its striving for some externally verifiable objective absolute 'truth', by distorting the original meaning of the word 'science', and with an exaggerated emphasis on so-called objective methodologies rather than on *knowing*, Western science became increasingly separative, materialistic, and divisive in nature. The totality of 'all that is' was reduced to subject / object. The more we explore things from this standpoint the further it takes us from the truth of our being. Yet if we simply return to the original meaning of the word 'science' as 'knowing' then it is perfectly possible, through subjective methodologies, to have a science of wholeness, integration, and unity. Indeed many spiritual and yogic traditions of the East have thousands of years of history and experience with such methodologies.

Can Astrology Be A Science of Oneness?

How can astrology inform us, give us knowledge, and be considered a true science of inner knowing? To answer that question we now need to look at astrology in itself. Unsurprisingly, true astrology has also been distorted by the dualistic mind. During the time of Pythagoras, astrologers and astronomers were one and the same. In the days before Isaac Newton the most important astronomers were astrologers by profession – Tycho Brahe, Johannes Kepler, and Galileo Galilei[88]. Medical students were even taught astrology

---

[88] *"Astrology and Astronomy"* online document at
https://en.wikipedia.org/wiki/Astrology_and_astronomy

because it was used in medical practice. This is still the case today with Tibetan Medicine.

With the advent of 'scientific method'[89] and the emphasis on absolute objectivity, by the end of the 18th century astronomy had become a new and distinct 'science', separate from astrology. The planets were considered to be 'out there' and separate. Astronomy came to be the science of choice for the study of planets because of it's perceived objectivity: we get to be 'over here', studying these things called planets which appear to be 'over there'. Subject – object.

As we shift our consciousness to increasingly embrace wholeness, we can begin to understand astrology as a science of wholeness, energy and interrelatedness. The more we perceive the Universe in it's oneness as a field of dancing, interrelated, energy and light, the more we value astrology as a language to describe our experience of that energy and light. More importantly, astrology is a body of wisdom already gathered over thousands of years by wisdom teachers and yogic masters such as Pythagoras who, *through their own experience and inner knowing*, developed a deep understanding of the *true nature of reality*, and left the science of astrology behind for us, as a map to follow in their footsteps.

"The Ancient Wisdom teaches that 'space is an entity.' It is with the life of this entity and with the rhythms, the cycles and the times and the seasons that "Esoteric Astrology" deals"

- The Tibetan, *"Esoteric Astrology"*

---

[89] "Scientific Method" from Wikipedia at
https://en.wikipedia.org/wiki/Scientific_method

Developing The Intuitive Faculty To Access Higher Mind

As mentioned in an earlier footnote the work known as *Esoteric Astrology* was received by Alice Bailey (A.B.) from a spiritual teacher who referred to himself as 'The Tibetan', later to become known as the Master DK. At the time he was thought to be the Abbott of a monastery in Tibet and he transmitted wisdom teachings by telepathic means to A.B. In itself, this is an exciting testimony to the power of a highly-developed and crystal-clear human mind!

One of the first questions I had upon reading *Esoteric Astrology* was how the teachings related to Tibetan Buddhism. Although there are clearly differences, there are also core truths that can be related not only to Buddhist teaching, but also to the teachings from other wisdom schools. They are in agreement about the presence and capacities of the higher mind, telepathy, the subject of reincarnation, and the interrelatedness of all things.

In the Pythagorean school, knowledge of reincarnation was also a fundamental principle. It seems that, irrespective of religious belief or tradition, there is a core wisdom that we in the West have forgotten how to access. Soul Astrology is giving us tools to access and understand this wisdom.

The Tibetan tells us that we exist within a living organism, with whom we co-create in every moment with our minds. Albert Einstein is reported to have said, "I want to know the mind of God". The Tibetan reminds us that we are not separate from God so this is possible, but first we have to develop our perception enormously to become aware of this.

Just as a cell in our big toe has no knowledge of our mind, this is the difference between the small capacity of our mind, and the mind of God! The cell in our toe cannot stand outside our body to understand it, it can only increase its awareness until it realizes there is a whole body, of which it is an intrinsic part.

The current state of Western science sends rockets to the moon and beyond to see what is 'out there', when indeed all of 'out there' is really 'in here'! This is like our toe sending a rocket to our head to see what is 'out there', when the best way to know and understand would be for the toe to simply expand its perception it can feel and thereby know its connectedness to the rest of the body!

The Tibetan does not ask us to accept the teachings in *"Esoteric Astrology"* on blind faith. He tells us to corroborate them and, if we cannot, then of course we must reject them. How do we corroborate[90] them? He tells us, that it can only be done through *developing the intuitive faculty* and accessing *'the illumined mind'*.

The human body is the only 'instrument' of perception that can corroborate these teachings, and while we seek for truth outside of ourselves we will remain in ignorance. This is where conventional science has done us the greatest disservice: by keeping our attention outside of ourselves it has denied us access to the greatest of mysteries - human consciousness. The true science of the future will increasingly be based on heuristic research – looking within. Only then will we develop the skills of expanded awareness that allow us to discern the subtle energies that were known to Pythagoras, countless mystics and yogis throughout the ages, and are described in *"Esoteric Astrology"*.

"Someday after we have mastered the winds, the waves, the tides and gravity, we shall harness the energies of love. Then for the second time in the history of the world man will have discovered fire."

- Pierre Teilhard de Chardin

---

[90] Corroborate: *confirm*, or *validate* (in this case from our own experience). See http://www.oxforddictionaries.com/definition/english/corroborate

Seven Creative Forces

The Pythagorean model of the Universe used music and color to illustrate seven creative forces, which issued forth from the mouth of 'the One'. Judaism tells us that seven creative 'lords' (Elohim) issued forth from the mouth of God. There are seven colors in the spectrum and seven notes make up the musical scale.

In *"Esoteric Astrology"* the Tibetan tells us that seven energy 'rays' issue from one. The one divides into two and from that issues forth a third, from which issue rays 4 to 7. We ourselves are energetic fields vibrating, resonating, within one larger energetic field. As we begin to stand in the truth of this and expand our awareness of these energies we will realize some of the deeper truths of which the ancient Masters spoke.

How do we recognize these energies? Through our perception. We may perceive them as positive emotions and sensations. Buddhist teaching refers to 'subtle winds' to describe the various forms of energy that flow through, and from, our body. There are seven chakras, or energy centers, in the human body, which correspond to seven chakras, or energy centers, in the solar system.

In *"Esoteric Astrology"* the first ray is known as the will of God, the second ray as love/wisdom and the third ray as active intelligence. This is similar to a Tibetan Buddhist prayer that asks for 'enlightened power' (will), 'enlightened compassion' (love/wisdom), and 'enlightened wisdom' (active intelligence).

The seven rays of which the Tibetan speaks are literally describing the fabric of the Universe in terms of loving, compassionate and powerful energies. The very energies that saints, mystics and yogis have told us are always there for us, if we know how to access them. Energy, Chi, Prana: although known by different names in different traditions, the nature of these fundamental energies remains the same and possesses the qualities of *love and intelligence*.

Quantum physics is amassing a wealth of evidence that supports these teachings. Nothing is solid, everything is energy, and there is no such thing as 'empty space'. After many attempts scientists have finally accepted that it is impossible to create a vacuum in a laboratory, because whenever they try, there are always at least photons (particles of light) present! In other words, there is no such thing as a vacuum, or space. Everything is connected and, more importantly, it is connected by light.

As we move away from the concrete literal-mindedness of early science, we are beginning to realize that everything in astrology - the Zodiac with its animal signs and the planets - is symbolic of an underlying energetic reality. The Zodiac signs as symbols made sense to an ancient people who were much more closely connected with nature than we are. Because they understood animals, the symbolism helped them to understand the energetic qualities of Aries as a ram, for example, or Scorpio as a Scorpion.

Soul-centered astrology is pointing us toward a deeper understanding of underlying energy, the differing energetic qualities that we command and receive, and the relationship dynamics between them. Soul Astrology teaches us about the nature of energy through metaphor and simile. When we say 'the Moon' is an accumulation of past learning, it is not so much to do with the physical, actual Moon but more a symbol of an energy dynamic in our energy field.

This is where confusion arose between science and astrology in the Twentieth Century. In astrology we are talking energetically. We are talking about a wave: an energy pattern that is in us and is reflected above in the constellations and planets. As in the ancient hermetic aphorism: "As above, so below".

"The Rising Sign might be called the 'straight and narrow path' for as long as one is on this path one is on the right path. We all deviate from this path as our minds, emotions and the physical pressures of life sway us to and fro.

*But we can refocus our energies by constantly recognizing our
Rising Sign, repeating its spiritual keynote and reorganizing our
lives accordingly."*

- Errol Weiner, Transpersonal Astrology

The Connection With Your Rising Sign

We can only understand these divine energies by coming to know
them intimately through personal experience. Many forms of healing
have arisen in recent years based on energy and vibration. We are
slowly beginning to recognize ourselves as energetic beings: living,
intelligent, energy fields. *"Esoteric Astrology"* gives us a blueprint
of the entire energy field. A personal Soul-based astrological reading
gives us the blueprint not only of the mind that created the physical
form that we have now, but what we are creating for our future lives,
and what we have the potential to change.

As we mentioned in earlier Chapters, the most important part of our
natal chart is the Rising Sign. The constellation that was 'rising' on
the horizon at the point of our birth indicates the dominant energy
that prevailed at that precise point in time. As above, so below.

You are a product and co-creator of this energy. It indicates the
nature of your Soul and therefore was a natural medium for you to
use as a gateway into this physical incarnation. In contrast, the
positions of the Sun and Moon indicate the dualistic nature of our
lower egoic mind. By 'ego' I mean the mind thinking of itself, or our
general sense of 'there is a me in here'.

The Moon represents what Carl Jung called our 'shadow', meaning
those aspects of our psyche which are in the dark: our unconscious
mind. The Sun represents that which is in the light, our conscious
mind. Neither one is our 'true' nature. The Moon is an accumulation
of conditioning, learned behavior and traits, from many past lives,
while the Sun can be thought of as the present.

Through self-observation we can not only come to know and recognize the subtle energy patterns in ourselves that lead us to repeat behaviors, but understand those thought-forms that we ourselves are perpetuating that create our future experiences.

The Tibetan and others have told us that, just like in the past and in Tibetan Medicine, physicians of the future will want to know a person's birth chart before treating them. Just like an electrician would need to see a wiring plan before detecting a fault in the system, doesn't it make sense that if blueprints of our whole system are available, then our physicians and therapists would need to be aware of them?

An awareness of the habitual energies dominating a chart can tell us which dis-eases that individual will re-create in this and future lifetimes. It is the ultimate in preventive medicine. Imagine being able to correct 'mis-fires' in your energy field now, to prevent illness in your future lives!

"Look you, Doubloon, your Zodiac here is the life of man in one
round Chapter. To begin: there's Aries, or the Ram,
lecherous dog, he begets us; then, Taurus, or the Bull,
he bumps us the first thing; then Gemini, or the Twins,
that is, Virtue and Vice; we try to reach Virtue,
when lo! comes Cancer the Crab,
and drags us back; and here,
going from Virtue, Leo, a roaring Lion,
lies in the path, he gives a few fierce bites and surly dabs
with his paw; we escape, and hail Virgo, the virgin!
that's our first love; we marry and think to be happy
for aye, when pop comes Libra, or the Scales,
happiness weighed and found wanting;
and while we are very sad about that, Lord!
how we suddenly jump, as Scorpio, or the Scorpion,
stings us in rear; we are curing the wound,
when come the arrows all round; Sagittarius, or the Archer,
is amusing himself. As we pluck out the shafts, stand aside!

here's the battering-ram, Capricornus, or the Goat;
full tilt, he comes rushing, and headlong we are tossed;
when Aquarius, or the Waterbearer,
pours out his whole deluge and drowns us;
and, to wind up, with Pisces, or the Fishes, we sleep."

- Herman Melville

Soul Astrology and Karma

Through deepening our understanding of energy, we begin to answer those really big questions about the very nature of our being, such as 'Who am I?', 'Why am I here?' and 'What am I supposed to be doing with my Life?'. In Soul Astrology we have a frame of reference that assists us in understanding the nature and causal relationships between karma, energy, and our experienced reality. It helps us to understand the bigger picture through a deeper understanding of ourselves, and our part in it. If our Sun, Moon and Rising Sign help us to distinguish between Soul-based and ego-based behavior, it can also help us to understand the complex nature of karma.

As mentioned earlier, 'ego' in this sense refers to our self-concept: who or what we have been 'conditioned' to believe ourselves to be, what we identify with, including all our beliefs, skills, talents, fears and limitations. Karma refers to that conditioning which has been carried over in our psyche from previous incarnations. In the Buddhist tradition it is often said that if you want to know your past actions, look at your present life, if you want to know your future life, look at your present actions. The Zen school teaches:

"Karma creates the body, and the body creates Karma"

- Zen Master Seung Sahn, The Compass of Zen

This is known in Buddhism as the wheel of samsara: the cycle of death and re-birth. The energy of our past thoughts, actions and behavior is mirrored in our Moon sign. A storehouse of karmic 'seeds', which we are unaware of, ready to ripen in any moment. It is not 'past' in the sense that it is gone, but rather that we created it with our past thoughts, words and actions. It indicates energy that we still carry and are unconscious of. We can see the metaphor of the physical Moon. The physical Moon is 'dead', in the sense that there is no life as we know it on the Moon. Yet it still has an effect on us: it interacts with the gravitational field of the earth, and has a powerful affect on the tides. So we can clearly see the analogy of something that is 'dead' connected to our past, which is exerting a 'pull' on our present life.

The Sun can be thought of as karma that is *currently ripening*. Although created in our past, it is coming into our conscious awareness in the present. Thought-forms that are currently expressed in our conscious awareness. The qualities of the signs in those positions tells us much about who we were and who we are currently becoming, as a living energy form. In this way, using our natal chart with a process of self-observation, we can distinguish our Soul's evolving nature from our individual and collective karma, and realize we are so much more than we currently experience ourselves to be.

Soul Astrology is a key to unlocking why we came in to this specific incarnation, what we are here to heal, and what we are here to grow. We may even have a conscious experience of our Soul, and realize ourselves as a Soul-based being. In observing ourselves, we deepen our understanding of the nature of 'mind' and karma, and adopt a very different approach to astrology. Soul Astrology in the future will include deep personal development, through observation, to cultivate intuition. Students of Soul-based Astrology will develop knowledge based on experience of their own individual journey. As we touch and come to know our own Soul, we naturally develop a deeper understanding of the nature of mind.

Our Dualistic Mind, and Our Oneness

What do we mean by mind? Tibetan Buddhists have no distinction between heart and mind as we do in the West. Emotions are also considered part of the mind. The Tibetan speaks of the plane of emotions as an aspect of 'lower mind' as distinct from the clear, higher mind we can access where the wisdom of the Masters can be found.

According to Buddha we are a continuous stream of mental moments. Practices such as meditation help us to slow down to the point where we can see the gap between thoughts, and discern what lies underneath. With deeper awareness we can see the relationship between our thoughts and the reality we experience. Understanding this distinction between 'lower' and 'higher' mind leads to a fundamental understanding in *"Esoteric Astrology"*.

In *"Esoteric Astrology"*, each Zodiac sign has a lower and an upper octave, a conventional and an esoteric ruler, indicative of our lower and higher mind. Buddhism again speaks of conventional and ultimate reality. Until relatively recently, Western psychology has approached understanding the mind from the perspective that we are our personality. We in the West tend to be attached to our personality as if it is a fixed thing, an intrinsic part of who we are.

Soul Astrology invites us to consider that the roles and behaviors that we attach to as our 'personality' are not inherently 'who we are' but are learned behavior, with which we have become identified (see social conditioning in Chapter 1). Although we may identify ourselves with our personality, we can also understand that we are part of something greater that is bigger than this small 'I', and understand that the two realities are really one. We understand that we have a dualistic nature.

Karma tells us something about why this is so, and how we experience at least two levels of being. Soul Astrology, in contrast to conventional astrology, addresses both our dualistic nature, and our oneness. It therefore has the potential to be a 'whole' science that integrates transpersonal psychology and explains the interrelated dynamics of the physical universe.

There is a direct connection between thoughts, emotions, and physical health and illness. Sigmund Freud, the father of modern psychology, based his psychodynamic theory[91] on 'thermodynamic theory'[92], which was popular at the time. The Victorian steam technologies (steam-powered ships, trains, factories) were all based on thermodynamic theory, which states that when water boils it becomes steam and as steam cools it returns to water.

Freud realized that energy doesn't go anywhere, it just changes shape and form, and that this applies to people. So he based his theory of psychodynamics on the same idea: that mental and emotional energy cannot go anywhere. It just changes its state, and can become physical illness. From this we can deduce that energy patterns, or past 'karma', can be locked into our patterning at birth.

Future students of Soul Astrology will be able to recognize energetic patterning in a natal chart that could be potential for dis-ease, and understand what needs to change for healing to happen. At this point we can only imagine our deep understanding of the nature of disease. The Tibetan tells us that all dis-ease is caused by separation. The solution is a return to wholeness.

"The most exciting and important journey one can make
is the involutionary quest of the Soul
and the evolutionary aspiration of the personality.

---

[91] "Psychodynamics" online document at
https://en.wikipedia.org/wiki/Psychodynamics

[92] "Thermodynamics" online document at
https://en.wikipedia.org/wiki/Thermodynamics

Soul Astrology

When they meet, you come Home.
In that Dwelling Place, the life Purpose is revealed;
knowledge becomes wisdom;
and Love becomes a reality at last. "

- Alan Oken, Soul-Centered Astrology

The Path Of Inner Transformation

Just as self-examination was a requirement for students of the Pythagorean school, so modern counselors, psychologists and psychotherapists are required to undergo their own inner process work. Heuristic research and 'self-examination' is now valued in any study of psychology, because Western science is beginning to realize the significance of what can be revealed to us by understanding the inner workings and patterns of our own mind.

"All around us we encounter the forces of greed, fear,
prejudice, hatred and ignorance. Those of us
who seek liberation and wisdom are compelled
to discover the nature of these forces
in our own heart and mind."

- Jack Kornfield

Through exquisite self-observation we undergo a transformative process whereby we can access higher truth. We begin to widen our perceptive capacity and can recognize the inner gateways to the Universe through our own intuition. These inner doors, sometimes referred to by mystics as the 'Bhagavat in the ten directions', are our gateway to the Universe through inner space. We have access to ultimate truth because we are not separate from it. We can expand our capacity to reach the place where, as the Tibetan said, 'The will of God is known'.

Once we go deeper with our experience of self-observation, we realize that there is much more than merely observing. This is what the mystics referred to as opening the "inner doors". We experience some very deep realizations about the nature of reality, and who we are within it. Our capacity for directly perceiving[93] energy increases. This opens and expands our intuitive capacity. We become more skilled at focusing our attention, or to be more precise, at bringing our awareness to something. We realize that the quality of awareness that we bring to something, can change it.

In his book *"A Path With Heart"* insight meditation teacher Jack Kornfield explains the healing power of awareness. He describes how we can heal ourselves by looking directly at our physical, emotional, and psychological pain and simply bringing our loving awareness to it. This isn't a metaphor it is a very real, tangible, and powerful process. When we have cultivated our perception to this degree we realize how our own awareness has the power to transform energy, not through anything we are doing, but simply by bringing loving awareness to it. This is true healing.

As we expand our perception through awareness, we will recognize and know what the Tibetan means by our being 'living cells within one larger living organism'. We will be aware of our own connectedness, and come to an intimate knowing of our individual Soul, its relationship to the group Soul and, in turn, the greater Being, of whom we are part.

Self-examination, allows us to compare and validate our experiences and personal truths. Through our own personal experience we come to understand the deeper truths contained in the Tibetan's teachings. We realize from our own experience, that at our core, at the heart of who we are, we really are 'good'! We realize that our true nature is peace, love, joy, and light, and that when we are not being that, it is simply because we are caught up in (and are acting out) conditioned behavior. We are like pure snowball that has picked up a few sticks

[93] Direct perception means perceiving purely, and clearly, without our mind imposing any labels or meaning upon what is experienced.

and stones. We may not seem to be 'pure' but the fact remains that who we are is pure - we are not the 'sticks and stones'.

We really are, as all the great wisdom teachings have told us, defined by our goodness and not by our 'bad' actions and reactions. We are not our anger, fear, greed, hatred, ignorance and prejudice. Who we really are, is the love and light that is underneath all that. How can we know this is true? Because all that will dissolve when we bring our loving awareness to it, and what remains IS who we really are - love.

We really do have an innate inner light at our core, and all our 'negativity' is not inherent in our nature, but rather the result of past conditioning. A very negative side effect of our modern age is that it leaves us stuck with all our negative feelings and doesn't give us a way forward. All the ancient wisdom paths (including Soul Astrology) are telling us that yes, we do have a core essence, a vital spark, a light, and we are moving, growing into something, evolving.

All our negative thoughts and emotions are learned and, as real as they feel to us right now, they are habitual patterns in our field of consciousness, which we have the power to change if we know how. Our natal chart tells us how to tell which is which. It gives us a personality tool so we can see what kind of personality we have, what the positive and negative traits are and what we can change, whilst letting us know that we are so much more than that.

The Buddha taught that the true nature of our mind is one of pristine clarity like a stream of crystal clear mountain water. From this place, our perception is exquisite: all is known. We are clairvoyant, clairaudient, and clairsentient because all is clear: nothing is in the way, we have clear sight, sound and knowing. We are omniscient, all really is known. For most of us the spiritual path is a way of returning to this utmost clarity.

It is my experience that by integrating Soul Astrology with meditation it can be developed to the point where it becomes an effective tool on our path: a map, or guide, that can assist us in understanding our true nature. The combined Sun / Moon 'personality' can indicate why we don't experience expanded perception. It reflects what stands in our way in the form of our social conditioning: habitual patterns of thinking, feeling, and expressing, which cloud the clarity of our perceptions. Through awareness we can use Soul Astrology to understand those patterns of thought and behavior that we need to release, heal or change so that we can experience our mind's true nature.

> *"Light is undiminishable, eternal and omni-present.*
> *In every religion that existed these qualities*
> *have been recognized as divine.*
> *So that we are forced to the conclusion that light,*
> *actual sensible light, is indeed the direct vehicle of divinity:*
> *it is the consciousness of God."*

- Rodney Collin, The Theory of Celestial Influence

When each one of us has become an exquisite observer of Self, with integrated knowledge from our personal experience and an intimate relationship with our own Soul, we will recognize our true nature as one of light, and Soul Astrology as a true science of inner knowing.

7. Your Journey Continues...

According to the Tibetan in *"Esoteric Astrology"*, your Soul began its journey in Aries as "a point of light in the mind of God".

We have seen in this book how your Soul is on a fantastic journey through each of the twelve signs of the Zodiac. It is a journey of self-exploration, self-discovery, self-knowledge, self-understanding and adventure. Most of all, it is a fantastic journey of light! Ultimately you are on a journey of discovering your own true nature as a being of love and light, in physical form. In its deepest sense Soul Astrology is the study of love and light, expressed as you.

> *"The energies represented by the four elements*
> *are ultimately the fundamental realities of life*
> *that are being analyzed with astrology"*
>
> – Stephen Arroyo

On your Soul's journey you pass through the many different terrains of the elements in the expression of your personality signs:[94]

- You understand the element of water by experiencing the highs and lows of emotions, from deserts to waves of tsunamis and to great bliss. This is the path of awakening awareness through mastery of emotions, which leads to the highest experience of compassion.

- You understand the element of fire through the experiences of your heart, from the deep fires of passion to the clarity of intuition. This is the path of awakening awareness through mastery of action, creativity, and passion, which leads to the highest experience of heart-centeredness, love and intuition.

- You understand the element of air through the experiences of your mind, from navigating the dense, fear-based, labyrinth of lower thought to the infinite vastness, wisdom and clarity of Universal Mind. This is the path of awareness through mastery of mind, which leads to the highest experience of wisdom.

- You understand the element of earth through the experiences of physical form, from meeting the everyday needs of the physical body to deep somatic awareness (body awareness). This is the path of awareness through mastery of physical form, which leads to the highest realization of 'emptiness', meaning that all forms are not solid but are also expressions light.

---

[94] Your 'personality' is the result of your conditioning in this and past lifetimes (see Chapter 1). It is expressed through the energy dynamics of the signs where personal planets are placed in your chart, in particular your Sun and Moon signs. Working on clearing this conditioning, by understanding these dynamics and changing long-standing reactive habit patterns, accelerates your journey towards personality-Soul fusion.

As our Soul continues through many physical incarnations, we get to experience all of the elements in their various forms of expression. Most of us are a blend of two or three elements, which dominate our personality experience in this lifetime. Some people have an equal balance of all four while others may only have one or two, which indicates a specific focus on those elements in this lifetime. Eventually we will all experience every element, which will contribute to our wisdom and Soul awakening.

Journey Within

The word esoteric comes from the ancient Greek word *eso*, which means 'within'. The word astrology comes from the ancient Greek words *astron*, meaning 'star', and *logia* meaning 'speaking of', so the term ' *"Esoteric Astrology"'* literally means '*speaking of the stars within*'. This means understanding at the deepest level, that the very same energies that move entire galaxies and star systems, are also present within you. You are on a journey of discovering the highest truths of the universe, by observing them at work within yourself.

There is a living intelligence to the universe that has the power to create mountains, move oceans, grow rainforests, and fill them with a myriad of living beings, while simultaneously keeping the solar system orbiting around the Sun and maintaining the delicate inner workings of your human body, from digesting your food to making sure the oxygen levels in your cells are in perfect balance.

This living intelligence is exactly the same as your own intelligence: your consciousness. It is not something outside of you. There is no separation. As mentioned in the previous Chapter, this is the deeper understanding of the hermetic aphorism "*as above, so below*" yet even that can be misleading because it implies that 'above' and 'below' are two separate things. In reality there isn't even any 'above' or 'below'! There is only an oceanic consciousness that we call by many names from Universal Mind, to Oneness, to God. You experience it as simply awareness. The part of you that is aware, right now, that you are reading this, is the same intelligence that permeates the whole of existence.

Your journey is one of discovering these universal truths for yourself. Not because anyone told you, but because you are awakening to the truth of your own reality, through your own experience. You are a conscious, intelligent, being and your true nature is one of light. Intelligent, aware, conscious, light. It is time for you to realize that truth for yourself.

Your True Nature

What do we mean by true nature? The true nature of something is a quality that remains constant no matter what other conditions may change. For example the nature of water is wet. It can be hot or cold. We can make tea with it, or soup. We can add salt to it, or sugar, but no matter what else changes the water is always wet. It's inherent nature of 'wetness' remains.

Likewise human beings are of the nature of *aware light*. Intelligent, conscious, light, is who you are. No matter what other forms you take, or roles you play, nothing changes the fact that you *are* light. No matter what else changes, your inherent nature of 'light' always remains. And because this is a universal truth, there is always the potential for you to discover this fact for yourself by simply looking within.

If water had the ability to observe itself, it could realize the fact that it is wet. Unlike water you, as a conscious human being, are gifted from birth with the most powerful quality in the entire universe: *self-awareness*. Unlike water, you do have the ability to self-reflect: to look back on yourself and observe yourself. To *be aware* of your Self. This one miraculous ability is what gives you the power to wake up to your own true nature as a spiritual being of light.

*"We must see that consciousness is neither an isolated Soul nor
the mere function of a single nervous system,
but of that totality of interrelated stars and galaxies
which makes a nervous system possible."*

- Alan Watts

Your journey has already begun. The fact that you are reading this means that you are already in a physical form on this planet! All that needs to happen now is for you to remain awake, and aware of the fact that you are awake and aware. Be more aware of your own consciousness. Because in reality there is no separation, this means that anything that happens in the entire Universe also has ripples in your own consciousness that you can become aware of.

Observe Yourself

Just as Pythagoras and many spiritual masters before him advised: observe yourself. This means (if you don't do so already) taking up some form of meditative or mindfulness practices whereby you learn to go within. You learn to observe your thoughts, feelings, motivations and actions as you go through your day. Notice what moves you. Notice what motivates you. Notice what energies drive your behavior, and your day. Start noticing (at first) which element they relate to.

When you're driving a car, you have to keep your eyes on the road, no matter what else is happening. You might be talking to passengers, and/or thinking about where you are going and what you need to do when you get there, but nevertheless you can't take your attention and your eyes off the road, not even for a second.

With a little practice self-observation can easily be integrated into your day in much the same way. No matter what else is happening, keep your eyes on 'the road' - and the 'road' is YOU. No matter what you are doing, always keep some of your attention on you.

Buddhists call this 'mindfulness' (watching your body, speech, and mind), but it is essentially the same practice of self-examination that Pythagoras advocated in his mystery school in ancient times.

Self-Realization

This beautiful journey is one of your own Soul Awakening, spiritual awakening, consciousness or (as the Tibetan Master puts it in *"Esoteric Astrology"*) *personality-Soul fusion*. Some call it enlightenment, but that might seem like a lofty or impossible goal, whereas what we are really talking about is realizing your highest potential as a human being. Once you realize that you are a living body of dynamic energy (and that astrology is a language of energy) then you understand the potential for astrology to precisely describe your experience and indicate your path of spiritual awakening.

The most important and significant thing any one of us can do with our life, is to show others what is possible. When you achieve your full potential as a spiritual being of light you become an inspiration to others, and your human family can aspire to follow in your footsteps. This is how we collectively evolve human consciousness.

Just as we can have a perfectly reasonable expectation that an acorn will (under the right circumstances) become an oak tree, so you too can have a perfectly reasonable expectation that, under the right circumstances, you *will* realize your spiritual potential and unfold into a fully Soul-Centered human being.

This is not a matter of 'becoming' something. An acorn doesn't need to change anything to turn into an oak tree, it only has to realize what is already there. Likewise, you are on the beautiful journey of simply realizing what is already there, by awakening your own self-awareness.

With time you may realize that your very being is in the nature of awareness itself. Who you are is pure awareness, like a crystal clear sky. You are awareness itself, aware of everything. Just as clouds can come and go, yet the sky remains untouched, so through many lifetimes the various ego-personalities that you have identified with, come and go like clouds, leaving your awareness untouched. With time and careful attention, you may come to realize this deep spiritual truth for yourself.

"Everything is like the sky - this is what I have to realize"

- Shantideva

This book has hopefully provided an overview of your Soul's journey. Soul Astrology provides some language that can be helpful in understanding your experience and your path. To follow your Soul path in everyday life you also need to be able to 'listen' to the energy of your Soul, and to know where it is guiding you, so that you can follow. This insight comes through self-observation, awareness, and your own experience.

Now it's over to you…

Further Reading

The following books support a deeper understanding of spiritual awakening and the principles of Soul Astrology:

A Path With Heart: A Guide Through The Perils and Promises of A Spiritual Life by Jack Kornfield

Awakening The Sacred Body by Tenzin Wangyal Rinpoche

Breaking The Habit of Being Yourself: How to Lose Your Mind and Create a New One by Dr. Joe Dispenza

Buddhist Astrology by Jhampa Shaneman

Esoteric Astrology by Alice Bailey

Esoteric Astrology: The Journey Of The Soul by Candy Hillenbrand Online document at http://www.aplaceinspace.net/Pages/CandyJourneyoftheSoul.html

Learn To Meditate: A quick start guide to meditation for beginners by Ruth Hadikin

Power vs Force: The Hidden Determinants of Human Behavior by Dr David Hawkins

Soul Centered Astrology: A Key to Your Expanding Self by Alan Oken

The Labours of Hercules: An Astrological Interpretation by Alice Bailey

The Natural Bliss of Being by Jackson Peterson

Transpersonal Astrology: The Astrology of Purpose by Errol Weiner

Waking From Sleep: Why Awakening Experiences Occur and How to Make them Permanent by Steve Taylor

Your Essential Guide To Soul Astrology by Ruth Hadikin. Short eBook. Free with Ruth's weekly newsletter at RuthHadikin.com

For professional astrologers and anyone who wants to learn astrological delineation techniques from a Soul-Centered astrology perspective I highly recommend Alan Oken's books and his webinar series' at **AlanOken.com**

Index

About The Author

Ruth Hadikin BSc. graduated with a first class honors degree (summa cum laude) in midwifery. She has Cancer Rising with Sun in Gemini and Moon in Leo. In addition to her many 'roles' in this lifetime she has been an ongoing student of astrology, esoteric, and spiritual teachings since she was 19 years old.

Author photo credit: ©Anya Sophia Mann

Ruth loves world travel, and has travelled extensively in the UK, Ireland, Spain, USA, Australia, Kenya, Egypt, India, Nepal and Tibet. She has lived in England, Scotland, Spain, and the USA.

She specializes in supporting you on your own greatest adventure: using Soul Astrology to explore your Soul Path and Life Purpose.

Web: **http://RuthHadikin.com http://Astrology-Symbols.com**

eMail: **Ruth@RuthHadikin.com**

Get *"Your Essential Guide To Soul Astrology"* free when you subscribe to Ruth's weekly newsletter "Life's Greatest Adventure" at RuthHadikin.com

Twitter: @SoulAstrologer @RuthHadikin
Facebook: http://www.facebook.com/SoulAstrologer

CPSIA information can be obtained
at www.ICGtesting.com
Printed in the USA
FSHW020614070219
55532FS